PENGUIN CLASSICS

SELECTED POLITICAL SPEECHES

ADVISORY EDITOR: BETTY RADICE

MARCUS TULLIUS CICERO (106–43 BC), Roman orator and statesman, was born at Arpinum of a wealthy local family. He was taken to Rome for his education with the idea of a public career and by the year 70 BC he had established himself as the leading barrister in Rome. In the meantime his political career was well under way and he was elected praetor for the year 66 BC. His ambitious nature enabled him to obtain those honours which would normally only have been conferred upon members of the Roman aristocracy, and he was duly elected consul for 63 BC. One of the most permanent features of his political life was his attachment to Pompey. As a politician his notable quality was his consistent refusal to compromise; as a statesman his ideals were more honourable and unselfish than those of his contemporaries. Cicero was the greatest of the Roman orators, possessing a wide range of technique and an exceptional command of the Latin tongue. He followed the common practice of publishing his speeches. In addition to the great influence these have exercised on subsequent European thought, they are of profound intrinsic interest, as the selected works in the present volume reveal. The information that they give us about contemporary social and political life is greatly increased by his letters, of which we have 900, published posthumously. They reflect the changing personal feelings of an emotional and sensitive man. His deeper thoughts are revealed by a considerable number of writings on moral and political philosophy, on religion and on the theory and practice of rhetoric.

MICHAEL GRANT has been successively Chancellor's Medallist and Fellow of Trinity College, Cambridge, Professor of Humanity at Edinburgh University, first Vice-Chancellor of Khartoum University, President and Vice-Chancellor of the Queen's University of Belfast, and President of the Classical Association. Writings: translations of Cicero's *On Government*, *On the Good Life*, *Selected Works*, *Selected Political Speeches* and *Murder Trials*, Suetonius' *The Twelve Caesars* and Tacitus' *Annals*, and he revised Robert Graves's edition of *The Golden Ass* by Apuleius, all for Penguin Classics; *Roman Literature* (Penguin); *The Climax of Rome*; *The*

SELECTED
POLITICAL SPEECHES
OF
CICERO

ON THE COMMAND OF CNAEUS POMPEIUS
AGAINST LUCIUS SERGIUS CATILINA (I–IV)
IN DEFENCE OF THE POET AULUS LICINIUS ARCHIAS
IN DEFENCE OF MARCUS CAELIUS RUFUS
IN DEFENCE OF TITUS ANNIUS MILO
IN SUPPORT OF MARCUS CLAUDIUS MARCELLUS
THE FIRST PHILIPPIC AGAINST MARCUS ANTONIUS

Translated with an Introduction by
MICHAEL GRANT

PENGUIN BOOKS

PENGUIN BOOKS

Published by the Penguin Group
Penguin Books Ltd, 80 Strand, London WC2R 0RL, England
Penguin Putnam Inc., 375 Hudson Street, New York, New York 10014, USA
Penguin Books Australia Ltd, 250 Camberwell Road, Camberwell, Victoria 3124, Australia
Penguin Books Canada Ltd, 10 Alcorn Avenue, Toronto, Ontario, Canada M4V 3B2
Penguin Books India (P) Ltd, 11 Community Centre, Panchsheel Park, New Delhi – 110 017, India
Penguin Books (NZ) Ltd, Cnr Rosedale and Airborne Roads, Albany, Auckland, New Zealand
Penguin Books (South Africa) (Pty) Ltd, 24 Sturdee Avenue, Rosebank 2196, South Africa

Penguin Books Ltd, Registered Offices: 80 Strand, London WC2R 0RL, England

www.penguin.com

First published 1969
Reprinted with revisions 1973
Reprinted with a new bibliography 1989

28

Copyright © Michael Grant Publications Limited, 1969, 1973
Bibliography copyright © Michael Grant Publications Ltd, 1989
All rights reserved

Printed in England by Clays Ltd, St Ives plc
Set in Monotype Bembo

CONTENTS

INTRODUCTION

CICERO'S political speeches remain immensely important for a variety of reasons. They are a mine of information about one of the most significant periods in the history of the world. They are transcripts of the most successful and persuasive oratory ever delivered, belonging to an age when oratory was the major activity of civil life and the nucleus of the educational system. They help to reveal the man who was this pre-eminent orator and who also played a prominent part in the seething, ominous political scene, a person of extraordinary character whom we are able to get to know intimately. Moreover, his works have continued to exercise a decisive influence on the minds of men throughout the intervening ages.

The following table indicates the principal landmarks in Cicero's life and the dates at which the speeches translated in this book were delivered.

106 B.C.	Cicero born at Arpinum, sixty miles south-east of Rome
c. 97 B.C.	Moves to Rome with his family
89–87 B.C.	Attends lectures on law, philosophy and rhetoric
c. 84 B.C.	First extant rhetorical work
c. 81 B.C.	First speech (under Sulla)
79–77 B.C.	Attends lectures at Athens and Rhodes
70 B.C.	First major political speeches[1]
68–44 B.C.	Letters to Atticus (XVI books)

1. The first speech against Verres (70) and the *Second Philippic against Antonius* (44) are translated in *Cicero: Selected Works*, Penguin, 1971 ed.

66 B.C.   *On the Command of Cnaeus Pompeius: In Support of the Manilian Law:* before the Assembly

63 B.C.   Consul. *Against Lucius Sergius Catilina* (four speeches; first and fourth before the Senate, second and third before the Assembly)

62 B.C.   *In Defence of the Poet Aulus Licinius Archias:* before a court

58–57 B.C.   Exiled (First Triumvirate had started 60–59)

56 B.C.   *In Defence of Marcus Caelius Rufus:* before a court

52 B.C.   *In Defence of Titus Annius Milo:* before a court

46 B.C.   *In Support of Marcus Claudius Marcellus:* before the Senate (after the death of Pompeius following the battle of Pharsalus against Caesar in 48)

44 B.C.   *First Philippic against Marcus Antonius:* before the Senate (after the murder of Caesar)

43 B.C.   Death of Cicero (proscribed by the Second Triumvirate)

These sixty-three years were fateful for the history of the world. The Roman empire had achieved a position which was unprecedented and has never been repeated: it had established control over the entire Mediterranean area. But Rome was showing itself more and more incapable of governing this vast territory. Administrators were corrupt, Italy itself was reft by an ever-deepening gulf between rich and poor and by a too grudging enfranchisement policy. The machinery of government at Rome, designed for a small Republic, had proved woefully inadequate for the guidance of a huge empire. Politics was a selfish and ruthless struggle among aristocratic groups and grandees and business concerns (knights), each with their hordes of hangers-on.

There was also an ever-growing tendency for successful

2. This was also the peak period of his philosophical essays (*Cicero: On the Good Life*, Penguin, 1971).

generals to become political leaders on their own account, with the backing of their soldiers and ex-soldiers and proletarian dependents who developed personal instead of patriotic loyalties. As each successive commander – Marius, Sulla, Pompeius, Caesar – asserted himself with increasing contempt for the constitution and the laws and the conservative 'Faction', as Caesar called it, a great act in the drama of western civilization was nearing its end. The Republic could not survive. Twelve years after Cicero's Philippics, the young Octavian, the future Augustus (who had acquiesced in the orator's violent end), became sole master of Rome and its empire. The Republic had shown itself unable to grasp the nettle; just as three hundred years later the not wholly illiberal principate founded by Augustus again proved insufficiently tough to cope with fresh threats, and a harsher totalitarian regime took shape.

Yet the dying Republic was full of talent, in the political as well as the literary field. The Romans were the most gifted race of politicians the world has ever seen; and the leading statesmen of late Republican times have never been outdone for versatility. Theirs was the age, before dictatorship clamped down upon it, to which the historian Tacitus was looking back when he observed 'rare is the felicity of the times when you can think what you like and speak what you think.'

This is the decisive epoch revealed by Cicero in his 774 surviving letters, in his treatises which attain the ancient high-water mark of a decent, practical attitude to life, and in the speeches of which fifty-eight survive (forty-eight are lost) and ten are translated in the present volume. Like his other literary works they are full of information not only about his times but about himself, and it is a gifted, distinctive and unique personality that emerges. As a result of all his writings that have come down to us, we know Cicero better than any other individual from the ancient world, and indeed better than almost any other historical figure at all until comparatively recent times. Those of us who study the ancient civilizations are sometimes tempted by the enigmatically sparse and biased nature of our material to regard our field of study as a fundamentally different one from more recent periods of history, since we still have comparatively little idea what most of the leading Greeks and Romans were really like. But a study of Cicero restores a more optimistic viewpoint. There is, of course, bias again, since so much of the evidence comes from his own highly egotistical self, but in compensation he is self-revealing, deliberately and otherwise, to an extraordinary degree.

The part he played as a politician will be discernible from his speeches. It was a part which he rated higher in his own mind than all his other activities; he was the sort of man not infrequently met with today, who once he has touched politics finds everything else dust and ashes in comparison. But unfortunately the political role in which Cicero cast himself was one in which he could not succeed. For what he wanted was unrealizable. His central interest (in very Roman fashion) being the state, he resembled his contemporaries in having no constructive ideas for its much needed reform. Instead he looked back longingly and conservatively to a stable and balanced Republic, with each of its parts keeping loyally to its proper functions in pursuit of the common good and submitting voluntarily to the guidance of a small élite of enlightened leaders. But the old order which Cicero saw in so rosy a light had never truly existed in this ideal form. More important, it certainly could not be brought into existence now. The noblemen were too reactionary, the businessmen too grasping, the poor too poor, Pompeius and Caesar too ambitious. So Cicero's political ideal, to which he devoted so much labour and tortuous ingenuity, and in pursuit of which he suffered such disappointments, was a nostalgic vision – a vision of a certain romantic grandeur, but far too deeply rooted in that venerable, quasi-legendary tradition which meant so much to Romans.

Yet Cicero was the keenest of observers of the contemporary scene, and it would obviously be an exaggeration to regard this highly intelligent man as nothing but unrealistic. For one thing, it was brought to his notice only too clearly that his ideal state was now bound, in practice, to be modified by the predominance of some single powerful individual. He therefore formed the ambition, derived from Greek models, of becoming the political, philosophical and ethical mentor of that individual. He never could quite bring himself, however, to offer these services to Caesar, since for all Caesar's brilliance, tactful clemency and courtesy – and for all his similarity to Cicero in culture and persuasiveness – the orator was left with an uncomfortable, ineradicable and perfectly accurate conviction that Caesar intended the death of the Republic. So, possibly, did Pompeius, but less certainly; and so it was to this tricky man, an excellent soldier but lacking in political sense, that Cicero, with frequently recurrent misgivings, attached himself. But any idea of becoming Pompeius' mentor was ruled out, because Pompeius would have scoffed at the idea. What infuriated him most was that after his phenomenal victories in the east (67–63 B.C.) Cicero did nothing but utter self-praise about his own achievement at home in putting down the Catilinarian conspiracy as consul.

This was a conflict between vanities. Readers will be appalled at the boastfulness of Cicero in these speeches. He blows his own trumpet with an unremitting loudness which can scarcely be paralleled. Its worst and most strident notes are due to the justified fear that his contemporaries, not to speak of posterity, might think that in his handling of the conspiracy of Catilina (and notably in the executions that followed) he had acted illegally and wrongly. This would not do at all, since it was a cardinal feature of his life, a psychological and political necessity, to believe he himself had behaved marvellously – and to persuade the world of this. We must remember that our particular conventions about modesty are not necessarily always the best – and indeed are sometimes irksome. For example, imagine you were a tennis-player of Wimbledon standard, about to play a friendly singles game and asked how good you were: if you replied, 'Not much good,' this would subsequently prove embarrassing for all. Besides, the conception which prompts such self-depreciation is localized in space as well as time. A brilliant western applicant for a Chair in a middle-eastern country failed to secure the post because, in reply to a question whether he knew a lot about the subject, he answered like the tennis-player I mentioned above. ('Well, if he himself says he doesn't know much about it, how can we appoint him?') These *autres moeurs* must be borne in mind when Cicero's immodesty horrifies us. So must the importance which Romans, like ancient Greeks and Renaissance Italians, attached to glory. The only way to defy mortality is to live on the lips of men: 'honour', as Aristotle declared, 'is the reward of excellence and it is assigned to the good.' Nevertheless, all this still remains insufficient justification for Cicero's self-praise, which seemed altogether excessive even to his own fellow-citizens and contemporaries. Their view is reflected in his *Life* by Plutarch, who said that 'this unpleasing habit of his clung to him like fate'.

But it was not mere vanity. Curiously enough, Cicero's writings about philosophy and rhetoric show him as a relatively modest man. His political boasting had a purpose, and that purpose was derived from the situation in which Cicero found himself. Holding, as he did, that it was necessary for his consulship and other political deeds to be praised, he found that there was a dearth of supporters prepared to say the same with sufficient loudness, frequency and eloquence. This was largely because of his crippling disadvantage of being a 'new man', whose ancestors had never held a consulship. In a city where some twenty families controlled Senatorial policy very few 'new men' broke into the charmed, exclusive circle; and Cicero pointed out that in the past thirty years he was the very first son of a knight (that is to say, not of a Senator) to reach the consulship at all. A new man lacked the immense sources of influence available to the great families; and Cicero, it must be admitted, became consul not through merit alone – as he liked to declare – but because a faction among the nobles, afraid of something worse, unenthusiastically and temporarily opened its gates. But Cicero was out of his league among these better born, far richer, desperately hard men whose shifting combinations had for so long dominated the state. He had to accept many humiliating failures and compromises, especially as he himself was far from tough – a vain, timid, mercurial character, with the lawyer's ability to see both sides of a question all too clearly.

But Cicero was also peace-loving, free from envy, extremely clever, sometimes idealistic and on the whole amiable (very few of his letters show any real bad temper). And it is impossible not to feel that his boasting is partly redeemed by an engaging tendency to laugh at himself. When Caesar, amusedly trying to discover just how much flattery he would take, expressed the most fulsome admiration of one of Cicero's poems, but added a little mild criticism, Cicero in surprise asked his brother to find out exactly what the criticism meant. But he added: 'Don't worry, however! It won't make me even a fraction less pleased with it!' Another of Cicero's jokes at his own expense relates to his quaestorship (deputy-governorship) of Sicily (76–5 B.C.) – one quaestor resided at Syracuse, but the other, Cicero, was stationed at Lilybaeum (Marsala). Cicero tells us that he came back to Rome thinking everyone was talking of his marvellous achievements at Lilybaeum. But the first man he met had no idea where he had been, and when Cicero provided a reminder that he had just come from his province, said, 'Ah, yes, Africa.' However, a second person corrected him – and depressingly added: 'Don't you know he was quaestor at Syracuse?'

Cicero's very marked sense of humour comes out strongly in the speech *In Defence of Caelius*. The melodramatic bath-house incident still seems funny, and so do quite a lot of Cicero's jokes – a great tribute when you think of the un-funniness of *Punch* of fifty or even thirty years ago. In his day he was an extremely well-known humorist, master of epigram, irony, satire, anecdote and *double entendre* (in addition, I fear, to the pun), and famous for his entertaining cross-examinations. Caesar used to have Cicero's current witticisms collected and brought to him, and Cicero (who analyses wit at length in one of his treatises) complained that everyone's funny remarks, including even those of the most ponderous of his fellow-citizens, were attributed to him. But the trouble was that this otherwise engaging quality of Cicero's was not a help to his political life; it was yet another hindrance. For one thing, a lot of the jokes were personal. Contemporary taste regarded moral and intellectual failings and even the crudest physical defects as fair game, and Cicero's shafts were sharp and wounding. When the aristocratic Q. Metellus Nepos asked Cicero the snobbish question 'Who was your father?' it was understandable, but not calculated to endear a great family towards him, for Cicero to reply: 'I can scarcely ask you the same question since your mother has made it rather difficult to answer.' Most irritating of all were the witticisms which flowed from Cicero during the Civil War, while he sat, a critical non-combatant, in Pompeius' un-successful camp. 'We still have seven Eagles left' (the Eagle being the standard of the Legion), said someone with an attempt at optimism after the great defeat of Pharsalus. 'Excel-lent,' remarked Cicero, 'if only we were fighting against jackdaws.' How not to make and keep friends!

So even his sense of humour was often yet another disadvantage. What, then, did Cicero have to recommend him as a politician – what made it possible for him to play a role on the competitive stage of Roman politics at all? One gift and one only, a tremendous gift in the circumstances of the time, and a gift which Cicero possessed to an exceptional degree: his genius as a public speaker. Oratory in the ancient world, and especially in the later Roman Republic, was a part of life several thousand times more important than it is now. This went back to the classical Greeks. Their society had relied heavily on oral expression (as it still does), their government was largely conducted by talk and argument in mass gatherings, and rhetoric became one of their principal interests, with as much significance attached to form as to content.

In the fifth century B.C. Corax of Syracuse wrote the first manual on rhetoric, which was defined as an art of persuasion; and he and Tisias taught the art at Athens. The Sophists called the study useful and legitimate, but Plato, although admitting that 'even the wolf is entitled to plead in its own defence', was its severest enemy, because according to Socrates (d. 399) truth was absolute and discoverable (by dialectic), while rhetoric meant trickery and superficiality. Plato was answered by Isocrates (d. 338) who affirmed that speech is what divides us from brutes; that 'nothing done with intelligence is done without speech, but it is the marshal of all actions and of thoughts, and those who have the greatest wisdom use it most';[3] and that rhetoric is the best way of discovering what is probable, and the supreme means of training the Whole Man for citizenship, political activity and life. Aristotle's *Rhetoric* added that those speaking the truth have an obligation to be persuasive, and that rhetoric and Plato's dialectic are not contradictory but related. This point of view won a large measure of acceptance, and later Greek experts, among

3. Isocrates, *Nicocles*, 5 ff.; cf. *Antidosis*, 253 ff.

whom Hermagoras of Temnos (*c.* 150 B.C.) was the most eminent, proceeded to formulate that staggering multitude of detailed rules, classifications and subdivisions which awakened some echo in Elizabethan England but nowadays leave us feeling we are in the presence of a totally alien way of existence.

In Republican Rome public speaking assumed the same vital and urgent role as in Greece, and when Rome became important the orator began to discuss increasingly vital issues and consequently to possess an immense personal power for good and ill. No activity more adequately reflected Roman ideals and aspirations, or was more highly esteemed for its practical effectiveness in law and politics. These were the only respectable civil careers open to the Romans, and advocacy was as honourable as fighting. There were also huge benefits to be won, not necessarily in fees, which were forbidden (though evasions were frequent), but in gifts, loans, bequests, favours and political advancement. Even under the emperors, when speech had become less free, Tacitus makes a spokesman in his *Dialogue on Orators* describe the profession in these superlative terms:

You cannot imagine any profession in the whole country more productive of practical benefits, or that carries with it a sweeter sense of satisfaction, or that does more to enhance a man's personal standing, or that brings more honour and renown here in Rome, or that secures a more brilliant reputation throughout the Empire and in the world at large. . . . Can there be any safer line to take than the practice of an art which gives you an ever-ready weapon with which to protect your friends, to succour those to whom you are a stranger, to bring deliverance to persons in jeopardy, and even to strike fear and terror into the hearts of malignant foes – while you yourself have no anxiety, entrenched as you are behind a rampart of inalienable authority and power? . . . Can vast wealth or great power bring with it any satisfaction comparable to the sight of grave and reverend seniors, men with the whole world at their feet, freely owning that, though in circumstances of the utmost affluence, they lack the greatest gift of all?[4]

More astonishing still was the extent to which the entire structure of Roman higher education, and the greater part of secondary education also, was geared to training in oratory. Greek rhetoricians, especially from Athens and Rhodes, had come to Rome during the second century B.C., and in c. 95–3 B.C. the first school for Latin rhetoricians was opened. Soon afterwards it was suppressed – because conservatives did not want these dangerous techniques to spread too widely – but the floodgates could not be kept closed, and within a very few years Roman education became dominated by speech training, consisting chiefly of tuition in declamation, both as a practical exercise and a social grace. The best pupil was the best speaker. This was a rhetorician's world, and its ideal was an orator.

There followed a whole array of textbooks, based on innumerable Hellenistic models but also reflecting specifically Roman concerns. The most notable are those of Cicero, which – although a valedictory tribute to a political order already passing away – are peculiarly valuable since it is so rare for a first-rate exponent to describe his own art so well; then came Quintilian who in the first century A.D. became the first salaried professor of rhetoric. These works reveal the fantastic thoroughness and intricacy of the instruction that was regarded as necessary. For instance, they indicate at length the profound significance attached to the smallest minutiae of delivery, including care of the throat (with exercises to avoid strain on a hot or wet or windy day), breath-control and voice-production (one orator shouted so loud he drowned the proceedings in neighbouring courts), tone variation (the beginning of the speech for Milo was quoted as an example), carriage, expression, eyebrow movement, bearing of neck,

4. Tacitus, *Dialogus de Oratoribus*, 5 f. (translated by W. Peterson).

chin and shoulders, gestures (the detailed doctrine, compared to acting on the stage, reaches a startling degree of elaboration), toga-arrangement, stance (not too much walking – an orator was once asked how many miles he had spoken), the production of tears at necessary junctures (Cicero managed this on behalf of Milo, but his client was much too stone-faced), and action of the lips ('do not twist them sideways until they nearly reach the ear'). No wonder the speaker was told that he must keep fit by walking, simple living and looking after his digestion.

No wonder also that Cicero remarks more than once in these speeches that an orator had no time left for social life. Cicero himself, it is true, managed to find time for many other activities, but his great strength lay in the fact that he had pursued all this oratorical training and preparation so meticulously, professionally and successfully that every time he opened his mouth the powers of persuasion he exercised upon his audiences were fabulous and unequalled. The ancients, who liked comparing Romans with Greeks, inevitably compared Cicero with Demosthenes (d. 322 B.C.). The literary critic known as Longinus (now usually ascribed to the first century A.D.) sees Demosthenes as a thunderbolt, Cicero as a steady blaze. Quintilian realizes that Demosthenes, having come first, could not have failed to influence him, but finds all the same that Cicero's excellences really 'spring from the outstandingly abundant fertility of his own superhuman genius – the greatest artist who ever played on the strings of men's hearts'.[5] That he possessed this astonishing persuasiveness is a matter not of conjecture, or of whether one regards Cicero as lovable or not, but of undeniable historical fact. He won a fantastic number of cases, often against the severest odds.

How did he do it? To begin with, he knows all the technicalities. Analyses of his speeches, notably the defence of

5. Quintilian, *Institutio Oratoria*, X, i, 108 f., XI, i, 85.

Milo and even (it now seems) the unorthodox oration for Archias, show every sign of them behind the scenes. He knows all about the five parts of rhetoric and the three styles – the plain designed to teach, the grand intended to move, the middle to give pleasure: the orator himself regarded his speech on Pompeius' command as a typical example of this last – another is the speech for Caelius, delivered with swift changes of mood and manner, before tired and irritable judges. But he also stresses that these are not watertight compartments, that there are many overflows, that a speaker must be a master of all three styles, that there are as many styles as speakers, and that the best speaker must be able to manage them all. Cicero did just this. 'Like a spreading conflagration,' said Longinus, 'he ranges and rolls over the whole field.' His impeccable, gorgeous, ever-changing language, with its elaborate, resounding, clanging rhythms which obey and exploit (to the surprise of moderns) rules as intricate as those of the most formal poetry, has in many or most epochs of subsequent European literature been regarded as the greatest of all Latin prose; and he himself has been described as the most consummate prose stylist who has ever lived, with the possible exception of Plato.[6]

Cicero, with an obliqueness which is all the modesty one ought to expect from such a peerless authority, expresses in his treatises the immense and varied qualities which gave him absolute mastery, when he describes those that were lacking in the orators he used to hear around him during his youth.

There was not one of them who gave the impression of having read more deeply than the average man, and reading is the well-spring of perfect eloquence; no one whose studies had embraced philosophy, the mother of excellence in deeds and in words; no one who had mastered thoroughly the civil law, a subject absolutely essential to

6. For more on this subject, and for the problems it sets the translator, see *Cicero: Selected Works*, pp. 20 ff.

equip the orator with the knowledge and practical judgement requisite for the conduct of private suits; no one who knew thoroughly Roman history, from which as occasion demanded he could summon as from the dead unimpeachable witnesses; no one who with brief and pointed jest at his opponent's expense was able to relax the attention of the court and pass for a moment from the seriousness of the business in hand to provoke a smile or open laughter; no one who understood how to amplify his case, and, from a question restricted to a particular person and time, transfer it to universals; no one who knew how to enliven it with brief digression; no one who could inspire in the judge a feeling of angry indignation, or move him to tears, or in short (and this is the one supreme characteristic of the orator) sway his feelings in whatever direction the situation demanded.[7]

Enough has been said above of the 'brief and pointed jests', but the rest of the passage shows clearly two especially important features of Cicero's approach to his job. In the first place, he rises far beyond the rhetoricians' rules and insists on a very wide range of knowledge. He worked incessantly to possess this himself, succeeding thoroughly (even, perhaps, in law, though here the consultation of experts remained necessary). This more generous interpretation was a return from narrow Hellenistic conceptions to the more versatile classical ideal of Isocrates' Whole Man. The wide and liberal qualifications on which Cicero insisted made him agree with Aristotle that the conflict between rhetoric and philosophy was unreal: 'to speak copiously and elegantly on the most important subjects is in itself the most important philosophy.' Furthermore, philosophy being ethical (especially to the morally minded Romans), this meant that the orator had to be not only a learned but a virtuous man: already in the second century B.C. Cato the Censor had described the orator as 'a good man skilled in speaking', and this congenial idea was at the back of all Cicero's theorizing. He was deeply conscious of the responsibility that orators could wield in the society of

7. Cicero, *Brutus*, XCIII, 322 (translated by G. L. Hendrickson).

his day – the equivalent of press, pulpit and university combined – and he felt they were better equipped than anyone else to preach the good life.

However, the concluding part of that quotation from the *Brutus* also lays great stress on a second and quite different thing that the Roman orator had to do. He had to arouse that emotion which the rhetoricians had already regarded as the function of one of their three styles. And Cicero's unprecedented capacity to do this, not by adopting any particular stylistic category but by playing on every human chord, was the real key to his success. These rock-faced Romans were wildly excitable – a disconcerting blend between highly efficient Prussians and the most volatile of southerners. Cicero, who possessed impressive looks and who although never really robust kept himself in good health, had a magnificent voice, which he cured of a tendency to speak too loud – though he could still be heard all over the Forum. He observed that an orator's power depended on three things, first delivery, second delivery and third delivery; and he knew and asserted that audiences decide more problems by emotion than by reason.

There is unanimous evidence of his learning his lesson so well that he possessed an almost uncanny power to exploit the electric atmosphere that surrounded him, whipping up the feelings of his audiences to an extraordinary and indeed abnormal degree. Often he displayed passion himself: 'Many a time,' he makes his brother Quintus say, 'I have seen in you such passion of look and gesture that I thought some power was rendering you unconscious of what you did.'[8] But whether the feeling was genuine or not, the demonstration was very deliberate. However much his enemies mocked at these tear-drops, his method was immensely successful, skilful and insidious; as Quintilian remarks, 'Cicero appears to obtain as a favour what he is really extracting by force, and the judge, in reality forcibly carried away by Cicero, does not

8. Cicero, *De Divinatione*, I, xxxviii, 80.

know that he is being swept away but thinks he is following voluntarily.'⁹ One of the greatest tributes to his powers – and there is no reason to doubt the story – was supplied, despite himself, by Caesar the dictator, whose extreme strength of mind must have made him relatively impervious to techniques he perfectly well understood. 'It is said that when Quintus Ligarius was being prosecuted as one of Caesar's enemies and Cicero was defending him, Caesar said to his friends: "Why should we not hear a speech from Cicero after all this time? As for Ligarius, we have long known him to be guilty and an enemy." But when Cicero began to speak, his words were incredibly moving; and as his speech proceeded, ranging in the most wonderfully charming language from one emotion to another, the colour came and went on Caesar's face and it was evident that every passion of his soul was stirred. And finally, when the orator touched on the battle at Pharsalus, Caesar was so deeply affected that his whole body shook, and the papers that he was holding dropped from his hand. So he was overpowered, and acquitted Ligarius.'¹⁰ Cicero's was a fabulous talent; but, unfortunately for him as a statesman, even this was not enough to counterbalance his political disabilities.

Unfortunately again – this time from the point of view of the moralist – there is no doubt that the very special talent evolved by Cicero clashed with his ethical ideals. Contemporary politics being what they were, he was frequently compelled or induced by circumstances to champion unworthy causes for short-term results; and his peculiar gifts often enabled him to guide them to success. Like Mr Jaggers in Dickens's *Great Expectations*, he believed – and he felt able to announce quite openly – that 'it is sometimes the business of the advocate to maintain what is plausible even if it be not

9. Quintilian, *Institutio Oratoria*, X, i, 105 ff.
10. Plutarch, *Life of Cicero*, 39 (translated by Rex Warner).

strictly true'. This is very relevant to the present volume, in which one of Cicero's clients, Milo, was almost certainly a murderer; and so perhaps was another, Caelius, maybe several times over – in the speech, such perilous matters are brushed quickly aside, and the orator dwells on safer trivialities at humorous length. Moreover, the same speech declares that Caelius' previous boss Catilina (abused in extravagant terms seven years earlier) had the makings of not such a bad fellow after all – whom Cicero had even once considered defending himself! And then again, in the speech on behalf of Marcellus, Caesar is fulsomely praised only two years before Cicero was applauding his murder, in equally vigorous terms. Startling inconsistencies abound. Surely the promising, reformed son-in-law Publius Dolabella of the First and Second Philippics cannot be the same unmentionable man as the sadist of the Eleventh? But Cicero is quite prepared to boast privately of hoodwinking judges ('Let me tell you that it was I who produced the necessary darkness in the court to prevent your guilt from being visible to everyone'), and in one speech opportunistic inconsistency is elevated into a principle. 'It is the greatest possible mistake to suppose that the speeches we barristers have made in court contain our considered and certified opinions: all those speeches reflect the demands of some particular case or emergency.'[11] Crassus wondered why Cicero, who disliked him and said so, had praised him earlier; the reply he received was that it is good practice for an orator to make a speech on a bad subject.

But this situation cannot, of course, be fairly judged except in the light of the circumstances of the time. Among his contemporaries Cicero was nearly the most high-minded of any (next to Cato and Brutus, who were both, however, capable of descending to considerable inhumanity). He also felt able to point out that his dishonest, or subjective, practice was in

11. Cicero, *Pro Cluentio*, L, 139.

keeping with public opinion as well as ordinary decency –
and with the doctrines of the austere Stoic Panaetius. The fact
of the matter was that a successful orator had to be able to
handle three horses whose tempers, though all refractory,
were refractory in different ways: the Senate, the Assembly
(both these for political cases), and the law courts (for criminal
actions). Of the speeches translated in this book, four were
delivered before the Senate (the first and fourth orations
against Catilina, the encomium of Marcellus, and the First
Philippic), three before the Assembly (the speech on the
command of Pompeius, and the second and third Catilinarians), and three before courts (the defences of Archias, Caelius
and Milo).

The Senate, a council of about 600 members, was technically
no more than advisory, but for centuries it had been the real
head of state, advising the officials – and in particular the two
annually elected consuls – on domestic and foreign policy,
finance and religion, and offering guidance on legislative proposals. Until the second century B.C. its civil authority was
accepted without question. Then this was weakened by the
emergence, in the now wealthy empire, of a strong business
interest outside the Senate, represented by the knights (*equites*)
who, in their way, exploited the provinces even more than Senators did.[12] As his speech about Pompeius' command indicates,
Cicero, a knight's son himself, championed the knights; and
by the end of the Catilinarian incident he had come to consider himself as the architect of a harmonious *Concordia* between the two long-estranged orders of Senate and knights.
This proved unrealizable, but it had been a good idea and
Cicero was not ill placed to bring it into effect, since even
before his loyalty to the knights came his devotion to the
Senate. It was an important part of his conformist traditional-

12. Many of the knights were men from the Italian towns who were
jealous of the Senate because they too wished to rise in the public
service.

ism that he should support this body which was so closely identified of old with the fortunes of the Republic; though many of the more aristocratic Senators never really accepted him as one of themselves, and still less (as he fondly believed after his consulship) as their leader. Sulla (d. 78) had tried to restore the Senate's waning power, but soon afterwards the tribunes of the people, who could veto motions in the anti-Senatorial interest, re-emerged – mainly through the influence of Pompeius and Crassus – and Cicero's enemy Clodius made violently effective use of the tribuneship (58).

The principal necessary qualification for admission to the Senate was tenure of the junior post of quaestor. To this extent membership was indirectly founded on popular elections – since quaestors were elected – though this did not by any means signify that those elected paid attention to their electors. The Senators, who wore tunics with a broad purple stripe and red leather shoes, met in the Senate House or some other consecrated place. Meetings took place between dawn and sunset. Sons and grandsons of Senators were admitted, though not the general public; but the doors were left open. No official record was published until 59, when Caesar, as consul, arranged this in the hope of discrediting his conservative adversaries.

It was customary for the president of the Senate, who was usually one of the consuls, to lay the business before his fellow-members, and ask them what action they desired. First he put the question to the consuls elect (this enforced initiative was embarrassing for Decimus Silanus in the Catilinarian trouble, and he later pretended he had not really meant what he said), and then to the exalted group of former consuls or consulars. Their weight counted more than any votes towards the eventual decision. By Cicero's time, members had formed the custom of leaving their places and moving over to sit with the speakers they supported, whether these were consulars or not. The nineteenth-century Italian artist Cesare Maccari painted a vivid picture of Catilina sitting isolated while Cicero thundered at him.

However, except on especially emotion-fraught occasions such as the Catilinarian plot, thunder was somewhat less in evidence before the comparatively hard-headed and educated Senators than in the Assembly of the Roman people. This was the law-making body of the state and elected the chief officials, voting by groups. It had been customary for the Senate's advice to be listened to – 'people' normally came after 'Senate' in the traditional formula S.P.Q.R. – but the radical or revolutionary statesmen and demagogues of the last century B.C. showed increasing signs of trying to arrange direct action through the Assembly, which earned them the name of *populares* (as against the *optimates* or best people, that is to say the supporters of the traditional order). In his early days, as the speech on Pompeius' command shows, Cicero was quite keen on this sort of shortcut in the interests of the great man whom he was supporting at the time, but later he came to regard the procedure as dangerous to the survival of the Republic. The attendance of any significant proportion of the Assembly's million potential members (or even theoretically two or three millions after the enfranchisement of Italy in the eighties) was clearly inconceivable. Still, a great throng often flocked to the Comitium, the open meeting-place in the Forum, and to the Campus Martius where the principal elections were held. The crowds included numerous residents of Rome (often of rural origin) or of areas not too far away, comprising especially gangs of clients employed by noble families, or toughs directed by leaders like Clodius or Milo. Powerful influence was also exerted by groups of men from the municipalities of Italy, dispatched to Rome by prominent politicians to record their votes; and by soldiers sent to the capital by generals in Cisalpine Gaul (North Italy) for the same purpose.

The Assembly (later to be reduced to total insignificance by Augustus) had never become a unified or truly democratic force. Its authority was theoretically sovereign, but it possessed no more real sovereignty than the English electorate in the eighteenth century. Yet the people were responsible for laws and elections, and it was vital for a public speaker to be able to sway these vast and formidable gatherings – and to sway also the informal popular meetings which the consuls could bring together to report, prepare, explain or solicit support. These audiences were highly excitable and irrational. The speeches Cicero addressed to them contain a good deal of religious emotion which did not come really from the heart; but if he thought it worth while to inject this element, then worth while it was, for no one can doubt his ability to handle the Assembly superbly. Some think Cicero may be the man to whom Virgil is referring when Neptune's power over the waves is compared to the control of a mighty concourse by an orator.

> As when in tumults rise the ignoble crowd,
> Mad are their motions, and their tongues are loud;
> And stones and brands in rattling volleys fly,
> And all the rustic arms that fury can supply:
> If then some grave and pious man appear,
> They hush their noise, and lend a listening ear:
> He soothes with sober words their angry mood,
> And quenches their innate desire of blood.[13]

Cicero was also king of the law courts, as Quintilian very justly described him. The first permanent criminal court (relating to extortion, with special reference to the corrupt misgovernment of provinces) had been set up during the second century B.C. Others, each concerned with a special field such as murder, violence, treason, etc., were established soon after 100 B.C.

13. Virgil, *Aeneid*, I, ll. 148 ff. (translated by John Dryden).

It is not certain which law court tried the action against Archias, whose defence by Cicero appears in this book – possibly the treason court, which possessed terms of reference vague enough to cover even a mere franchise case such as this. Caelius, whom Cicero also defended, was before the tribunal concerned with violence, a number of apparently inappropriate charges being lumped together because this law, too, had wide scope, and in any case a variety of courts could not be mobilized as it was holiday time. The prosecution of Milo was brought, in the first instance, before a special new court created for an emergency by Pompeius, much to Cicero's disapproval.

These courts gave the Romans an opportunity to exercise their unrivalled talent for law. However, the contents of some of the speeches, and particularly their invective and irrelevance, will surprise modern jurists; and it must be added that corruption was far from impossible. Every court consisted of thirty or more judges or jurymen, under the presidency of one of the praetors, the state officials who stood next to the consuls in rank. By long tradition the judges had been Senators, but Gaius Gracchus (d. 121) gave these positions – and the extensive source of influence and patronage that they represented – to the knights, thus admitting that criminal justice had a political character. Sulla reversed the process, and between 70 and 46 the task was shared by Senators, knights and a third category known as the tribunes of the treasury, who were similar to the knights but less wealthy – still, they needed to possess a certain minimum amount of property to attain their rank, so that no one could be a judge unless he was a person of substance. As will be seen from the First Philippic, Antonius was credited with a revolutionary intention of removing the property qualifications of judges and admitting ordinary soldiers; though this may only have been a rumour, or an extremist policy to which Antonius had not fully committed himself.

Judges were agreed by the parties concerned, or chosen from a qualified panel; normally they were proposed by the plaintiff, but could be rejected by the defendant. The verdict was by majority vote, with no right of appeal – the president had no vote but inflicted the statutory penalty. Any citizen could initiate a prosecution (tribunes of the people sometimes did so in political cases). The accused might have one or more advocates to speak on his behalf.

It was very unusual for Cicero to act as prosecutor in the courts; his indictment of Verres in 70, which made his name, is a conspicuous exception. He preferred defending, because, as he said, 'briefs for the defence are most likely to bring glory and popularity to the pleader'. When there was more than one speaker for the defence, he chose to speak last, because he had an unrivalled talent for rousing the pity and sympathy of the judges; he made hay with them. In his speech for Archias, he scarcely bothers to talk about the charge at all, yet clearly won his case. His defence of Caelius, though it concerns, among other things, accusations of multiple murder, is scintillating and light-hearted, and was again evidently successful. Only his oration on behalf of Milo did not do the trick, not only because his client was evidently guilty but because Cicero felt intimidated by an armed and exceedingly hostile audience, and did not deliver, or at least did not deliver in full, the brilliant, fantastic collection of implausible arguments that have come down to us.

This brings us, in conclusion, to an awkward but inescapable question. Do any of the speeches bear any real resemblance to what Cicero really said at the time, in Senate or Assembly or court?

We know that some of his most famous orations, such as the Second Philippic and the greater part of the attacks on Verres, were not delivered at all. But most of the others, including all those in this volume with the partial exception of the defence of Milo, were published versions of what he had actually delivered. Usually publication of a speech, if he was satisfied with it, followed almost immediately. But the attacks on Catilina were not published until 60, three years after their delivery. Their anxious and at times defensive tone, unlikely in the euphoric days of the consulship, is indicative of the later date, when euphoria had been swamped by criticism; and our other sources implant a suspicion that the fourth in the series, as delivered, was not really quite so dramatic. Moreover, it is difficult to believe that the Senate, faced with a worrying problem, would have sat through the elaborate appeal by Our Country inserted in the first oration. Admittedly, the Catilinarians represent rather a special case because of the extensive time-lag, but every other published speech, too, was obviously revised, polished and corrected before it was allowed to see the light of day. Sometimes they were enlarged into what almost amounted to brochures. Sometimes, too, speeches were abbreviated. Moreover, they undoubtedly include matter transferred to them from cross-examinations or slanging matches which, on the day, had been quite separate from the speeches (if only we knew what the other side said! The few scathing sentences attributed to Catilina only whet the appetite for more).

Evidently then the works we have before us are not the speeches as they were actually delivered: and so yet another is added to the hideously difficult detective tasks of the ancient historian. Indeed, when Cicero delivered an oration, he had no complete version before him. His method, assisted by the rhetoricians' great emphasis on memory training (still greatly stressed in the east today), was to learn an elaborate introduction and peroration by heart, but to rely on rough notes or skeleton for what came in between. Indeed, more thorough preparation would not have been possible for harangues like some of the Catilinarians, which were stop-press affairs, delivered at a few hours' notice. So they had to be written afterwards – as Cicero himself records. But it is going much too far to say, like a spokesman quoted by the Greek historian Dio Cassius,[14] that Cicero, like persons who fashion generals and cavalry leaders out of clay, had never delivered the beautiful speeches he published. He did deliver them; but thereafter, it is true, they underwent transformation into the literary essays, political manifestos, apologias, eulogies or slanders that were subsequently given to the world.

That is certainly a pity from the point of view of personal immediacy, dramatic excitement, and historical evidence. But the ancients would not have understood our feelings of disillusionment or disappointment about the matter. For, unlike us, they regarded oratory not merely as public speaking but as a magnificent branch of literature. And Cicero's speeches, in the form in which we have them, are the most scintillatingly and perfectly constructed examples of this literary form that have come down to us. Indeed, by their splendour they have swamped almost all other Latin speeches out of existence.[15] They have therefore exerted a massive prolonged influence (punctuated by the contrary reactions which are the penalty of excellence) upon the culture of the western world throughout the two millenniums that have followed.[16]

I owe thanks to Mr A. E. Douglas and the editors of *Greece and Rome* for allowing me to have an advance view of Mr Douglas's survey of Cicero. I am indebted to the Harvard University Press and Messrs Heinemann Ltd, as publishers of the Loeb Classical Library, and to Messrs W. Peterson and G. L. Henrickson the translators, for the excerpts from Tacitus' *Dialogus de Oratoribus* and Cicero's *Brutus* in this Introduction, and to Penguin Books Ltd and Mr Rex Warner

14. Q. Fufius Calenus in Dio, XLVI, 7, 3.

15. The much later *Apologia* of Apuleius and *Apologeticus* of Tertullian are also very brilliant, but in quite a different way.

16. For particulars of this, see *Cicero: Selected Works*, pp. 24 ff.

for the quotation from Plutarch's *Life of Cicero*. I am also deeply grateful to my wife and my son Patrick for unfailing and indispensable assistance in the preparation of this book.

MICHAEL GRANT

CHAPTER ONE

ON THE COMMAND OF
CNAEUS POMPEIUS
(*In Support of the Manilian Law*)

The name Cicero gave this speech is uncertain; perhaps it was called
About the Manilian Law. *It was delivered before the Assembly of
the Roman People in 66* B.C. *Its subject was the war against King
Mithridates VI of Pontus in Asia Minor (Anatolia). During the
previous century Rome had added enormously to its wealth by the
annexation of the western part of that peninsula, the province of
Asia, which was bequeathed to the empire by the last king of
Pergamum (133). But in 120 the region of Pontus to its north-east,
the property of a partially Hellenized Iranian dynasty, had passed
into the hands of its last and most remarkable representative,
Mithridates VI 'the Great'. He seized huge areas of Asia Minor,
and caused many Roman citizens to be assassinated; by the time of
Cicero's oration, he had remained a bitter and dangerous enemy of
Rome for no less than twenty-two years.*

*A succession of Roman generals had failed to put an end to him,
and now Lucius Licinius Lucullus, after initial victories (72), was
being recalled following a severe defeat suffered by one of his lieutenants at Zela. An impressive strategist and administrator, Lucullus
was hampered by unpopularity among his own troops owing to his
excessively disciplinarian attitude, which was out of keeping with the
times. He also alienated the Roman knights by severely restricting
their financial gains in Asia. Conservatives (optimates), including
an influential section of the aristocracy, lined up in his favour, and
those who liked to by-pass the Senate and deal direct with the
Assembly (populares) became his opponents. People of the latter
tendency, suspected by their enemies of a desire for radical innovation, had an obvious candidate for the command in Cnaeus Pompeius,*

33

who had struck against the Senate while consul by enabling the tribunes to recover the powers Sulla had taken away from them, and by reducing senatorial representation on panels of judges to one third (70). Next, in one of the most sensationally efficient campaigns in Roman history, Pompeius terminated the very grave and long-standing pirate menace in the Mediterranean (67).

At that juncture a not particularly reputable tribune of the people, Gaius Manilius, proposed to the Assembly that Pompeius should be appointed to the command against Mithridates, with extremely wide powers; and here we have the published version of the speech which Cicero delivered in support of Manilius' proposal. The ancient historian Dio Cassius, followed by Theodor Mommsen in the nineteenth century, declared that it showed Cicero deserting the nobles for the commons. But probably he had never committed himself deeply to the conservatives, some of whom had, indeed, suffered from his prosecution of Verres in 70. Besides, one of the most interesting features of the speech is the almost acrobatic care with which Cicero, while supporting, as so often, the welfare of the knights from whom he had originated, sought to sugar the pill as far as Lucullus and his 'optimate' friends were concerned.

His motives may be described as enlightened self-interest. From a national point of view he had an excellent case; the prolonged war was a scandal, which Pompeius was the obvious man to terminate, as he did. And from Cicero's personal standpoint the moment was ripe for a political success, since he had just been elected to the office of praetor which entitled him to bring motions before the Assembly. The next step would be the consulship, and in his candidature for that office the support of Pompeius would be invaluable. Besides, the wife of Pompeius, Mucia Tertia, was linked with the great family of the Caecilii Metelli who had helped and employed Cicero in earlier stages of his career.

This, then, was a turning-point in Cicero's fortunes, because from now onwards (though with occasional lapses, as will be seen) his principal allegiance was given to Pompeius – though sometimes to an ideal Pompeius who bore little relation to that gifted but ungracious *hero himself. For Rome, too, the speech was a turning-point, for a bitterly ironic reason. The great command which Cicero's speech caused Pompeius to acquire – and which Caesar also, significantly, supported – became a forerunner of others which within a few years had destroyed the Republic that Cicero was genuinely so eager to preserve. The praise is piled on in a panegyric style which had later offspring (notably the speech for Marcellus) and is more fashionable in the east than the west today. But these deeply significant political circumstances, and the information which Cicero gives us about them, are what makes his speech something of a landmark in the history of Rome and the world. It also contains observations about the sensitivity of national finance which retain their relevance today.*

To face the crowded ranks of your Assembly has always given me a very special satisfaction. No place, it has seemed to me, lends greater dignity to the proposal of a motion, no environment is more impressive for a speech. You provide here, citizens, a road to fame which has always been wide open to every man of merit. And yet to me it has been barred – not indeed by any wish of mine, but because of a plan of life I adopted from the first days of my youth. For at an earlier stage of my life, I was too young to intrude on this imposing place; and I formed the determination never to bring you anything but the maturest and most carefully worked out contributions. Besides, I felt that my entire time ought to be made over to my friends in their hours of peril. Here, on the other hand, people competent to champion your interests were not in short supply.

Besides, my defences of private cases, conducted with all the scrupulous disinterestedness of which I am capable, were honourably rewarded by your approbation. For during successive postponements of the elections to praetorships,[1] I

1. The elections in 67 for the praetorships of the following year were twice interrupted by disturbances.

was on three consecutive occasions pronounced the leader of the poll by the unanimous decision of the voting groups. From this I could see very clearly, citizens, that you intended to pass a generous verdict upon myself, and that you commended a similar course of behaviour to others. And now the influence which you indicated – by entrusting me with this office – that you desired to place in my hands, is mine. Whatever capacity for public speaking I may have been able to derive from almost daily experience and close attention in the courts is mine also. As to the influence, I am happy to exercise it in front of the men who bestowed it upon me. And if I have any ability as a speaker, this, too, I shall be especially glad to display before those very people who decided that oratory was one of the qualifications that deserved to be rewarded by public office.

I am very conscious that there is one special aspect of the matter on which I have reason to congratulate myself. I know I am not accustomed to delivering the sort of oratory which is appropriate to this platform. On the other hand, the cause which I am called upon to support today is one which could leave nobody at a loss for words. For that cause is the outstanding, pre-eminent genius of Cnaeus Pompeius. A speech on such a subject is harder to stop than to start. Finding material is no problem at all; the question is how to keep it within bounds.

I will begin at the point where this whole situation also began. A large-scale war is being conducted against you by two formidable kings, Mithridates and Tigranes,[2] and it gravely menaces not only your allies but your own revenue as well. Mithridates has been left quite free to pursue his own devices – and to Tigranes, on the other hand, we have offered active provocation. For these two reasons, different though they are, both monarchs believe that this is their opportunity to seize the province of Asia. Every day, letters are coming in

2. Tigranes I the Great (*c.* 94–56) was king of Armenia.

from Asia to the good Roman knights[3] whose fortunes, invested on a large scale in the collection of your dues, are now imperilled. I, who am so closely associated with the knights, have been chosen as the recipient of their representations concerning this hazardous threat to their own personal resources: which is, at the same time, an equally grave menace to the interests of our country.

In Bithynia, now a province of yours, numerous villages are reported to have been burnt to the ground. The kingdom of Ariobarzanes,[4] bordering upon your tributary states, is said to be wholly in enemy hands. Lucius Lucullus, after all the fine things he achieved, is withdrawing from the field, and his successor, I am told, is not equipped to conduct a war of this magnitude. One man and one man only, they declare, is universally and insistently wanted for the command. Allies and citizens are unanimous in calling for him; he, and he alone, fills the enemy with fear.

You see the situation. Now consider what ought to be done. I propose to speak first about the nature of the war, then about its importance, and finally about the general who should be chosen to conduct it. The nature of the war is one which ought to stimulate and inspire you to a quite exceptional determination to carry it through to the end. For nothing less than the glory of Rome itself is at stake. This is the mighty heritage that has been handed down to you by your fore-fathers – mighty in every field, but mightiest of all in war. Endangered, too, is the safety of our allies and friends, on whose behalf those ancestors fought so many important wars. And solid, substantial sources of national income are also involved. If you let these go, not only will the funds needed to

3. The knights (*equites*) controlled the corporations which farmed the taxes of Asia, giving the government a fixed sum and keeping what was left over for themselves. See also p. 24.

4. Ariobarzanes I Philoromaeus (95–62) was king of Cappadocia.

pay for the war be lost, but your own peace-time comforts will go as well. And the same peril hangs over the personal property of many of our individual citizens – whom you are under an obligation to protect, both for their own sakes and in the national interests of Rome.

No country has ever equalled yours in its appetite for glory, its passion for renown. It is therefore imperative that you should wipe out the blot which stained Rome's reputation in the first war against Mithridates and has now been left untouched for so long that the blemish is deeply ingrained.

For in many different cities throughout the province of Asia, on one and the same day, by one single order and communication, Mithridates marked down every man who was a citizen of Rome for murder and massacre.[5] And in spite of this, he has totally failed so far to pay any penalty corresponding to the crime. Twenty-two years have passed, and he is still upon the throne – and not only upon the throne, but by no means even content to lurk in his own native hide-outs of Pontus and Cappadocia. On the contrary, out he bursts from his hereditary kingdom in order to occupy states that pay you tribute; while the whole of Asia watches what he does.

For up to now our generals have fought against Mithridates in the sort of way which produces the outward signs of victory, but not victory in any real sense. Lucius Sulla celebrated a Triumph over him, and so did Lucius Murena.[6] Both were brave men and distinguished commanders, and the Triumphs of each of them left the enemy routed and conquered – yet still in possession of his kingdom. All the same, it is proper to compliment those two generals on what they accomplished, and to excuse what they left unaccomplished, because both of

5. In 88 Mithridates' order for the massacre of all Roman citizens in Asia was estimated to have resulted in 80,000 deaths in one day.
6. The Triumphs of L. Cornelius Sulla and L. Licinius Murena were in 83 and 81 respectively.

them were summoned back to Italy. Sulla was recalled by a national emergency; and Murena was recalled by Sulla.

Ever since then Mithridates has been engaged, not by any means in helping to banish the unpleasant memory of the old war, but in preparing for a new one. For he has spent the entire intervening period constructing and fitting out enormous fleets, and raising huge armies from every nation that would help him. His pretext was a war against the neighbouring kingdom of the Crimean Bosphorus. Yet Mithridates also sent envoys all the way to Spain with messages for the Roman commanders against whom our government was then fighting. What he proposed to do was to organize hostilities on land and sea, conducted by widely separated enemies of Rome, operating far apart but closely coordinating their plans – so that you would have to face a world war with your forces split between two distant fronts.

The western menace from Sertorius in Spain,[7] which presented much the more formidable problem of the two, was eliminated by the inspired strategy and exceptional military gifts of Cnaeus Pompeius. In the east, where the eminent Lucius Lucullus[8] was fighting, the course of the campaigns suggests that his conspicuous initial successes must be attributed to his own merits rather than just to good luck, whereas these recent, concluding events, on the other hand, were evidently due to ill-fortune rather than to any deficiencies of his own. About Lucullus I shall be saying something later on, and my words will be framed, gentlemen, in a way calculated neither to diminish the glory he has truly earned nor to magnify it by any fictitious exaggeration.

The point I mentioned first concerned the honour and renown of your empire. May I now, therefore, request you to con-

7. Proscribed by Sulla, Q. Sertorius led an anti-governmental movement in Spain in 82–81 and from 80 until his death in 72.
8. L. Licinius Lucullus conducted the Third Mithridatic War (74–66).

sider the feelings by which you should deem it proper to be guided when these great considerations are at stake.

Whenever, in the past, Roman traders or ship-owners had been treated somewhat high-handedly, our ancestors often went to war for their protection. With this in mind I have to ask you to reflect how you yourselves ought to react when, at one and the same time and on one man's single order, thousand upon thousand of Roman citizens have been slaughtered. Because their emissaries had been rather insolently addressed, your forefathers ordained that Corinth, the shining light of all Greece, must suffer annihilation.[9] Surely you, therefore, will not let off the king who compelled a Roman general of consular rank to endure imprisonment, beating, every kind of torture and finally death.[10] Your ancestors refused to tolerate the slightest restriction upon the liberty of Roman citizens. Will you, on the other hand, remain indifferent when their very lives are taken away from them? The verbal infringement of an envoy's privilege caused those ancestors of yours to retaliate. *Your* envoy, on the other hand, has been subjected to multiple agonies culminating in actual murder – and are you going to pay no attention? Your ancestors won themselves glory by the magnificent empire they handed down to you. See to it that you do not earn a corresponding load of shame by failing to protect and safeguard the heritage you have received as their gift.

And then again, when the safety of your allies is terribly endangered, what should be your response? King Ariobarzanes, the ally and friend of Rome, has been ejected from his kingdom. The entire province of Asia is menaced by two kings who hate your allies and friends as bitterly as they hate yourselves. The danger is so appalling that every community in all

9. The Romans destroyed Corinth in 146.
10. Mithridates defeated and killed Man. Aquilius (88).

Asia and Greece is compelled to look to you for help. To request you to send a particular general would be more than they would dare to do. Indeed, they would regard such a course as highly perilous – especially as you have already sent someone else. And yet, like yourselves, they quite clearly appreciate that there is one man and one man only who possesses all the necessary qualifications, and possesses them in the highest degree. And they see he is near at hand: which makes them miss him all the more. The mere fact of his proximity, as well as his outstanding reputation – even though it is a war not on land but at sea from which he has come – already gives them the optimistic feeling that the attacks of their enemies have been beaten off and relegated to a distant date.

So these people cannot speak out openly. But, mutely, they beg you to treat them at least as well as you treat your allies in every other province; in other words, to deem them worthy of having their safety entrusted to this great man.

Their plea is all the more pressing because of the kind of governor whom we usually send to administer a province. These are generally the sort of people whose defence of their territory against external enemies takes the form of descents upon allied cities which are barely distinguishable from hostile assaults. Whereas this other man, as the provincials had already heard and now see with their own eyes, is so moderate, lenient and kindly that the longer he makes his residence at a particular place the more fortunate its inhabitants are accounted to be.

For the sake of their allies, Romans of earlier generations fought wars[11] against Antiochus, Philip, the Aetolians and Carthage – even though they themselves had received not the slightest injury from any of these foes. By the same token, your own keenness to defend your allies, as well as your own imperial prestige, ought to be intense. For you have been subjected

11. These wars were against the Seleucid Antiochus III the Great (192–188), Philip V of Macedonia (200–197), the Aetolian League (191–189), and Carthage (the three Punic Wars).

to the most damaging provocation, and your principal sources of income are menaced with reduction to nothing. Other provinces, gentlemen, produce so little for us that it is scarcely worth our while to defend them. But Asia, on the other hand, is so extraordinarily wealthy and fertile that the productiveness of its soil, the diversity of its crops, the dimensions of its pasture-land and the volume of its exports exceed those of any other country upon earth.

If therefore, gentlemen, you regard either your success in time of war or your advantage in time of peace as of the slightest importance, it is imperative for you to protect this province from catastrophe – and from the fear of catastrophes to come. In other spheres, loss is not felt until the actual moment of disaster; but where revenue is concerned, the blow does not await the actual onslaughts but falls as soon as people become afraid that they are coming. For the mere approach of a hostile army, even if no attack has yet taken place, already leaves pastures deserted, fields untilled, sea-borne trade at a standstill. That means that harbour duties, tithes and grazing dues all dry up, and so it often happens that a single rumour of peril, a single alarm of war, has the result that an entire year's income is lost.

You can imagine the feelings of the people who pay us taxes, and the men who levy and collect them, when two kings and their enormous armies are in the neighbourhood. A single cavalry raid may carry off a whole year's intake in a moment; and our tax-farmers feel that their substantial staffs in the salt-works and fields and harbours and forts can only be kept there at the gravest possible risk. You surely do not suppose that you can still continue to enjoy all these assets when the men who are working to maintain them for you are no longer accorded your protection and salvation from impending calamity – and, as I said before, from the fear of similar calamities in the future.

There is also another matter which must not be forgotten: when I set out to examine the character of the war I decided to leave it to the end. This relates to the property of all those individual Roman citizens – whose interests, gentlemen, you have the good sense to realize you must take into careful account. For one thing, the respected and well-to-do personages who contracted to collect your taxes have transferred their business and their funds to the Asian province, and they are entitled, in their own right, to look to you for protection of their resources and possessions. We have always understood that our revenues are the sinews of the state. And that being so, we shall be right to maintain that the class which farms them is the mainstay of every other part of the community.

However, there are also further classes of the population which likewise have energetic, hard-working members in Asia, carrying out commercial activities on the spot; and their interests, too, ought to be your concern while they are abroad. And there are many other people besides who have huge sums of money invested in the province. The very least you can humanely do is to rescue this numerous body of Roman citizens from ruin – and, besides, your intelligence will enable you to see that the ruin of a large number of citizens cannot fail to involve the state. The possibility that we may, by a subsequent victory, win back the revenues that the tax-farmers had lost is hardly relevant. The men concerned will be too impoverished to offer another bid for the taxes, and everyone else will be too nervous to feel inclined to make the attempt.

Besides, how can we forget the lesson which this same province of Asia and this same Mithridates taught us at the time when the war in Asia first started?[12] It was a lesson learnt amid direst trouble, since the loss of numerous large fortunes in Asia was immediately followed by a collapse of credit at Rome due to the widespread non-payment of debts. For it is

12. The Romans under L. Triarius were defeated at Zela (67).

not possible for many members of a community to be deprived of their property and fortunes without dragging down still larger members in their downfall. That is the peril which it is your duty to avert from our country now. Believe me when I tell you – though indeed you can see it for yourselves – that this whole system of credit and finance which exists here in the Forum at Rome is directly linked and bound up with the money that is invested in Asia. If that is lost, then our Roman finances, too, are inevitably involved in the same process of upheaval and collapse.

It is your duty, then, to prosecute the war with all the earnestness within your power. Your glorious prestige must be defended; and so must the safety of your allies. You have also got to protect your principal sources of income, and the fortunes of a large number of individual citizens – which cannot be separated from the interests of the state.

Now that I have said something about the character of the war, it remains for me to add a few words about its dimensions. This is to counter possible suggestions that, while the nature of the war admittedly makes it necessary to fight, the operations are nevertheless not significant enough to be really formidable. My most important task here is to ensure that you should think it worth while to show the requisite amount of foresight. And indeed to avoid failure in this respect ought to be your principal concern.

I should like to make one thing clear to everyone. I maintain that Lucius Lucullus deserves the credit due to a brave soldier, a wise man and a fine general. At the time of his arrival, as you know, the armies of Mithridates were of considerable size and thoroughly well equipped and prepared. The king in person, with an extremely substantial force, had invested Cyzicus, the finest city in Asia and a very good friend to ourselves, and had vigorously pressed home his assault. It was the gallantry, perseverance and skill of Lucullus which relieved the place from the desperate perils of that siege. Moreover, let me remind you that, at the same time, a large and well-appointed fleet, commanded by supporters of Sertorius, was speeding against Italy filled with all the savage rancour which party feeling can foment. That fleet was defeated and sunk by Lucullus. He also fought numerous land-battles, in which he destroyed big enemy forces. This gave our legions access to the kingdom of Pontus, which had hitherto been completely closed to Roman troops. The conclusion of the matter was that, at the very first instant of Lucullus' approach and arrival, Sinope and Amisus – which contained the king's extravagantly well-provided palaces – fell straight into his hands, and so did numerous other cities of Pontus and Cappadocia. Thereupon the king, stripped of the realm that had belonged to his father and grandfather before him, fled to foreign monarchs and peoples and sought refuge as a suppliant. And all this was achieved without the smallest damage to Rome's allies or financial expectations. Gentlemen, this is surely high praise of Lucullus. Indeed, none of the men who oppose the cause and measure for which I am speaking have stood here and praised him as highly.

Yet perhaps it will now be asked how, after all this has been done, any significant part of the war can still remain uncompleted. Now this point, gentlemen, is clearly a reasonable one, and I will give you the answer. Let me start by saying that the way in which Mithridates escaped from his kingdom is reminiscent of the flight in which Medea, according to the myth, once betook herself from this selfsame country of Pontus. As she fled, the story goes, she scattered the limbs of her brother along the route where her father was likely to follow, with the intention that his pursuit should be slowed down and delayed by fatherly sorrow, as he collected each successive piece of his son's body in one place after another. That is very much what Mithridates did. As he went, he left behind him in Pontus an enormous quantity of gold and silver and all the beautiful things which he had inherited from his ancestors and which he himself during the earlier war had plundered from all parts of Asia and accumulated in his own kingdom. Our soldiers were too intent upon picking all this up; and meanwhile the king slipped through their hands. Medea's father Aeetes had been delayed by grief – but our men were slowed down by more pleasurable experiences. And so the terrified fugitive found asylum with Tigranes, the king of Armenia, who comforted his desperate guest and gave him new strength and life when all seemed lost.

As Lucullus next proceeded to enter Armenia with his army, a number of fresh states erupted into hostile activity against our commander: for all these nations, which Rome had never thought of directly attacking or even provoking by unfriendly acts, had taken fright. Besides, the barbarian communities had formed a powerful and fanatical conviction that the purpose of our army's arrival in these regions was to plunder a certain extremely wealthy and holy shrine. In consequence of this idea, many large tribes became a prey to quite unprecedented terrors and alarms. Our own troops too, although they had captured one of Tigranes' towns and had gained victories in the field, began to feel upset because they were so far from home and missed their own people. That is all I shall say at this juncture; for the end of the story was that our men became less keen on extending their advance than on withdrawing from the country as early as they possibly could. Meanwhile Mithridates had not only rallied his own forces, but had secured the support of large foreign contingents from many kings and nations. This, one sees, is what almost always happens – kings in trouble easily attract pity and help from many quarters, and particularly from people who are either kings themselves or, because they live in kingdoms, respect and venerate the name of king.

And so Mithridates, after his defeat, looked like accomplishing more than he had ever dared to hope for before he had been defeated. He made his way back to his own kingdom. Once there, the wholly unexpected achievement of returning to the homeland from which he had been driven was by no means enough to content him, and our army, for all its distinguished and victorious record, was subjected to his attack. At this point, gentlemen, I must be allowed to employ the licence usual to poets writing about Roman history, and to pass over the disaster which now overtook us. It was so complete that no messenger even came from the battle-field to tell the general what had happened. He learnt of it from rumours that were passing from mouth to mouth.

At this juncture, in the hour of disaster and total rout, you ruled, gentlemen, that in accordance with ancient precedent a limit should be set to the long duration of Lucullus' command. Accordingly – although he might perhaps have been able to some extent to remedy the deplorable situation – he was compelled by your orders to demobilize a number of his soldiers who had already served their time, and he handed others over to Manius Glabrio. There are a good many points about which I am deliberately saying nothing at all. But please try to imagine what they are, and thus appreciate the formidable range of a war coordinated by two powerful kings, resuscitated by a seething mass of tribes, taken up by whole countries that had up till now been wholly unconnected with the fighting: and recently entrusted, on our side, to a new general – just at the moment when our former army has been overwhelmed.

I think I have said enough to explain, first, why the character of this war means that it is inevitable, secondly, why its dimensions make it dangerous. Next, I feel I should speak about the commander whom we ought to choose to conduct the campaign and assume responsibility for all the major issues involved.

Gentlemen, I only wish the supply of brave and honest generals at your disposal was so large that the selection of a man to put in charge of these major operations and all that they involve presented some problem. In fact, however, Cnaeus Pompeius is in the unique position of not only exceeding all his contemporaries in merit but even eclipsing every figure recorded from the past. That being so, surely there is no reason whatever to feel the slightest misgivings about such a choice.

The ideal general, I submit, should possess four qualities – military knowledge, talent, prestige and luck. In knowledge of military affairs Pompey has never been surpassed, nor has anyone ever been in a position to do so. For here was a man who moved straight from school and the classroom into the practical study of war: and this took place in his father's own army, while it was engaged in a terrible struggle against the bitterest of foes.[13] When Cnaeus Pompeius was scarcely more than a boy he served under a general of outstanding distinction, and after he had only just become a man he himself commanded a mighty army. Take anyone else's disputes in the law courts, against his own private enemies: the engagements fought by Pompeius on the field of battle, against the national enemies of Rome, outnumber them all. He has waged more wars than other people have read about, held more public offices than anyone else has even dreamt he might possess. As a young man, he learnt the art of war not from what others taught him but from the high commands he occupied himself. He had no need of years of service and military adversity to teach him what to do. His instructors were his own victories, the Triumphs he had earned for himself.

The varying fortunes of Rome have given him experience of every conceivable sort of fighting. The Civil War, the

13. Pompeius was with his father Cn. Pompeius Strabo in the Marsian War (89–88).

African, Transalpine and Spanish Wars, the war against the slaves, the naval war against the pirates,[14] were campaigns involving the greatest possible diversity of conditions and opponents. They were conducted and won, all of them, by his own unaided endeavours – and they proclaim that the entire range of military experience contains nothing beyond the scope of what this man knows.

The abilities of Cnaeus Pompeius are too vast for any words to do them justice. No imaginable compliments would be worthy of him, or new to you, or unfamiliar to any single person. The talents a general needs are numerous. Among them are some which are well known – meticulous organization, courage in danger, painstaking execution, prompt action, foresight in planning. In each and every one of those qualities Pompeius excels all other generals we have ever seen or heard of. Italy bears witness to this, for the conqueror Sulla himself admitted the great debt its liberation owed to the valiant support of Pompeius. Another witness is Sicily,[15] where a variety of dangers beset the island on every side; but he dispelled them all, not by the terrors of a prolonged war but by tactics of lightning rapidity. Gaul, too, can show evidence of Pompey's talents as a commander, since it was by the elimination of obstructive Gaulish tribesmen that access to Spain was opened for our legions. From Spain also comes a testimonial of its own, since the foes of Rome who in that land were overcome and laid low by Pompeius could be numbered in multitudes. And then, over and over again, it is Italy which testifies to the genius of Pompeius. For when the country was in the toils of a shameful and menacing slave rebellion, it called to him for aid, although he was far away. The mere

14. These wars were the Civil War in Italy (83–82), campaigns in Africa against Marians and Numidians (81), in Gaul on his way to Spain (76) and in Spain (73–72), the last phase of the Slave War against Spartacus (71), and the Pirate War (67).

15. Pompeius recovered Sicily from the Marians (81).

expectation of his coming reduced the war to insignificant proportions, and his actual arrival sank it without a trace.

But indeed every place upon earth can give comparable evidence, and every foreign nation and state, and all the seas as well – their open expanses tell the same story, and so do the creeks and harbours of each separate stretch of coast. During recent years not one single point along the entire seaboard was strongly enough defended to be safe, or sufficiently well hidden to escape the onslaught of the pirates. Every man who went out in a ship risked death or slavery; unless he sailed in winter, the only alternative was to embark on a pirate-infested sea. It seemed unimaginable that a war which was so formidable, so humiliating, so prolonged, so extensive and so widespread could be brought to an end in a single year, even if any number of Roman generals took a hand; and if there were only one general, he surely could not finish it in all the years of his life. For throughout this whole period of years there was not a single province which you managed to keep free of pirates. There was no part of your revenue that you could feel was safe. Not one of your allies enjoyed your protection, and your fleet was no help to anybody at all. It is common knowledge that island after island was left deserted, and city after city evacuated in a panic or captured by pirate fleets.

But there is no need for me to talk of events that took place so many miles away. In past times it was the peculiar character-istic of the Romans that their wars were fought at a distance from the homeland. In those days the bulwarks of our country had no call to defend the habitations of its own citizens; it was their task to protect the property of our allies instead. But as for the years just past, on the other hand, what need is there to remind you that the sea has been closed against your allies, seeing that your own armies, too, never even dared venture upon the crossing from Brundisium except in the depths of winter? Emissaries on their way to you from foreign nations have been seized. But what is the use of complaining about that, when the ambassadors of Rome itself have been held to ransom? Nor would there be much point in lamenting the perils of the sea for businessmen, in circumstances which actually allowed the pirates to capture two Roman praetors; and to complain about the loss of famous cities such as Cnidus or Colophon or Samos, or any number of others, would be a waste of time when you are fully aware that your very own harbours, which are the breath of life to you, have been in the pirates' hands. The illustrious port of Caieta, as you well know, was raided by pirates right under the eyes of a praetor,[16] at a time when it was crammed with ships: while a man who had earlier fought against the pirates at Misenum had his children kidnapped by them at the very same place. And a particularly scandalous blot on our reputation was the disastrous raid on Ostia. Yet even this scarcely merits a protesting word, when almost before your own eyes a naval contingent important enough for a consul of Rome to be its commander was captured by the pirates and sunk to the bottom of the sea.

In contrast to that sad story the talent of this single individual has achieved what would surely have been regarded as beyond the bounds of all possibility and human capacity.[17] Within an extraordinarily brief space of time, he has brightened our national situation to such an extent that, in place of your recent experience of sighting an enemy fleet immediately off the mouth of the Tiber, you now have news brought to you that there is no longer one single pirate ship anywhere this side of the Atlantic Ocean. You know the amazing rapidity with

16. This praetor may have been M. Antonius Creticus (74), and the kidnapped girl ('children') his sister. Their father was M. Antonius Orator who celebrated a Triumph against the pirates in 102.

17. The reference is to the appointment of Pompeius to the command against the pirates in 67.

which he accomplished all this; but all the same I cannot resist saying something about it. For nobody at any epoch – not even the keenest or most profit-loving trader – has ever managed to move so speedily from place to place, or to cover the immense distances traversed by Pompeius' fleet when the mighty shock of his attack swept over the seas. The fact that it was not yet the season for navigation did not prevent him from crossing to Sicily, exploring the shores of Africa, landing in Sardinia and planting powerful units of the army and navy to secure these three granaries of Rome. Returning next to Italy, he dispatched military and naval detachments to strengthen the two provinces of Spain and Transalpine Gaul, and sent ships along the Adriatic seaboard of Illyricum and on to the Peloponnese and every other part of the coasts of Greece. And so the two seas of Italy were fortified with mighty fleets and impressive garrisons.

He himself, however, left from Brundisium, and within forty-nine days thereafter he had added Cilicia to the Roman empire. All pirates, wherever they might be, were either taken prisoner and put to death, or surrendered themselves into his unaided hands. When pirates from Crete sent envoys all the way to Pamphylia in order to see him and plead for mercy, he indicated that the prospects of surrender were not hopeless, and requested them to hand over hostages.[18] And so this immense, long-drawn-out war, extending over an enormous area and weighing heavily upon every country and nation, was planned by Cnaeus Pompeius at the end of a winter, tackled in earliest spring, and carried to its conclusion before midsummer of the selfsame year.

Such is his incredible, immortal genius as a commander. But a little while back I was beginning to speak of his other qualities

18. Q. Caecilius Metellus Creticus conquered Crete (68–66), but Pompeius accepted its submission and unsuccessfully sent two representatives to occupy the island.

as well; and they too are as superlative as they are numerous.

In the consummate, perfect general, military ability is by no means all that we have to look for. On the contrary, such gifts need to be accompanied and supported by a variety of other notable talents. In the first place, a general needs to possess complete integrity. He must also be a man of moderation in all that he does. He has to be trustworthy; and he has to be accessible, intelligent and civilized as well.

Let me now review these characteristics as they are found in Cnaeus Pompeius. Gentlemen, he has them all – in the highest possible degree. Compare him with other men, and you will recognize and appreciate his possession of such qualities even more easily than if you consider them by themselves. The sort of commanding officer who has sold, and still sells, centurions' commissions cannot be held in the smallest esteem. Nor is it possible to ascribe noble, elevated patriotic sentiments to the kind of man who is so eager to retain his provincial command that he doles out to Roman officials the money he drew from the treasury for the conduct of the war – or who, alternatively, is so acquisitive that he has left these funds profitably invested at Rome. Gentlemen, I hear from your disapproving murmurs that you do not fail to identify the functionaries who have acted in this way. But I name no names, and in this way anyone who resents what I have said will be visibly admitting how well the cap fits. For it is common knowledge that this grasping behaviour by generals has caused our armies to spread devastation wherever they go. Think of the tours they have made in recent years all over Italy, among lands and municipalities that are the property of Roman citizens. Then you will find it easier to imagine how such men act among foreigners. Ask yourselves which, in these years, have reached the larger total – enemy towns destroyed by your soldiers, or allied communities ruined by the rapacity those same troops have shown when they requisition winter quarters. A leader who does not restrain himself cannot restrain his army; if his own conduct will not bear exacting criticism, he is in no position to censure others.

When this is the situation, it is not in the least surprising that Pompeius so completely excels all other generals without exception. For when he and his legions arrived in Asia it was said that not one single peaceable individual suffered the slightest damage from the hand, or even the passing footsteps, of any single man in all of that great army. Furthermore, verbal and written reports are reaching us every day with accounts of the excellent behaviour of our army in its winter quarters. Far from any local inhabitants being forced to incur expense on a Roman soldier's account, they are not even allowed to do so if they want to. This is in keeping with the practice of our ancestors, who ordained that the homes of our allies and friends should serve our troops as refuges from the cold of winter – but not as places where they can indulge their acquisitiveness unchecked.

And Pompeius, you will note, shows equal restraint in everything else he does. How do you suppose he managed to attain that extraordinary speed on his astonishing journey? Now, what bore him so rapidly to the ends of the earth was no exceptional rowing power in his fleet, no hitherto un-discovered method of navigation, no unique combination of winds. No, the fact rather was that he did not allow the things which keep other men back to stand in his way. No greed for gain inspired thoughts of loot to seduce him from his ap-pointed course. Lust failed to lure him into self-indulgence; the beauties of nature never tempted him to relax. For Pompeius the sights of famous cities offered no distraction; his mighty labours left him with no inclination to take a rest. And as for the statues and pictures and other works of art in Greek towns, which no one else can resist picking up and carrying away, he did not even see fit to give them a glance.

The result is that everybody in those parts considers Cnaeus Pompeius not so much an envoy of Rome as some visitant from heaven itself. At last they begin to believe that, once upon a time, Romans with this sort of self-control really existed, a thing which foreigners were coming to regard as an unbelievable and mythical tradition. And so now the splendour of your empire really does begin to cheer all these peoples with its radiance! Now, finally, they are starting to understand how their ancestors, in bygone days when our officials showed such exemplary moderation, thought it a more desirable fate to be the subjects of Rome than to rule over other nations for themselves.

Pompeius is known for his readiness to be approached by ordinary people, and for his willingness to hear out their complaints about wrongs they have suffered from others. Indeed, although he himself ranks higher than the highest, he is as accessible as any humble individual. His political wisdom too, and the dignity and fluency of his oratory – with its note of authority appropriate to a general – are characteristics which you, gentlemen, have often had occasion to appreciate in this very place. And as to his reputation for good faith among our allies, you can estimate how high this stands when you recall that even our enemies, without exception, and to whatever race they belong, have judged it utterly inviolable. Pompeius is also a thoroughly humane man: it is hard to say which is the more impressive, the dread his valour inspired in his foes while they were fighting against him, or their gratitude for his mercy after they were defeated. How can anyone hesitate to entrust such a man with the direction of this formidable war? Surely some special design of the gods must have brought him into being for the express purpose of successfully terminating all the wars of our time.

Another important quality in the conduct of warfare and command of armies is prestige. And in this respect, again, no one could feel a shadow of doubt concerning the absolute pre-eminence of this general whom we are discussing. It may well be true that people are moved to terror, scorn, hatred or love by mere impression and rumour quite as much as by any rational process of thought, but at all events there is no denying the extent to which the success of a campaign depends on what our enemies and our allies think of the commanders we appoint. Well, throughout the whole history of the world, no name has ever been more illustrious than the name of Pompeius; and indeed, in his case, this renown is based on achievements that have never been equalled.

Now, nothing enhances prestige so greatly as the marks of esteem conferred by your Assembly, and those you have bestowed upon Pompeius, gentlemen, have been the most superlative and honorific of all. Nowhere upon earth, believe me, is there a region so desolate that news has not reached it of that solemn day when the entire Roman people packed the Forum, and crammed every available corner in each of the temples which overlook this platform, in order to demand that a war involving all the nations in the world should be placed under the charge of Cnaeus Pompeius alone.

But I do not propose to offer a long discourse on that subject; nor, in order to demonstrate the importance of prestige in military operations, is there any need for me to cite the careers of other men. For the record of Cnaeus Pompeius himself is enough to provide examples of every conceivable kind of distinction. For instance, that appointment to the naval war against the pirates followed a period when corn had been extremely scarce and expensive. But on the very day when he was given the command, the hopes inspired by his reputation were in themselves sufficient to cause a sudden reduction of grain prices to a low level which could only barely have been attained even after the most prolonged period of peace, when land was at the height of its productivity.

I referred very reluctantly, a little earlier, to the disastrous battle in Pontus. It left our allies in a panic and the enemy bursting with strength and confidence. At that juncture, gentlemen, you would have lost the entire province of Asia, had not the good fortune of Rome, at the very height of the emergency, providentially brought Cnaeus Pompeius into the area. Mithridates was exulting in the unusual experience of victory, and Tigranes menaced Asia Minor with a powerful force. But Mithridates was checked, and Tigranes held back, by the mere appearance of Pompeius upon the scene. Since he has accomplished all this by means of his prestige alone, just imagine what will be the results of his bravery in the field! His mere name and reputation have been enough to defend our allies and revenues. So when he is actually commanding operations, at the head of his army, their salvation will be secured beyond any doubt whatever.

The prestige of Pompeius among the enemies of Rome is again made manifest in the unanimity with which the pirates, although they came from countries an enormous distance away and apart, surrendered to him and him only, after the briefest possible lapse of time. Although there was another Roman general in the area, commanding an army in Crete, a deputation from that island's Assembly came almost to the ends of the earth in order to find Cnaeus Pompeius, since it was to him, they declared, that all the Cretan cities wanted to surrender. And then again this very Mithridates himself had sent an envoy all the way to Spain to see Pompeius (for Pompeius always regarded him as an envoy – although some people, who resented his being sent expressly to Pompeius, preferred instead to consider the man a spy). All this, gentlemen, makes it possible for you to estimate the enormous effect on those two kings, and on foreign countries in general, that will be exercised by prestige of this degree of magnitude, heightened as it has been still further by many subsequent exploits and by outstanding proofs of your own high esteem.

It remains for me to speak of his good luck – though I shall do so in the brief and guarded terms that are necessary in discussing what, after all, depends upon the gods; for this is, indeed, something which no one can guarantee that he himself will be able to acquire. Yet we are at liberty to remember and record instances when it has attended others. For merit, I am sure, was not the only reason why Fabius, Marcellus, Scipio, Marius and other eminent generals[19] were repeatedly entrusted with army commands. Another important factor was their luck. Certain very distinguished men have undoubtedly been helped to achieve their honour, glory and imposing success by a sort of providential good fortune. Now, when I come to speak of luck in connexion with the man of whom we are now speaking, I propose to be somewhat cautious since, as I say, I do not want to give the impression that luck is a matter that lies within his control. Nevertheless, recollection of what has happened in the past surely cannot fail to make us optimistic for the future. In saying this, I trust that the immortal gods will not regard me as guilty either of over-confidence on the one hand or of ingratitude on the other. For I do not intend to enumerate all the great deeds of Cnaeus Pompeius at home and in the field, on land and at sea, and all the good fortune that has brought his enterprises the support of his fellow-Romans, the concurrence of our allies, the obedience of our enemies, and even the cooperation of wind and weather. But this I will very briefly assert, that no one in this world has ever had the presumption to ask the immortal gods, even silently in his own heart, for all the mighty favours they have showered upon Pompeius. And not only on his own personal behalf, but for the sake of our common good and our empire, it should be your most earnest desire (as I am sure it is) that this luck should remain his special and permanent prerogative.

The war under discussion, then, is so necessary that it cannot

19. The heroes mentioned are Q. Fabius Maximus Cunctator (Second Punic War), M. Claudius Marcellus, who conquered Syracuse in 211, P. Cornelius Scipio Africanus the younger (Aemilianus) (d. 129) and C. Marius (d. 86).

be avoided and so important that it requires the utmost care. But you are in the happy position of being able to entrust its conduct to a commander whose remarkable military knowledge is only equalled by his extraordinary personal gifts, outstanding prestige, and pre-eminent good fortune. It is inconceivable, then, gentlemen, that you should hesitate to utilize, for the preservation and greater glory of our country, this exceptional blessing which heaven has placed in your hands.

Indeed, even if Pompeius at this juncture were in Rome and out of office, it would still have been incumbent upon you to select him and send him out to a war which is so grave as this. But as things are, all other supreme qualifications are united with the remarkably fortunate coincidence that he is actually on the spot with an army of his own: which, moreover, he can immediately supplement by taking over the forces of other commanders. What more, then, are we waiting for? Surely we must follow the direction of providence and allocate the conduct of this war against Mithridates to the man who has already, to our enormous national advantage, been entrusted with so many other great commands.

Opposition, I know, comes from Quintus Catulus, the patriotic recipient of many marks of your approval, and from Quintus Hortensius[20] whose distinguished career and wealth are only equalled by his virtues and talents. I am aware that the authority of these personages has on numerous occasions carried great weight with you; and so indeed it should. But on the present issue, for all the authority, determination and distinction one cannot fail to recognize in my opponents, we have to disregard this factor and arrive at the truth, instead, by a logical consideration of the facts. This is less difficult than

20. Q. Lutatius Catulus jun. (consul 78) was the leader of the conservative group in the Senate, and Q. Hortensius Hortalus (d. 50) Cicero's chief rival as an orator.

it might have been because these gentlemen themselves admit the truth of everything I have so far said, namely, that the war is massive and unavoidable, and that Cnaeus Pompeius is the only man with first-class qualifications.

So what is Hortensius' argument? He agrees that if the supreme command needed to be given to a single man, that man should be Pompeius. But he maintains that no such need exists. Yet surely that line of argument is now completely out of date. Facts, much more than words, have proved it wrong. When the resolute Aulus Gabinius introduced a law proposing the appointment of a supreme commander against the pirates, you, Quintus Hortensius, employed all your matchless eloquence and fluency to oppose him in the Senate, and in this Assembly too you argued at length against the measure. And yet, if the people of Rome had on that occasion paid more attention to your authoritative advice than to their own welfare and true interests, heaven knows, our glorious renown and our world empire would not be in existence to-day. For what sort of an empire could you call it when Roman envoys, quaestors and praetors were kidnapped, when we were cut off from all private or official communication with every one of our own provinces, when the total closure of every sea to our ships made it utterly impossible to attend to our personal or national business overseas?

Has any state ever before – and I am not talking of important places such as Athens, with its extensive control over the sea, or Carthage, with its naval and maritime power, or Rhodes, whose nautical science and renown have lasted down into our own times – but has *any* state in previous history been too weak a unit or too small an island to be capable of defending its own harbours and fields and a stretch of surrounding country and coast? And yet, for a consecutive period of years before the law of Gabinius, it has to be admitted that the mighty Roman nation, which down to our own times had never ceased to be famous for its unfailing invincibility in every naval engagement, was actually deprived of an over-whelmingly large proportion of its own resources – so that it lost every trace of impressiveness as an imperial power.

Our forefathers were very different. They routed King Antiochus and King Perseus[21] at sea, and even against people with the unique seafaring experience and equipment of the Carthaginians there was not a single sea-battle that our own side failed to win. But now look at us on the other hand, totally unable to hold our own against pirates. In former times we not only protected the whole of Italy but succeeded, through the prestige of our imperial name, in securing the safety of all our allies right to the very ends of the earth. Consider, for example, Delos, far away from Rome in the Aegean Sea, thronged with traders bringing merchandise and cargoes from every quarter, a tiny defenceless island crammed with riches. In those days even Delos had nothing whatever to fear. But now see ourselves, on the contrary. During these recent times we have been ejected from our provinces and the seaboard of Italy itself and from our very own harbours. And we have actually been chased off the Appian Way! While such things were happening, how on earth could any Roman official forbear to feel shame, when he mounted this rostrum[22] inherited from our ancestors who adorned it with the trophies of naval victories and the spoils of captured fleets?

When you, Hortensius, and those who felt like you, said what you thought about the pirate war, Roman audiences appreciated your good intentions. But all the same, when the safety of the entire community was at stake, our people preferred to be guided by its own distressed feelings rather than by any pronouncements you had made. The consequence was that one single law, one single individual, one single year were enough to eliminate every trace of our humiliation and

21. Perseus of Macedonia was defeated by the Romans at Pydna (168).
22. The rostrum (beak) was so called because it was adorned with the prows of ships captured in the war against Antium (338).

affliction. And so it came about that our dominion over all the peoples and nations of the world, by land and sea, really seems to have come true at long last!

This, in my opinion, lends a singularly ungracious air to objections opposing the emphatic request of Pompeius that his second-in-command should be Gabinius[23] – whether the objection is directed against Gabinius or against Pompeius or, more probably, against them both. Surely one cannot suppose that the general who, in a war of this importance, asks that he himself should be allowed to choose his own deputy is not entitled to have his request met! Other military leaders have been permitted to take out with them the lieutenant of their own choice although they have had no other purpose in their minds except to rob our allies and plunder our provinces. Does it not, then, seem an extraordinary suggestion that the man who moved a law which actually brought salvation and honour to Rome and all other nations should be refused the smallest part in the glory of the commander and the army which he risked his career to bring into existence? Gaius Falcidius, Quintus Metellus, Quintus Caelius Latiniensis and Cnaeus Lentulus, whose names I mention with due respect, were allowed to accept appointment to similar secondary posts although they had served as tribunes of the people in the previous year. Is this present degree of punctiliousness going to be applied to no one but Gabinius? Surely the situation rather is that he above all others deserves our very special favour, since the whole war is being conducted on the basis of the law that he himself introduced, and undertaken by the general and army that you created on his proposal.

I hope the question of Gabinius' appointment as second-in-command will be referred by the consuls to the Senate. If the consuls hesitate or make difficulties, I declare I will refer the

23. A. Gabinius proposed the law which entrusted the pirate war to Pompeius in 67.

proposal to that body myself.[24] I shall not allow any unfriendly action by any official whatever to prevent me from relying on your support and safeguarding your right to appoint whom you will. I am not prepared to tolerate any interference short of an actual veto – and I surmise that the men who threaten to impose one will reflect with a good deal of care how far they can go. In my judgement, gentlemen, Aulus Gabinius has a unique justification to be associated with Cnaeus Pompeius in the triumphs of the naval war, seeing that whereas the latter took it over, mastered it, and brought it to a conclusion, Gabinius had been the man who, supported by your own vote, was responsible for the allocation of the campaign to this single, supreme commander.

Next I ought to say something about the pronouncement which carries the authority of Quintus Catulus. If you decided to place your entire dependence upon Cnaeus Pompeius, he wanted to know, on whom would you be able to rely if anything happened to him? Your answer to this question took the form of a high compliment to the character and position of the man who had asked it, when you were virtually unanimous in declaring that if such circumstances arose you would put your trust in himself. And indeed the qualities of Catulus are so exceptional that, however vast or difficult an enterprise might be, his wisdom would see to its efficient management, his integrity would guarantee it was kept on the right lines, and his ability would ensure its successful completion. Nevertheless, in this particular instance I disagree with him. Mortal life is fleeting, and full of uncertainties. All the more imperative, then, is the necessity that the state should make the most of a great man's life and genius while heaven still allows this to be done.

Innovations, it is objected, must not be made contrary to the

24. As praetor Cicero was entitled to bring motions before the Senate, though these were subject to vetos by equal or superior officials.

precedents and principles of our ancestors. I will refrain from pointing out, in reply, that whereas our ancestors respected tradition when Rome was at peace, they were invariably guided by expediency in time of war, constantly meeting new emergencies by fresh devices. I will say nothing about how two wars of the highest importance, the Punic and Spanish wars, were successfully terminated by one and the same general, at that time when two most formidable cities, Carthage and Numantia, each a terrible menace to our empire, were both destroyed by Scipio Aemilianus. I refrain, likewise, from reminding you of the more recent occasion when you and your fathers decided to vest the entire hopes of the Roman world in Gaius Marius, so that this single individual was loaded with a multiplicity of commands against Jugurtha, the Cimbri and the Teutones.[25]

And finally, let us pass on to Cnaeus Pompeius himself. Here is the man for whom Quintus Catulus objects that no new precedent ought to be established. But just consider how many new precedents have already been created in his favour – with Catulus' full approval. That someone of extreme youthfulness,[26] who held no public office, should raise an army in a time of national crisis was a complete innovation. Yet that is what Pompeius did. For this same young man to be made its commander was equally novel. However, that is what he became. That he should succeed so triumphantly in the enterprise was equally unparalleled. Nevertheless, such was his achievement. It was wholly contrary to custom that a youth of very tender years, who was far below the minimum age even for admission to the Senate, should be given a command

25. Scipio Aemilianus (Africanus the younger) destroyed Carthage (146) and Numantia (133), and C. Marius defeated Jugurtha of Numidia (106) and the Teutones and Cimbri (102–1).

26. Pompeius was twenty-four when he went to Sicily (82). His triumphs were in 81 and 71.

and an army, allocated a sphere of action comprising Sicily and Africa, and entrusted with the conduct of a war within those territories. But the integrity, dignity and ability he displayed in that capacity were outstanding. In Africa, he terminated a very serious campaign, and brought his army home victorious. For a Roman knight to be awarded a Triumph was unheard of. Yet the people of Rome not only witnessed the conferment of such an award but saw fit to throng the proceedings in huge and universally enthusiastic crowds.

Next, it was totally unprecedented, when two eminent and gallant consuls were available,[27] for a Roman knight to be sent out with consular powers to wage a grave and terrible war. All the same, he was sent. There were members of the Senate, on that occasion, who maintained it was wrong that the man we dispatched, with the authority of a consul, should be just a private individual. But Lucius Philippus is said to have remarked that if he had his way Pompeius should be sent with the powers not of one consul but of the two of them. And so enormous were the hopes of success which were placed in him that this single young man was, in fact, virtually invested with the combined functions of both of our consuls.

It was equally without parallel, again, that he should be exempted from the laws[28] by a resolution of the Senate, and elected to a consulship actually before he had the legal right to hold any office at all. And that he, not yet a Senator but only a knight, should celebrate a Triumph, not once but twice, in pursuance of senatorial resolutions, might seem incredible. If you count up every single departure from precedent since the very beginning of Roman history, they add up to a smaller

27. When Pompeius was sent to take command against Q. Sertorius (77), the consuls were Dec. Junius Brutus and Mam. Aemilius Lepidus Livianus.

28. Pompeius' early consulship infringed upon the Lex Villia Annalis and the Lex Cornelia.

total than those which have been lavished upon the career of this single man. And all these remarkable and revolutionary innovations, directed towards one and the same individual, were brought about as a result of enactments by distinguished national leaders – of whom Quintus Catulus was one.

And those proposals, recognizing the merits of Cnaeus Pompeius, consistently received the approval of this Assembly. In order, therefore, to prevent an intolerably unjust situation, the least that Catulus and the other leaders can now do is to support *your* present initiative – the initiative of the Roman people – in favour of the same man. The point is particularly valid at this time, when the Assembly is in an excellent position, by its own right, to justify what it proposes for Pompeius against anyone in the world who might choose to object. For, in spite of protests from similar sources, it was you who made the choice of this selfsame single individual to command in the war against the pirates.

If you did this ill-advisedly and without due regard for the national interests, the men who opposed the measure are justified in their attempts to moderate your partisanship now. But if, rather, the patriotic foresight was on your own side, seeing that it was you who despite their opposition were responsible for bringing glory to our empire and salvation to the world, the eminent men in question should no longer be reluctant to admit that they, like everyone else, are obliged to bow to the unanimous authority of the people of Rome.

I might add that a war fought against a king, in this Asian setting, needs a commander with many outstanding qualities in addition to the military talents which are so conspicuously to be found in Cnaeus Pompeius. It is hard for any Roman general fighting in Asia, Cilicia, Syria or the kingdoms of the interior to limit his attention to the enemy and to successes in the field. Even if there are some commanders whose decency and self-control makes them behave with greater moderation, no one is prepared to believe this of them, because the rapacious are such a large majority. Words cannot express the hatred, gentlemen, in which we are held in countries overseas because of this scandalous, extortionate behaviour of the persons we have sent out to govern them. In all those lands it would be impossible to find a shrine which they have held sacred, a city they have left unviolated, or a home that has proved able to withstand their encroachments. Such men, to satisfy their lust for plunder, search out rich and prosperous cities capable of furnishing them with a pretext – and then deliberately make war on them.

I should like to discuss this matter face to face with the distinguished and illustrious Quintus Catulus and Quintus Hortensius. They must be perfectly well aware of the sufferings of our allies, whose miseries are before their eyes and whose lamentations sound in their ears. When you send an army you do not imagine, surely, that it is going to help your allies and fight your enemies! What it will do, instead, is to use the enemy as a mere excuse for savage onslaughts upon your own allies and friends. In all Asia there is no city large enough to slake the insolent pretensions of one single Roman military tribune. I say nothing of commanders-in-chief and their lieutenants.

Even, therefore, if you possess a general who seems qualified to defeat the royal armies in a pitched battle, he will only be suitable for this war against the Asian monarchs on certain definite conditions. That is to say, he must also have the self-control to keep his hands and eyes and thoughts off the money, wives and children of allies, the artistic masterpieces of temples and cities, and the gold and treasures of the kings. For a city to be 'at peace with Rome' and yet also to have retained its wealth is a contradiction in terms. Indeed, if it still possesses such resources there is little chance of a governor of ours treating its citizens as if they are at peace at all.

The people of the coastal territories, gentlemen, requested

the appointment of Cnaeus Pompeius against the pirates not merely because of his military renown but also because of his restraint. For they were easily able to observe that with very few exceptions provincial governors make large fortunes every year out of public funds, and that all our hypothetical fleets had achieved was to lose battles and thus add still further to our disgrace. Those who say that the supreme command ought not to be given to a single individual seem to be unaware of the avarice of the men who set out to govern provinces, the sums they lay out in bribes, the intrigues they enter into. Even if Cnaeus Pompeius did not have to be called Great on his own merits, he would deserve the name in contrast to the appalling faults of the rest.

So you must hesitate no longer. Give this man the supreme command. For of all the generals, throughout all these years, who have entered the cities of our allies with an army, he is the only one whose arrival among them is actually a cause for self-congratulation.

If however, gentlemen, you feel that my case needs the support of authoritative witnesses, you have the authority of Publius Servilius Vatia,[29] whose long experience in warfare of every kind as well as in important public affairs entitles his opinion to carry unique weight in your current deliberations on this military issue. You have the authority of Gaius Curio,[30] whose exceptional ability, judgement and achievements have been recognized by your conferment of the highest offices. You have the authority of Cnaeus Lentulus,[31] in whom you have all had occasion to appreciate the wisdom and high

29. P. Servilius Vatia was given the name Isauricus for his victories over the pirates as proconsul of Cilicia (78–74).

30. C. Scribonius Curio obtained a Triumph for his victory over the Dardani and Moesi (71).

31. Cn. Cornelius Lentulus Clodianus served with Pompeius against the pirates and had earlier been censor (70).

principles befitting the ample dignities you have bestowed on him. You have the authority of the honourable, excellent, unwavering Gaius Cassius.[32] The authority of all these men makes it possible to give a more than adequate answer to any and every opposing argument.

In these circumstances, Gaius Manilius, first of all I profoundly approve and applaud your law and your intention and your proposal. And, secondly, I urge you, with the Roman people behind you, to stand by your motion undeterred by violence or by threats from any quarter. As to my first point, I know you are not lacking in the necessary courage and determination. And with regard to the second, as we now see this vast crowd gathered here to repeat the conferment of a supreme command on a single personage, how can we have the slightest doubts either about the merit of the proposal or about our capacity to carry it through?

For my part, whatever keenness, intelligence, energy or ability I may possess; whatever I may be enabled to accomplish in the course of this praetorship, bestowed upon me by the favour of the Roman people; or whatever I can achieve by means of any influence, loyalty and resolution of my own, all these assets, I swear, will be put at the disposal of yourself and Rome, and dedicated to the task of bringing this purpose of ours into effect.

I appeal to the gods – and especially to those who watch over this hallowed place and gaze into the hearts of all who engage in public life – to confirm that my plea is not prompted by orders from any other man. Nor do I argue this issue with the intention of winning the favour of Cnaeus Pompeius; my purpose is not to make use of any man's great position to win myself protection in danger or support towards advancement. For against danger, in so far as it lies with a human being to be assured of such a thing, the justice of my cause will be adequate

32. C. Cassius Longinus passed an agrarian law, and was defeated by Spartacus in the Slave War (72).

defence; and my advancement will come, if such is your pleasure, not from the favour of any single individual, or from what I say on this platform, but as a result of the unremitting hard work in which I spend my life.

Throughout all the endeavours then, gentlemen, that I have devoted to supporting this cause, I declare that my one thought has been for the interests of Rome. Of trying to win popularity for myself there can be no question. On the contrary, I am only too well aware that the case has gained me numerous enemies, some clearly apparent and others lurking secretly. I could easily have avoided their hostility; but then you would have been the losers. And so, gentlemen, holding this high office and enjoying all the favours you have conferred, I have decided I must regard my own private interests and advantages as insignificant in comparison with your will, and the welfare of our country, and the safe preservation of the provinces and allies of the Roman state.

CHAPTER TWO

AGAINST
LUCIUS SERGIUS CATILINA

*Lucius Sergius Catilina, who was about two years older than
Cicero, belonged to an ancient but impoverished patrician family. He
had become a supporter of Sulla in the Civil War of the late eighties
and the bloodstained dictatorship that followed, obtained the praetorship in 68, and then became governor of Africa (Tunisia). He returned in mid-66 to find that the consuls-elect for the following year,
Publius Cornelius Sulla and Publius Autronius Paetus, having been
found guilty of bribery during the elections, had been disqualified from
office, the defeated candidates Lucius Aurelius Cotta and Lucius
Manlius Torquatus being elected in their place. Catilina conceived
the idea of offering himself as a candidate in opposition to these
substitutes, but was not allowed to do so, since (as happened to many
governors) he was facing a prosecution for illicit financial gains
(extortion) in his province.*

*Then followed an affair, shrouded in mystery, which is known as
the First Catilinarian Conspiracy. It appears that there was a plot to
murder the two incoming consuls Cotta and Torquatus in the interests
of the two men who had been disqualified. The historian Sallust and
the commentator Quintus Asconius Pedianus (of the first century
A.D.) believe Catilina was involved in the plot, but make another
poverty-stricken nobleman, Cnaeus Calpurnius Piso, the prime
mover. Suetonius on the other hand (writing in the second century
A.D.) says that the main conspirators were Crassus and Caesar, who
hoped to emerge as dictator and master of the horse respectively, with
the intention of rearranging things according to their pleasure and
then restoring the disqualified pair to the consulship. Suetonius says
nothing about any part played by Catilina, whose name may perhaps
have been introduced into the record in place of Publius Sulla's, as a*

result of a tradition going back to Cicero – since he had defended Sulla in the courts and wanted to keep his name clear. But the true facts are still highly obscure; and in any case the plot, if it ever existed, was first postponed and then finally abandoned (February 65).

Catilina was acquitted on the provincial charge, and proceeded to stand for the consulship twice more, in successive years. He was defeated on both occasions, the first time by Cicero and Gaius Antonius Hybrida and on the second by Decimus Junius Silanus and Lucius Licinius Murena.[1] Supporters of the calibre of Crassus and Caesar (who was a recipient of Crassus' financial support) had been scared off by Catilina's increasing tendency to adopt a policy of abolition of debts and redistribution of land, which threatened property owners. This was the chance of Cicero; 'new men', such as he was, very rarely reached the consulship, but now he seemed preferable to Catilina in conservative eyes, and in July 64 he was elected consul for 63 – a proud moment of his life to which he subsequently referred over and over again. Accordingly, at the next consular elections (late summer 63 for 62), he himself as consul was the presiding officer; and this was the occasion on which Catilina made his second attempt to win the consulship. Cicero later claimed that his life was in danger at the election, which is unlikely. However, Catilina was again defeated, and it was probably at this point that he abandoned constitutional methods and decided to achieve the headship of the state – and freedom from his debts – by conspiracy and revolutionary violence. How the situation then unfolded will be seen from the four Catilinarian speeches of Cicero which followed.

What was Catilina really like? Cicero's picture of his personal character, although admitting energy, talent and charm, is too classically frightful and diabolical to be true (and is somewhat modified in the speech for Caelius); the grammarians had good reason to call these orations the Invectives. On the other hand, there can be little doubt that after his second electoral defeat Catilina did intend to

---

1. Between his Second and Third Catilinarian speeches Cicero had to defend Murena on a charge of bribery brought by an unsuccessful candidate, the jurist Servius Sulpicius Rufus.

bring down the Republic by force. He was, of course, not alone in this ambition. The whole of the last century B.C. saw a rapidly augmenting process of dissolution, as one powerful figure after another used private armies and strong-arm political methods to subvert the oligarchic caucus which had proved so incapable of governing an empire. Lucius Sulla succeeded but abdicated, Pompeius was at this moment holding a perilously large command, fourteen years later Caesar was to assume a dictatorship which only ended with his murder; and Octavian then became the emperor Augustus. Where Catilina fell short of them was probably not so much in the ethical qualities so vigorously found wanting by Cicero as in success and skill; the old idea of redistributing property, though by now a social revolutionary commonplace, was not the best way to win influential supporters. The most that can be said of Catilina (apart from his capacity to keep devoted supporters) was that his own poverty and political disappointments inspired him with a rather vague anger against the injustice of things in general. And this was, indeed, flagrant, in a corruptly mismanaged Italy and empire where the distribution of wealth had become more and more glaringly uneven. In the words of Plutarch: 'Only a spark was needed to set everything on fire, and, since the whole state was rotten within itself, it was in the power of any bold man to overthrow it.'

Unfortunately Catilina's own statement of his point of view, has not survived, except in a few phrases. So with the exception of the hostile Sallust, we have to rely for our evidence upon the thundering, sparkling, totally one-sided vituperation of Cicero. The orator always believed that his suppression of the Catilinarian conspiracy was not only the greatest thing that he himself had ever done but the greatest thing that had ever happened in Roman history. That was not true, and its reiteration became boring and ludicrous. It was true, however, that Cicero, for all his hesitant nature, had played the principal part in saving Rome from a real and nasty coup d' état, though this is sometimes difficult to believe when he tells us so often how wonderful he was. Yet, at the time, his series of speeches carried the day (though the fourth speech may not have been so *effective as the published version). For the conspiracy gave him a unique opportunity to deploy his incomparably persuasive eloquence in a field worthy of the central part which oratory played in ancient culture and Roman life.*

THE FIRST SPEECH
Delivered to the Senate

On 21 October 63 B.C. Cicero's excellent intelligence service – including the mistress of one of the conspirators – enabled him to inform a startled Senate that six days later a rebellion under Catilina's henchman Gaius Manlius would break out at Faesulae (Fiesole) in Etruria; that on 28 October there would be an extensive massacre at Rome, and that on 1 November the rebels would attempt to take Praeneste (Palestrina) by surprise. He profited by the alarm caused by this news to persuade the Senate to pass the formal Emergency Decree, charging the consuls to see that no harm befell the Republic; and of this more will be heard in connexion with the Fourth Speech.

Cicero's consular colleague Gaius Antonius Hybrida did nothing, and was indeed strongly suspected of Catilinarian sympathies. Cicero also did nothing much at first, for he was not by nature a man of action. But then events enabled, or forced, him to move. First, Crassus brought him an anonymous letter he had received: it gave warning that a massacre was indeed imminent. Then another Senator, Lucius Saenius, read out in the Senate a letter indicating that Manlius had taken the field at Faesulae on precisely the day which Cicero had foretold. Military counter-measures were taken, and Cicero recruited a large and vigorous bodyguard of the knights who were his strong supporters.

Cicero now convened an extraordinary meeting of the Senate for 7 November. He was able to provide a sensational new piece of information. For he had learnt that on the previous night Catilina, still in Rome, and ostensibly in voluntary custody (to disarm suspicion), had summoned a secret conference of the conspirators, at which according to the orator – who is no doubt, as usual, exaggerating, but probably this time not too much – the most treasonable and violent designs were formed. The Senate's meeting was particularly dramatic because Catilina thought it advisable to attend in person, as a bluff to display his good intentions, and so he sat listening to Cicero's violent abuse.

The speech was a triumph because it convinced the Senate, whose members (though unwilling to sit anywhere near Catilina) had at first been incredulous of the plot and reluctant to act, that the danger was a real one; and as open hostility broke out against Catilina, he got up and walked out. But before leaving the meeting, according to Sallust, he spoke up for himself, at first quietly denying all charges and recalling his family's services to the state, then sneering at Cicero as an upstart 'resident alien', and finally, when faced with angry cries, shouting back ferocious threats in a fury and rushing from the temple where the meeting was held. But it is, in fact, doubtful whether Cicero and Catilina each delivered a single speech in turn. Probably there was much excitable give-and-take, what the Romans called altercatio: *the oration which has come down to us being a written-up version of the points which Cicero made during this exchange, perhaps with a few more added by hindsight after the event.*

Nevertheless, the speech as we have it still ends with something of an anti-climax, because after a recital of Catilina's allegedly horrible record and intentions Cicero concludes with a rather tame suggestion that he should relieve Rome of his presence. Probably, however, the anti-climax was an authentic feature of what he had actually said, and was calculated: the Senate was supposed to reply, 'No, no, arrest him immediately!' But when it was clear that the Senators were not going to react in this way, Cicero managed, as practised orators do when they see they are not going to achieve their first aim, to score another success instead. For Catilina, bated beyond endurance and no doubt alarmed that his movements might soon be restricted, not only left the meeting but immediately departed from Rome altogether and moved off to join his associates in Etruria, thus convincing many who had previously been sceptical that his plans

were as treasonable as Cicero maintained, and inducing the Senate to
declare him a public enemy.

In the name of heaven, Catilina, how long do you propose to
exploit our patience? Do you really suppose that your lunatic
activities are going to escape our retaliation for evermore?
Are there to be no limits to this audacious, uncontrollable
swaggering? Look at the garrison of our Roman nation which
guards the Palatine by night, look at the patrols ranging the
city, the whole population gripped by terror, the entire body
of loyal citizens massing at one single spot! Look at this meeting of our Senate behind strongly fortified defences[2], see the
expressions on the countenances of every one of these men
who are here! Have none of these sights made the smallest
impact on your heart? You must be well aware that your plot
has been detected. Now that every single person in this place
knows all about your conspiracy, you cannot fail to realize it
is doomed. Do you suppose there is a single individual here
who has not got the very fullest information about what you
were doing last night and the night before, where you went,
the men you summoned, the plans you concocted?

What a scandalous commentary on our age and its standards! For the Senate knows about all these things. The consul
sees them being done. And yet this man still lives! Lives? He
walks right into the Senate. He joins in our national debates –
watches and notes and marks down with his gaze each one of
us he plots to assassinate. And we, how brave we are! Just by
getting out of the way of his frenzied onslaught, we feel we
are doing patriotic duty enough.

But yours was the death which the consul should have
ordered long ago. The calamity which you have long been
planning for each one of us ought to have rebounded on to
yourself alone. The noble Publius Scipio Nasica,[3] who was

2. The Senate was meeting in the Temple of Jupiter Stator.
3. He initiated the attack on the reformer Ti. Gracchus (133).

chief priest but held no administrative office, killed Tiberius Gracchus, although his threat to the national security was only on a limited scale. Shall we, then, who hold the office of consuls, tolerate Catilina when he is determined to plunge the entire world into fire and slaughter? Upon precedents that go too far back into antiquity, such as the act of Gaius Servilius Ahala[4] who with his own hand slew Spurius Maelius for plotting a revolution, I shall not dwell: except to say that at former epochs, in this country of ours, brave men did not lack the courage to strike down a dangerous Roman citizen more fiercely even than they struck down the bitterest of foreign foes. Moreover, we have in our hands, Catilina, a decree of the Senate that is specifically aimed against yourself; and a formidable and stern decree it is.[5] From this body, then, the state has no lack of counsel and authority. I tell you frankly, it is we, the consuls, who are not doing our duty.

The Senate once ordained that Lucius Opimius,[6] who was at that time consul, should *take measures to protect the state from harm*. Thereafter, not one single night was allowed to elapse. Because of a mere suspicion of treason, Gaius Gracchus, the son, grandson and descendant of highly distinguished men, was put to death. A man of consular rank, Marcus Fulvius, was also killed, and so were his children. A similar resolution of the Senate entrusted the national safety to the consuls Gaius Marius and Lucius Valerius; and thereafter not one day went by before the vengeance of the state brought a violent end to the tribune of the people Lucius Saturninus and the praetor Gaius Servilius.[7]

4. C. Servilius Ahala killed Sp. Maelius for selling cheap corn with alleged revolutionary intentions (439).

5. The Senate had passed the *senatus consultum ultimum* against Catilina on 21 October 63.

6. L. Opimius was responsible for the death of C. Sempronius Gracchus (121).

7. L. Appuleius Saturninus was killed after using violence and committing murder in support of the candidature of C. Servilius Glaucia for the consulship (100).

But look at us, on the other hand. For the past twenty days we have allowed the powers which the Senate has given into our grasp to become blunt at the edges. We have an entirely appropriate decree – but it is left buried in the archives like a sword hidden in its sheath. According to this decree, Catilina, it is evident to all that you should have been instantly executed. And yet you are still alive – and living with an effrontery which bears not the smallest sign of subsiding and is indeed more outrageous than ever.

Members of the Senate, my desire is to be merciful. Yet in this grave national emergency I also do not want to seem negligent; and as things are I blame myself for culpable inaction. Inside Italy, within the passes of Etruria, there is a camp occupied by men who plan the destruction of the Roman people. The number of these enemies increases every day. But as for the real commander of that camp, the leader of the hostile force, he is to be seen within our own walls and even inside the Senate itself, plotting every day, from this interior vantage point, some form of ruin for our country. If, therefore, Catilina, I order your arrest and execution, surely all honest men will complain, not that I am acting with undue brutality, but that I have delayed too long.

Yet there is a particular reason why I still cannot bring myself to do what I ought to have done long ago. For I intend that your execution shall be timed to coincide with that day when even the most abandoned rascals, the people most resembling yourself, will be admitting one and all that this is your just fate. As long as one man exists who can dare to defend you, you will continue to live – and live as you are living now, surrounded by large numbers of my trusty guards whose duty it is to ensure that you make no move against the government. Although you may not know it, many eyes and ears will be paying you their alert attention. They have been doing so already.

For now, Catilina, your hopes must obviously be at an end.

The darkness of night no longer avails to conceal your traitorous consultations. A private house does not suffice to keep the voices of your conspiracy secret.[8] Everything is patently apparent. It all bursts out into the open; you are forced to give up the whole outrageous design. So do as I say: dismiss all those projects of carnage and conflagration from your mind. You are hemmed in on every side. All your schemes are more glaringly evident to us than the light of day.

Let us just go over them together. Do you remember how I said in the Senate on the twenty-first of October that Gaius Manlius, your henchman and satellite in this frightful project, would take up arms on a particular date, and that the date in question would be the twenty-seventh of October? Was I mistaken, Catilina, in prophesying this significant, deplorable and unbelievable event? And, more remarkable still, was I wrong about the day? I also informed the Senate that you had put off the massacre of our national leaders until the twenty-eighth of October, although by that time many of the chief men in the state had fled from Rome, less from a desire for self-preservation than in order to thwart your plans. But you went around saying that, in spite of their departure, you would still be content with the slaughter of the rest of us who remained. After that admission of failure, you cannot very well deny that my guards and my vigilant attentions encompassed you so completely that you were quite unable to take any effective revolutionary action. When you were confident you would be able to seize Praeneste on the first of November by a night attack, you had no idea that the town was defended, on my orders, by my police and garrisons and protective forces. No single thing you do, nothing you attempt or even contemplate, escapes my notice. I hear and see and plainly understand your every move.

Review with me what happened on the night before last,

8. According to Sallust, Cicero's informant was Fulvia, mistress of one of the conspirators, Q. Curius.

and you will appreciate that I watch for the safety of our country far more keenly even than you watch for its destruction. I am able to report how on that night you came into Scythe-makers' Street (I will be perfectly specific) and entered the home of Marcus Laeca: and many of your accomplices in this lunatic, criminal enterprise joined you there. Do you dare to deny it? What can be the reason for your silence? But indeed, if you attempt a denial, I will prove that it is true. For here in the Senate today I can see with my own eyes some of the men who were with you in that house.

By heaven, Senators, it is difficult to imagine where on earth we can be, or what sort of a system of government is ours, or what kind of a city we inhabit, when there are men sitting here among ourselves, in this most solemn and dignified of all the world's assemblies, who are actually plotting the destruction of every single one of us, and of all Rome, and of everything upon the face of the earth! I, the consul, am gazing upon them now; they are taking part in this national debate. They ought to have been put to death by the sword. And yet, so far, I have not even succeeded in marking them with a verbal wound.

So you were at Laeca's house that night, Catilina. You parcelled out the regions of Italy. You decided where you wanted each of your agents to go. You chose the men to leave at Rome and the men you would take with you. You divided up the city into sections for the benefit of the incendiaries. You confirmed that you yourself would be leaving, and added that the only thing which still held you back for a bit was the fact that I was still alive. But two Roman knights[9] were found to relieve you of this worry. They promised they would kill me in my bed during that same night, a little before dawn. However, almost before your meeting dispersed, I knew about all these projects. Thereupon

9. According to Sallust the assassins were C. Cornelius and a (former? Senator L. Vargunteius.

I proceeded to strengthen and fortify my home with an increased number of bodyguards; and the individuals you had sent me, to convey the morning's greetings, were refused admission. I had foretold the arrival of these visitors to many leading personages. And the men made their appearance at the very hour I had indicated.

Since that is the position, Catilina, I call upon you to leave for the destination you already have in mind. Depart, at last, from our city! The gates are open; be on your way. Your camp run by Manlius has been waiting all too long for you to take over its command. And take all your friends with you, or as many as you can – clean the city up. Once there is a wall between you and ourselves, you will have delivered me from grave anxiety. With us, you can remain no longer. I find it unendurable that you should still be here: unendurable, intolerable, impermissible.

Profound thanks are owed to the immortal gods, and particularly to Jupiter the Stayer in this very place, the most ancient guardian of our city, because we have already on so many occasions proved able to ward off this most ferocious and appalling and deadly menace to our country. But there is a limit to the number of times when one can allow the supreme national safety to be imperilled by a single individual. All the time you were intriguing against me while I was consul elect, Catilina, I employed no official guard to defend me, but only my own private security measures. And then after I had become consul, when at the last consular elections[10] you wanted to kill both myself and your own rival candidates in the Campus Martius, I thwarted your murderous scheme by the assistance and resources of my friends, without raising any public alarm of war. In a word, every time that you attacked me, although I was well aware that my death would be a

10. The reference is to the elections of 28 October 63, in which Catilina was again defeated.

disaster to our state, I employed only my own unaided endeavours to frustrate your plots.

But now it is different: for now you are openly attacking our whole existence, and calling down destruction and devastation upon the temples of the immortal gods, the habitations of our city, the lives of every citizen, and Italy in all its parts. Even so, I still do not venture to perform what ought to be my very first action, the action most in keeping with this authority I hold and with the traditions of ancient times. But instead I shall adopt a course which is at the same time more lenient and more expedient to our common welfare. For if I order you to be killed, the rest of your conspirators will still remain embedded in our public life. But if you leave Rome, as I have long been urging you to do, the city will be relieved of those copious, pestilential dregs of the community who are your accomplices. Well, Catilina? That is what you were just going to do in any case, of your own accord; so I am unable to see why you take your time in going, when that is precisely the course which I, too, propose that you should adopt. The consul orders a public enemy to leave the city. Into banishment? you ask. That is not part of my order. But, if you ask my opinion, it is what I advise.[11]

For within this city today, Catilina, there is nothing that could give you satisfaction any more. Apart from your own degraded band of fellow-conspirators, no man exists who does not hold you in fear and detestation. Your life is marked with every sort of scandalous blot. There is no imaginable form of dishonour which does not stain your private affairs. No bounds can be set to the lecheries your eyes have witnessed, the atrocities your hands have committed, the iniquities into which every part of your body has been plunged. Your insidious seductions, that trapped one young man after another, have left them well equipped for a career of dreadful

11. Cicero as consul did not possess the power to order exile, which was not an official sanction according to Roman Law.

crime, or thoroughly stimulated to pursue a life of unrestrained sensuality. And then again, think of the time when by means of your former wife's death you ensured that your house should be vacated and free for a further marriage. You supplemented that ghastly deed by another so appalling that it is scarcely believable.[12] But I pass the incident over and gladly allow it to be veiled in silence, because I cannot bear people to say that such a horror could have been perpetrated in this country – without receiving the smallest retribution of any kind. I say nothing, either, about the financial ruin into which you will be plunged upon the thirteenth of this month.[13]

Instead, I shall turn to the matters which relate not to the squalor of your personal depravities, not to the sordid tangle of your personal affairs, but to the supreme interests of our commonwealth, and the life and safety of every one of us. It is hard to see, Catilina, how you can derive any satisfaction from this daylight that you see around you, this air you breathe. For you must realize that, out of all these men seated here, not one single person is unaware how during the consulship of Lepidus and Tullus, when you took your place in the Assembly on the last day of December,[14] you were illegally carrying arms. You had got together a group determined to strike down the leading men of the state, including the two consuls themselves; and what prevented this mad crime from being carried out was no sanity or nervousness of yours, but the good fortune that favours the people of Rome.

Of other offences I say nothing, because they are well known, and in any case many more have been added since they

12. Shortly after Catilina's marriage with Aurelia Orestilla, his son by his previous marriage died.

13. The Kalends (1st) and Ides (13th or 15th) of each month were the days on which debts fell due.

14. This was 31 December 66, the day before Catilina's alleged plan to murder the incoming consuls L. Aurelius Cotta and L. Manlius Torquatus.

were committed. There are all your attempts, for example, to kill myself, when I was consul elect, and again when I had assumed the consulship. Many of your thrusts were so lethal that it seemed they could not fail to hit their mark. All the same, by some sort of sideways movement or dodge, I managed to elude them. For your plans, in fact, do not work; you achieve nothing. But that does not seem to stop you from trying and hoping. Many a time, already, that dagger has been swept from your hands, and many a time, too, it has slipped out of them and fallen by some mere chance. And yet you still cannot endure to be parted from the weapon for one single day. I do not like to think of the rituals you must have performed in order to hallow and dedicate the blade for its appointed task: the task of being plunged into the body of a Roman consul.

And now let us speak of this life you are leading. I shall show, by what I say, that I am not impelled by hatred – although I ought to be. On the contrary, I am moved by pity, which you do not deserve. A little while ago, you walked into the Senate. Here was this large gathering of members; here were many friends and relatives of your own. And yet, out of all these men, which one offered you a single word of greeting? Within all human memory no one else has been treated in such a way. When this is what happens, do you have to wait for the hostility to be expressed in words as well? The blow against you has already been struck – by that terrible verdict of silence.

And then again, when you arrived inside the Senate, every seat anywhere near your own was promptly vacated. As soon as you took your place, all the former consuls, whom you have repeatedly marked down for assassination, left that entire area of seats unoccupied and empty. Well, how does this make you feel? I really believe that, if my slaves were as scared of me as all your fellow-citizens are scared of you, I should be forced to leave my home altogether. Do you not have a comparable feeling – that you ought to go away from the city? If I saw that my fellow-citizens held me in such suspicion and loathing, even unjustly, I should not be able to face their hostile looks; I should depart outside their range. As for yourself, you know your own crimes well enough to understand that the universal hatred which men feel for you is justified, and has long been no more than your due. How, then, can you hesitate to flee from the gaze and presence of the men who are the victims of your persecution and torment?

If your parents feared and hated you, and you could find no way to pacify them, surely you would withdraw somewhere out of their sight. And now you are feared and hated by your country, the common parent of us all: for, indeed, she is convinced that your one idea is her assassination. Can it be that you feel no reverence at all for her authority, or deference to her judgement – or, for that matter, fear of her strong hand? Imagine her pleading with you in silent eloquence. 'For years past,' she will say, 'there has not been one single abomination or outrage for which anyone has been responsible apart from yourself. By your own agency you have slain many Roman citizens. You have harassed and plundered our allies.[15] And you have done all this in freedom and with impunity. Indeed, you have contrived not merely to ignore our laws and courts altogether, but to beat them down and shatter them into fragments. I ought not to have tolerated your earlier offences; yet I did. But now that I am stricken through and through with terror, entirely because of yourself, now that every sound I hear inspires me with dread of Catilina, now that your evil spirit is behind every sort of conspiracy against my life, I can bear it no longer. Therefore be gone, and relieve me of anxiety. If there is reason for my alarm, your departure will save me from destruction – and even if it is baseless, once you are away I shall at long last be freed from my fears.'

15. After his governorship of Africa (68–6) Catilina was due to be prosecuted for extortion.

If our country spoke to you in such terms, ought not her plea to be granted, even if she did not have the power to back it with force?

It is significant that you actually gave yourself voluntarily into custody, declaring that you wished to live in the house of Manius Lepidus in order to avoid suspicion. When he refused to receive you, you even had the audacity to come to myself and ask me to keep you at my house. But I replied that, since I was in the utmost peril while the two of us were even inside the same city, I should feel the very opposite of safe if we were together within a single house. Accordingly you went on to Quintus Metellus the praetor. When he likewise rebuffed you, your next visit was to your own marvellous associate Marcus Metellus.[16] How convinced you must have been that he would guard you most diligently, eye you with the very keenest suspicion, and intrepidly enforce against you the full rigours of the law! But when a man is himself so sure that he deserves to be under arrest, it is evident enough that prison chains ought not to be very far away.

So, then, Catilina, if you cannot die with a good grace, you ought at the very least to take yourself off with great alacrity to some other land, and having thus saved your life from a host of just and amply merited penalties, resign it to a future of exile and solitude.

'Refer the matter to the Senate,' you say. That is your demand, and if the Senate decides you should go into exile[17] you declare you will obey. I shall not refer it to them, for a step as rigorous as that would be against my principles. And yet all the same I propose to let you see what the Senators think of you. Get out of Rome, Catilina. Spare our country this feeling of panic. Go into exile, if that is the word you are

16. M. Metellus is unknown but was evidently a friend of Catilina.

17. The Senate did not, in fact, possess the authority to send anyone into exile, any more than the consuls (n. 11).

waiting to hear. Note and mark well how silent the Senators are. Their silence means that they agree; and when you see their wishes expressed without a sound, what need is there to wait for the spoken word?

If I had addressed the excellent Publius Sestius or the gallant Marcus Marcellus in these terms, the Senate would have been entirely justified in laying violent hands upon me in this very temple, consul though I am. But since it is yourself who are concerned, Catilina, their absence of words means approval, their acquiescence amounts to a formal resolution, their silence is the equivalent of a mighty cry. Nor does this apply only to the Senators, whose opinions you plainly value, though you rate their lives low. For the same is true also of the loyal, honourable Roman knights and other staunch citizens who are standing round outside this meeting. You had a sight of their large numbers just now. Their passionate feelings were paraded before your eyes; and you also heard clearly enough what they were shouting. For quite a time I have been hard put to it to keep their hands and weapons off you. When you quit the places which you have so long been planning to destroy, I shall have not the slightest difficulty in persuading them to escort you to the gates.

But why do I say all this? For nothing is likely to deter you from your purpose; nothing will make you mend your ways or contemplate flight or think of going into exile. If only the gods might incline you in that direction, what a wonderful thing it would be!

And yet, if you did by any chance take fright at my words and decided to go away into banishment, I am well aware that a storm of unpopularity would then fall upon myself, not perhaps now when the recollection of your crimes is still fresh, but in the years to come. However, I judge that prospect amply worth while, provided only that my ruin remains personal to myself and does not at the same time imperil our country.

But it is evidently no use expecting you to be disturbed by your own crimes, or to stand in awe of legal penalties, or give way to a national emergency. For you are by no means the man, Catilina, to let shame deter you from evil-doing, or fear from perilous adventures, or reason from acts of madness. I have urged you repeatedly to get out. If, as you proclaim, I am your enemy, if you want to stir up hatred against me, the very best thing that you could do would be to go straight into exile. For if that becomes your decision, I know I shall have a difficult time enduring all the criticisms that will descend upon my head; if your banishment should be due to the consul's orders, the odium falling upon myself, the consul, will be hard indeed to bear. But if, instead, your aim is to increase my reputation and glory, take your degraded herd of rascals and go with them to Manlius. Stir up, by all means, the dregs of our community, and alienate every honest man. Make war on your own country; behave like a godless brigand, and revel in the fact. For then it will be abundantly clear that I have not driven you into the arms of strangers, but that you have merely responded to an invitation to join your own friends.

And yet I do not see why I should be urging this course upon you, because I am well aware that you have already sent armed men ahead to wait for your arrival at Forum Aurelium. I know you have fixed a day with Manlius. I know you have sent ahead your silver eagle,[18] the one which you housed in a blasphemous shrine in your home – and may it bring ruin and annihilation upon you and all your friends! When you were about to set forth to commit a murder, you used to bow down before this object; upon its altar rested your god-forsaken hand before you lifted it to massacre Roman citizens. Where your eagle has gone, you yourself will assuredly soon follow.

18. The eagle was reputed to be the standard used by Marius in the war against the Cimbri.

And so, at long last, you will have made for the destination to which your unbridled, deranged ambition has all this time been dragging you. Nor does the prospect cause you a bit of grief. No, it fills your heart with a kind of unimaginable delight. This is the lunacy for which nature has brought you into the world and your own will has trained you – for which destiny has kept you alive. You never wanted peace; and the only war you wanted was a horrible one. Around yourself you have collected a depraved gang compounded of ruffians utterly abandoned by fortune and even by hope. Among them you will be able to indulge in every excess of gloating and exultation and debauchery, since among all the number of your associates you will not hear the voice or see the face of one single decent man. For that kind of life these exertions of yours, of which men speak, have been excellent practice – lying on the bare ground, well placed to tackle the object of your lusts or commit a variety of evil deeds; and keeping wakeful watch by night, to take advantage of some husband's sleep or rob peaceful citizens of their property. Now you have every opportunity for exhibitions of your famous endurance of hunger, cold and every discomfort. Indeed, soon you will be experiencing a good deal too much of them all. And so, by preventing you from becoming consul, here at any rate is one thing that I have achieved. For I am at least able to ensure that your attacks on our country are made in the capacity of an exile rather than a consul, and that it is abundantly clear, from the nature of your foul enterprise, that you are no fighter and nothing but a bandit.

And now, Senators, I want to avert and fend off a protest which my country, almost with some justification, might address to me. So I urge you to listen carefully to what I am going to say, and to store it in your innermost hearts and minds. For let us imagine that this land of ours, which is far dearer to me than my life itself, let us imagine that all Italy and our entire nation addressed me in some such terms as these: 'Marcus Tullius, what are you doing? You have discovered that this man is a public enemy. You are well aware he will be the leader of your foes in the war. You know the enemy camp is waiting for him to take command. You have learnt that he is the planner of this criminal enterprise and the instigator of the plot, a mobilizer of slaves and of the most disreputable citizens he can find. Are you really going to let him go? If you do, it will by no means look as though you are ejecting him from the city; it will seem as though you are letting him loose for its destruction. It is surely your duty to bid him be cast into chains and hurried off to supreme retribution and death. What can be preventing you? Is it our ancestral custom? And yet, in this country, even private individuals have inflicted the capital penalty upon treasonable citizens. Is it the law about punishing Roman citizens that deters you?[19] But Rome has never accepted that rebels against the state enjoy the rights of citizens.

'Or are you afraid of censure from posterity? Now, in your career, you have had nothing but your own deeds to recommend you. There were no distinctions won by your ancestors to give you a start. Nevertheless, at an early age, the Roman people advanced you from one post to another, at every level, up to the highest office of the state. A fine return you are giving them if the fear of incurring dislike, or indeed if any kind of danger whatever, makes you neglect your fellow citizens' security! If the question of inviting disapproval arises at all, the unpopularity resulting from firmness and determination is no more to be dreaded than the opprobrium produced by culpable failure to act. For when Italy is to be ravaged by war, when cities are assaulted and houses gutted by fire, do you not see how utterly the flames of hatred will consume you then?'

To those solemn remonstrances addressed to me by our

19. According to the Valerian, Porcian and Sempronian laws only the Assembly could condemn a Roman citizen to death.

country – by the men whose feelings such reproaches reflect – I will offer this brief answer. Had I thought it best, Senators, that Catilina should be put to death, I would not have given that gladiator the enjoyment of one single further hour of life. For seeing that our most eminent and distinguished citizens of earlier times, when they shed the blood of Saturninus and the Gracchi and Flaccus and many others, did not by any means stain their reputations but even enhanced them, I certainly had not the smallest reason to fear that the execution of this murderer of Roman citizens would cause me to be blamed by posterity. And indeed, even if this were a serious danger, I have always been convinced that unpopularity earned by honourable actions is not unpopularity at all, but renown.

And yet there are some men here in this Senate who either genuinely fail to see, or make a pretence of not seeing, the disasters by which we are menaced. Their mildness has fostered Catilina's hopes, and their refusal to believe in his growing conspiracy has given it strength.

Had I punished Catilina, their influence would cause many persons, some of them malignant but others merely ignorant, to say that I had acted with tyrannical brutality. True, it is clear enough that if he joins Manlius' camp, for which he is now bound, no one will be too stupid to realize that a conspiracy has come into existence or too dishonest to admit it. Yet if, on the other hand, Catilina is executed and nobody else dies with him, it is very clear to me that the disease which is eating into our country may be checked for a short time, but cannot be completely cured. But if, instead, he removes himself, and takes his friends away too, and concentrates in one single place all the derelicts who have joined him from every quarter, not only will this pestilence which rages in our nation be obliterated and stamped out, but the very roots and seeds of the plague will also be eradicated.

Senators, we have been living for a long time among the

perils and snares of his conspiracy. But somehow or other it was reserved for my consulship to witness all these incurable manias and outrages and horrors coming to a head and breaking out into open view. If the horde of looters is diminished by the removal of this single man, we shall perhaps have the brief illusion of finding a respite from our anxieties and fears. But the danger will still be here, lurking deep within the veins and vital parts of our nation. When a very sick person, tossing about in a burning fever, takes a drink of cold water, at first he thinks it has made him better, but afterwards he feels much more seriously and violently ill than he did before. In just the same way the disease that afflicts our nation will at first seem relieved by the punishment of this single individual, but later it will get much worse: since the others will still be alive.

Therefore let all bad citizens be gone. Let them separate themselves from the good, and gather together in a single place – segregated, as I have often suggested before, by a wall. Let them no longer lay snares for the consul in his own home, stand around the tribunal of the city praetor,[20] besiege the Senate House with their swords, and mobilize their fire-bombs and brands to plunge the city into flames. Finally, let every man's political views be written on his brow for all to see. I swear to you, Senators, that we consuls are going to display such vigour, you yourselves to carry so much weight, the knights to display so great courage, and all patriotic men to act with such a single and unanimous accord, that once Catilina has departed you will see everything brought out clearly into the light of day, and the time of suppression and punishment will be at hand.

So these are the omens, Catilina, with which I bid you get off to your wicked and traitorous war. Your departure will be the cause of supreme salvation for the state. It will cause your own ruin and downfall, and the extermination of those who

20. The city praetor who apparently had a permanent tribunal in the Forum, was in charge of cases involving debt.

have been your accomplices in every one of your murderous atrocities. And you, Jupiter, who were set up in this place by Romulus under the selfsame auspices as our own city itself, who are justly named by us the Stayer[21] of this city and its empire, you will keep this man and his associates away from the dwellings and walls of Rome, away from the lives and properties of all its citizens. And as for these rogues whom every patriot hates, the enemies of our country and ravishers of Italy, united in their infamous alliance by a compact of abomination, you will immolate them, dead or alive, in retribution without end.

THE SECOND SPEECH
Delivered to the People

Even if Cicero had really hoped for Catilina's arrest, his 'voluntary' departure for the rebel camp at Faesulae on the very night following the First Speech gave the orator plausible and real grounds for self-justification in this second speech, pronounced on the next day (9 November) before the wider and less knowledgeable audience of the Assembly, convened in the Roman Forum. The written version of the speech retains much of the verve and vividness of its original delivery, and the account that it gave of the conspiracy clearly exercised a profoundly persuasive effect. The portrait of Catilina is an exaggerated set-piece of abuse in the grand satanic style, displaying the bogey-man who was the projection of every property-owner's bad dreams; but the analysis of his backers is an acute and fascinating contribution to contemporary history. Yet Cicero, in spite of his desire to emphasize the importance of the conspiracy, finds it desirable, at this juncture, to underestimate the range of supporters available to Catilina (for example, he says nothing of his success with society ladies), since the orator wanted to stress their disreputable character.

21. Jupiter Stator, the Stayer, was supposedly so called because he had stayed the flight of Romulus' army from the Sabines.

And there is little to be learnt, except by reading between the lines, about the appalling social and economic evils which made many besides outcasts feel restive at the harsh and unimaginative rule of the traditional governmental class: the class whose failures and weaknesses, revolted against by a series of powerful generals, were soon to bring down the Republic which Cicero was so proud of having served during this consulship of 63.

At long last, citizens, Lucius Catilina, blazing with insolence, breathing forth blasts of every audacious rascality, outrageously plotting to overthrow his country, menacing yourselves and our city with fire and sword, has been expelled from Rome by our action – or allowed to leave, or bidden farewell as he took his departure. Gone, retired, run away, broken out – express it how you will. At all events, this unnatural monster will no longer enjoy the shelter of our walls while scheming to hurl them to the ground.

And we, for our part, have indisputably vanquished the supreme initiator of this civil war. No longer will that dagger of his be brandished within an inch of us. Whether on the Campus Martius, or in the Forum, or within the Senate House, or inside our own homes, we can throw off our tormenting fears. When Catilina was driven from the city he lost his point of vantage. Now we shall be carrying on a regular war against a national enemy, and no one shall get in our way. By flushing the man out of his secret hiding-place into open brigandage, we have unmistakably brought about his destruction. It was a brilliant success.

He had hoped to take with him a sword dripping with blood. But this he did not do. For he departed without depriving us of our lives; we had wrested the sword from his hands! He has left behind him the citizens of Rome, alive and safe, and the city itself still undestroyed. This, believe me, distresses him deeply. Romans, he is prostrated. He knows he is a ruined outcast – and we may be sure that he often turns his gaze back upon this city and laments that it was snatched from his jaws. And Rome has corresponding reason to rejoice, because it has brought up and spewed forth this pestilential object from its system.

Yet I fully expected to be attacked and censured – with truly right-minded severity – for the selfsame thing upon which I am now triumphantly congratulating myself: namely, because I decided to send this deadly enemy away rather than place him under arrest. The answer, however, is, gentlemen, that the blame does not lie with me, but rather with the circumstances. It is indeed true that Lucius Catilina should long ago have been put to death by the solemn supreme penalty. The custom of our ancestors, the sternness incumbent upon my office, and the interests of our nation, alike demanded this of me. But there were quite a number of people, you know, who did not believe what I was telling them. There were men who were actually prepared to speak up for Catilina – people too stupid to see what the situation was, or even malevolent enough to become his supporters. If I had believed that his removal would free you from all danger, I should long ago have eliminated Lucius Catilina, at the risk of my own popularity or even of my life.

But it became clear to me that even you yourselves were not unanimous in approving this course of action, and that, if I had put him to the death he deserved, the consequent outcry against myself would have made it impossible to go on and tackle his accomplices. That being so, I instead arranged matters so that you would be able to see the enemy undisguised and fight him in the open. And you will appreciate how little danger I now see in Catilina, once he has gone away from the city, when I tell you I am actually sorry that so few of his associates accompanied him when he left. It would have been far better if he had taken all his forces with him. Certainly, he took Tongilius, whose lover he had been since the creature was a mere boy, and he took Publicius and

Minucius. But their unpaid bills at eating-houses could scarcely overthrow the constitution; whereas think of all the debt-ridden, aristocratic heroes he has left behind to make trouble here.

In comparison with the legions in Gaul this side of the Alps, and the troops raised by Quintus Metellus in Picenum and the parts of Gaul on the near bank of the Po,[22] in addition to the forces we are mobilizing every day, I regard Catilina's soldiery as beneath contempt. It is a mere rabble of elderly down-and-outs, rustic debauchees, bankrupt country bumpkins, and characters who find it less trouble to forfeit their bail than to desert from Catilina's ranks. Men of this type will collapse if I show them the praetor's edict, not to speak of a line of troops. But these creatures whom I see hovering about the Forum and lounging around outside the Senate House and even walking into the Senate, individuals glistening with scent and glittering with purple, I do wish he had taken them to be his warriors too! For if they stay here, mark my words, we shall need to be more anxious about these deserters from his army than about the actual army itself. And they are the more to be feared because they realize – though this does not seem to bother them – that I am aware of all their inmost thoughts. For I know who has been allotted Apulia, and Etruria, and the Picenum country, and Gaul our side of the Po, and who on the other hand has claimed for himself the metropolitan part of the plot with its plans for massacre and conflagration. These men realize perfectly well that full reports of their machinations of two nights ago came into my hands. After all, I revealed them in the Senate yesterday. When I did so, Catilina himself took fright and fled. So what are his accomplices waiting for? If they cherish hopes that my earlier leniency will last for ever, they are profoundly mistaken.

22. Cispadane Gaul approximately corresponded with the present Emilia.

What I have been aiming at, I have now finally achieved: namely, that it may be clear to every one of you that a conspiracy has been openly formed against the state – unless, indeed, there are still people who refuse to see that men who share Catilina's character will inevitably share his political views as well. There is no place, now, for mercy. Rigorous sternness is what the situation demands. And yet one thing I will grant even at this late stage. They can still get out! Let them vanish from the scene; let them not allow poor Catilina to pine away because he misses them so much. I will show them the route – he went by the Via Aurelia, and if they choose to hurry they will catch him up by evening. What happiness for Rome if it really could succeed in eliminating all this load of waste! Even after the purge of Catilina and no one else, heaven knows, the city is beginning to look relieved and revived already.

For imagine every type of criminality and wickedness that you can think of; he has been behind them all. In the whole of Italy there is not one single poisoner, gladiator, robber, assassin, parricide, will-forger, cheat, glutton, wastrel, adulterer, prostitute, corrupter of youth, or youth who has been corrupted, indeed any nasty individual of any kind whatever, who would not be obliged to admit he has been Catilina's intimate. Whenever, all through these years, there has been a murder, the murderer has been he. Not one single act of filthy lechery has been committed without him being its guiding spirit. For no one has ever had such a talent for seducing young men. He himself became the lover of a number of them, in the most repulsive fashion; and he disgustingly allowed others to make love to himself. The incentives he offered varied from the mere satisfaction of lust to the murder of their parents, a path along which he not only encouraged these youths but personally lent a hand. With astonishing speed he collected around him a great crowd of ruffians, from the country as well as the city. Neither in Rome nor in any other corner of Italy was there a single debtor whom he failed to enlist in this incredible league of crime.

And note well the diversity of his interests, the wide range of his activities. If a training-school for gladiators contains an inmate with criminal inclinations, be sure he will claim he is Catilina's close friend. Or, take any light-weight actor of lowish principles; he is certain to declare they have been going around together. Here was a man whose endurance of cold and hunger and thirst and sleepless nights was the product of his sexual enormities and evil deeds. These degenerate outcasts declared him a brave man. He had, it is true, the qualities that make for physical energy and moral strength. But, instead, he dissipated them in orgies of sex and violence.

If his accomplices go where he has gone, if these infamous swarms of desperate men depart from Rome, how happy we shall be, how fortunate our country, how enthusiastic the compliments about my consulship! For theirs are no ordinary dissipations; their scandals have passed every limit of humanity and tolerance. All they think of is assassination and arson and loot. They have squandered their inheritances, mortgaged their properties. Their money has long since run out, and recently credit has begun to fail them too. And yet the filthy tastes they indulged when there were funds to spare are still very much in evidence. Now, if during their drinking and gambling bouts they merely caroused and whored, they would be hopeless enough cases, it is true, yet they could be put up with all the same. But what is unbearable is that these spiritless, stupid, drunken, somnolent brutes should be plotting to cut down citizens who are pre-eminent for their courage and wisdom and sobriety and energy. For as these individuals recline at their banquets and embrace their harlots, dazed by wine and stuffed by food, garlanded with wreathes and smothered with scents and riddled with every sort of lewdness, the vomit which issues from their mouths consists of talk about massacring every loyal citizen and burning the city to the ground.

I believe they are doomed. I am convinced that the punishment long since due to their iniquity and vileness and lust is by no means far away. Indeed, it may already be right on top of them. If my consulship succeeds in getting rid of these men whom it has found no means to cure, it will have extended the life of our state not just by some trivial duration but by the space of many centuries. There is no foreign nation which need cause us alarm, no monarch capable of making war on Rome. On land and sea, one single valiant man[23] has brought universal peace. What a contrast to this civil war in our midst! Here, set deep inside the country, are conspiracy, danger and a deadly foe. Degeneracy, madness and evil are the enemies we have to fight. In this war, Romans, it is I who offer myself as your commander. The hostility of these criminals I take upon myself. What can be healed I will somehow contrive to heal, and what must be cut away I shall not allow to spread and involve our country in mortal peril. And so let these creatures remove themselves. Or let them, instead, be at peace. If, on the other hand, they remain in the city and persist in this purpose of theirs, then they must expect the retaliation they deserve.

It is being said, citizens, that I am the man who has driven Catilina out into exile. Now the people I should like to drive out, if this could be done by word of mouth alone, are precisely those who make this sort of allegation. I suppose you will tell me that the retiring, bashful Catilina was too sensitive to endure an utterance by the consul – when he was ordered to go into exile, he straight away did just exactly what he was told!

Consider what happened yesterday. After I had almost been murdered in my own home, I convened a meeting of the Senate at the temple of Jupiter the Stayer, and gave its members a comprehensive report. When Catilina entered, not one single Senator spoke to him, or offered a greeting. Without

23. The reference is to Pompeius.

exception they regarded him, not merely as a debauchee, but as a public enemy of peculiarly dangerous character. Why, the leading Senators actually left that whole area of seats where he had taken his place entirely empty and deserted! Then I – this tough consul whose pronouncements drive citizens into exile – asked Catilina whether he had been at the meeting in Marcus Laeca's house the previous night or not. But he, his impudence momentarily quelled by awareness of guilt, remained silent. Then I went on to reveal the rest of the story. I disclosed what he had done that night, what he plotted for the following night, how he had designed the entire operations of the war. And then, seeing he was evidently trapped and at a loss, I asked what was delaying his departure for the destination he had long since proposed for himself: since, to my certain knowledge, weapons, ceremonial rods and axes, trumpets and military standards had already been sent on – as well as the silver eagle which he had cherished in that shrine of profanity within his home. How could I be driving into exile the man who I knew perfectly well had already launched out into war? You cannot surely suppose that Manlius, the centurion who has pitched his camp in the territory of Faesulae, was declaring war upon the Roman people on his own account. You are not going to tell me that the idea of Manlius' people waiting for Catilina to arrive and take over the command is a fiction – and that the banished citizen is really off to Massilia,[24] and not to the camp at all.

It is indeed a grim task, not only to govern the country, but even merely to ensure its survival. For suppose that Lucius Catilina, feeling hemmed in and disabled by all the measures and endeavours for which I have been responsible at such great personal risk, suddenly takes fright, reverses his intentions, deserts his friends, gives up his plans to start a war and abandons his nefarious martial projects in favour of flight and

24. According to Sallust, Catilina had written to various friends saying he was leaving for Massilia.

exile. If that happens, not everyone will applaud me for taking his insolent weapons away from him, dazing and terrifying him by my vigilance, frustrating him in all his hopes and schemes. Some people will say instead that here is an unconvicted, guiltless citizen who has been driven into banishment by a threatening, violent consul. If, that is to say, he behaves as I am suggesting, there will be men ready to treat him not as a criminal at all but actually as a martyr, and myself not as a consul who is doing his duty but as a tyrant of the cruellest kind.

And yet, gentlemen, I am perfectly prepared to endure this storm of unjustified, undeserved hatred if only the menace of a horrifying and iniquitous war can be averted from all of you. Let it, therefore, by all means be said that I have driven him into exile – if only that is where he goes. But, believe me, he will do nothing of the sort. No desire to spare myself hostility will ever be enough to make me actually *hope* you will be told that Lucius Catilina is commanding an enemy force and marching from place to place under arms. Yet in three days that is exactly what you will have heard – and I am much more afraid that in time to come I shall be detested for letting him go rather than for expelling him from Rome. And as for the people who, now that he has departed, complain he was driven out, whatever would they have said if he had been put to death instead?

In any case the persons who keep lamenting that Catilina is on his way to Massilia are showing a sympathy that is distinctly misplaced. It is true that they do not desire him to go to Massilia. What they want, out of their goodwill towards him, is that he should join Manlius. But this is the strangest way to show their generous feelings for the man: though he himself, admittedly, even if he had never contemplated his present evil projects at all, is precisely the sort of person who would rather die an outlaw's violent death than live in banishment. Indeed, for Catilina, everything has gone exactly according to his desires and designs – except only that I was still alive when he withdrew from Rome. As for ourselves, instead of complaining that he has gone into exile, we can only wish he would!

But it is wrong to speak at such length about one single public enemy – an enemy who is self-confessed, and causes me no alarm because the wall I have always wanted to have between us is now there. Something must also be said about the conspirators who are concealing their intentions and staying on with us in Rome. If at all possible, I do not want to punish these offenders. I want, instead, to reconcile them with their own selves and hearts, and with our country; and I see no reason why this should not be done, if they are willing to listen to what I have to say. I will show you, gentlemen, the various types of men from whom their ranks are filled. And then I will apply to each in turn such therapeutic treatment as my advice and persuasion are capable of providing.

The first class consists of those who have large debts but even larger property, from both of which they are so inseparable that nothing can tear them loose. These men have an air of respectability, for they are wealthy, but their ambitions and intentions are scandalous. Let me speak to them and ask them this: since you are so abundantly endowed with lands and residences and silver plate and every sort of material goods, what holds you back from selling some of your property to make yourselves solvent again? What are you waiting for? War? But surely you cannot imagine that amid the general devastation those possessions of yours will be in any way sacrosanct. Or are you hoping for a general list of cancelled debts? Anyone who expects that from Catilina is going to be disappointed. Certainly – and this will emerge from a beneficial measure I myself have in mind – there are going to be lists. But they will be lists of goods up for auction; for that is the only way in which these property-owners can ever pay back what they owe. If they had been willing to act in this way earlier instead of stupidly struggling to pay the interest on their debts out of the produce of their estates, we should now find them better and more prosperous citizens. But this is the least formidable among the various categories of people involved, because they can be induced to change their attitudes – or even if they remain impenitent, they are more likely to assail the government with petitions than with force of arms.

The second class is composed of men who are again heavily in debt, but who expect to come into power. For they propose to seize control of the state. They believe that when the country is in a chaotic situation they will be able to win the official posts which they despair of gaining under peaceful conditions. However, in the hope of making them give up the idea of ever achieving such a purpose, I suggest that they (and for that matter all the rest as well) should be made aware of certain plain facts. First of all, they should know that I myself am on guard: the interests of our country are in my watchful care. And in the second place it should be clear to them that there is a magnificent spirit, a total unanimity, among our loyal citizens – they are exceedingly numerous, and they dispose of a substantial body of troops. And finally, the immortal gods, by their active presences, will give succour to this invincible people, this glorious realm, this most beautiful of cities, against all such abominable intentions. Besides, even if, despite all, these madmen achieved what they are after, they need entertain no hopes that amid the ashes of Rome and the blood of its citizens, for which they have such a perverted and infamous longing, the consuls or dictators or even kings would be themselves. For surely they must see that they would be compelled to surrender these objects of their desire to some runaway slave or gladiator instead.

The third class of Catilina's followers comprises men who are already showing the effects of age but still remain vigorous from constant physical exercise. In this category is the fellow Manlius from whom Catilina is just taking over. These are the settlers from the towns colonized by Sulla. I am well aware that most of the people who live in such foundations are worthy and gallant citizens. But they do, all the same, also include a certain number of individuals whose sudden, unexpected riches have plunged them into immoderately expensive habits. While they are treating themselves to wealthy men's building programmes and taking pleasure in their choice estates and vast slave-households and elaborate dinner-parties, they have borrowed such a lot of money that the only way to achieve solvency again would be to raise Sulla from the dead. They have also excited a number of insignificant, poverty-stricken countryfolk to share their optimistic belief that loot will again be forthcoming as in times gone by. I classify these rustics, like the colonists, in the category of plunderers or robbers. But I give them this warning. They must get rid of their insane ideas of proscriptions and dictatorships. The misery of the times when such things were among us is so indelibly branded on the memory of our country that I truly believe neither the human race nor even the beasts of the field would tolerate their horrors again today.

The fourth class is varied, mixed and tempestuous: the men who went under long ago, who never get their heads above water, whose laziness, incompetence and extravagance combine to send them reeling beneath their perpetual debts. Wearied by bankruptcy summonses and court cases and compulsory auctions, large numbers of these individuals are reported to be converging on that camp from city and rural areas alike. I reckon that such people are not eager soldiers at all; they are nothing but indolent defaulters. If they cannot keep themselves going, the best thing would be for them to collapse as promptly as possible, and with so little noise that the incident is kept quite private from their fellow-citizens and even from their nearest neighbours. For I cannot see why, if they are unable to live decently, they should also have this passion for a shameful death. Why should they think it less painful to die in a large company than by themselves?

The fifth class includes the people who have murdered their parents, and assassins in general, and vile characters of every kind. Of my detaching these from Catilina there can be no question, because they have not the slightest desire to be prised apart from him. Let them perish in their villainous enterprises, say I, since they are far too numerous for any prison[25] to be large enough to hold them.

The last class ranks lowest not only in numbers but in its way of life. This is Catilina's special treasure, his picked elect, formed from his own beloved cronies and bosom friends. You can see them about, lovely young men with elegantly combed hair, either beardless or bearded to excess, wearing tunics that reach down to the wrists and ankles, and togas which look more like veils. Their entire interest in life and all the alertness they can muster are squandered on parties that last all night long. In these gangs are to be found every gambler, adulterer, debauchee and sensualist who exists. These soft and pretty boys are experts at making love and having love made to them, and they know how to dance and sing; but they have also learnt to wave daggers about and sprinkle poisons. Unless they depart from this city, unless they die (and this remains true even if Catilina himself should die), you can rest assured that this hotbed of future Catilinas will continue to fester in our midst.

Yet what are these wretched characters after? I cannot believe that they are really proposing to bring their fancy women into the camp. Yet how on earth will they be able to get on without them, especially on nights like this? How will they manage to endure the Apennines and all that frost and

25. At this time Rome only had one prison, with two cells, of which the lower, the Tullianum, was used for the execution of death-sentences.

snow? Or perhaps they imagine that their habit of dancing naked at parties will give them useful experience for enduring winter conditions? Catilina's praetorian guard of pansies is certainly going to add to the terrors of the war.

Now as for you, citizens, you must counter these remarkable troops of his with your own defences and armies. Against the shagged and damaged gladiator himself you can pit your consuls and commanders. In opposition to his enervated gang of outcast wrecks you are able to marshal the flower and strength of all Italy. The tangled upland lairs where Catilina lurks will be dealt with as they deserve by the cities that are your colonies and municipalities.[26] There is no need for me to compare all your resources and war materials and garrisons with the shabby penury of a gangster, or to list all the things that we possess and he does not – the Senate, the order of knights, the people of Rome, the city, the treasury, the revenue from taxation, the whole land of Italy, all the provinces of the empire and every one of our allies.

Indeed, even if we leave all these assets aside and limit ourselves to contrasting the merits of the rival causes, their hopeless inferiority again becomes utterly clear. Our cause is respectable, theirs disreputable; ours decent, theirs obscene; ours trustworthy, theirs fraudulent; ours patriotic, theirs traitorous; ours determined, theirs hysterical; ours honourable, theirs infamous; ours a model of self-restraint, theirs given up wholly to lechery. On one side of the confrontation are justice, moderation, courage, wisdom and all that is good: on the other the contestants are injustice, over-indulgence, cowardice, recklessness and everything that is bad. Prosperity fights against destitution, right against wrong, sanity against madness, fairest hope against bottomless despair. In a conflict

26. At this period all self-governing Italian boroughs were called *municipia*, other than the 'colonies' to which settlers had been sent at various epochs.

and battle of this kind, even if the hearts of human beings may flag, surely the immortal gods themselves would ordain that this mass of hideous vices must fall before such an array of immeasurably glorious virtues.

Nevertheless, gentlemen, take my advice and set watchmen and guards to protect your houses. To ensure that the city itself shall have safe protection, I have taken all the necessary steps – without involving you in any upheaval or inconvenience. I have notified all your colonial towns and municipalities about Catilina's nocturnal break-out, and they will have no difficulty in defending their walls and their territories. The gladiators, too, whom he expected to have as his firmest supporters (and indeed they have more spirit than some of the patricians) will be kept under control by my authority. When I foresaw what has now happened I sent Quintus Metellus to Picenum and Gaul this side of the Po, and he will either strike Catilina down or at least forestall every one of his movements and manoeuvres. All the other arrangements that need to be planned, expedited and pursued I shall refer to the Senate, which as you see is being convened.

To the men who have stayed behind in Rome or, rather, who have been left here by Catilina with the intention of wiping out the city and every single individual among you, I offer and reiterate this warning: for although they have become enemies, they were, after all, born Roman citizens. If anyone has felt I have shown excessive leniency up to now, I was holding back precisely for this – I was waiting for what lay hidden to burst out into the open and be revealed. As for the future, it is impossible for me to forget that Rome is my country and that I am the consul of all you people who are assembled here – with whom I will live, if you live, or die on your behalf! At the gates there are no sentries, on the road I have set no ambush. If there are those who desire to take their leave, I can connive at it. But if, on the other hand, there is a single move inside Rome itself, if I detect any move against

our government or even the first beginnings or attempts at
such a move, its instigator will have good reason to discover
that this city of ours is not lacking in vigilant consuls, reliable
officials, a courageous Senate, all the weapons that are needed –
and the prison which our forefathers appointed as a place
where the gravest convicted crimes receive their due.

And all such measures will be taken, citizens, in such a way
that these mighty issues be settled with the least possible
disturbance. The dangers will be dispelled without dramatic
alarms. The most formidable and horrifying civil war in
human memory will be disposed of under the sole and single
leadership and command of myself – wearing the clothes of
peace. Indeed, if it can be done, gentlemen, I will so arrange
matters within the city that not one single man, however vile
he may be, shall pay the penalty his wrongdoing deserves.
And if, all the same, an open revolutionary outbreak – menacing our country with annihilation – makes it inevitable that I
should modify this merciful spirit, there is nevertheless one
thing which I shall continue to promise: though it almost
seems beyond hope when so far-reaching and hazardous a war
is concerned. That is to say, even if such circumstances arise, I
still propose to ensure that not one loyal citizen shall lose his
life, and that the penalties imposed shall fall on the very
smallest number of people compatible with the salvation of
you all.

This assurance, Romans, comes from no wisdom of my
own, and indeed from no merely human processes of reason-
ing. No, it is derived rather from a number of manifest
intimations received from the gods themselves. It is they who
have directed me to formulate the hope and purpose which
guide my actions. In bygone times they were wont to protect
us, from afar, against our foreign enemies, who were also far
away. But here and now, it is their own temples they are
defending, and the dwellings of Rome itself. Their divine
power and aid are with us; they are here by our side. From

these heavenly beings comes the ordinance that has made our city more beautiful, more splendid and more powerful than any other upon earth. Wherefore, citizens, it is your bounden duty to pray and implore and beseech the gods that this city of ours, which has vanquished all the hosts of our foreign foes on land and sea, should be defended from this outrageous conspiracy plotted by Roman citizens of the most loathsome character.

THE THIRD SPEECH
Delivered to the People

When Cicero came before the Assembly of the Roman people again on 3 December he had received an absolute godsend. A deputation from the Allobroges, a tribe living in Dauphiné and Savoy which now formed part of the Roman province of Gallia Narbonensis, had been tampered with by the Catilinarian leaders who had stayed on in Rome after Catilina's departure. In spite of their extreme discontent with the oppressive rule of Rome these Gauls had, after reflection, given (or sold) this information to their Roman patron Quintus Fabius Sanga, who in turn conveyed it to Cicero. In this speech the whole exciting story was told, and any remaining doubts about the reality of the conspiracy were dispelled.

These representatives of Catilina in Rome had made a sorry mess of the plot, and Cicero was justified in pointing out that his success in ejecting Catilina from the city had left a not very formidable collection of traitors behind; though this was a somewhat two-edged argument, since although it showed how wise he had been in getting rid of Catilina it later made it difficult to stress how important the urban conspiracy had been as well. And its leaders in fact, although they behaved so indiscreetly, were not such insignificant figures as might be inferred from this speech. Publius Cornelius Lentulus Sura was an imposing and popular orator with a fine voice; angry because, like others, he was expelled from the Senate for misconduct, he had *recovered to hold a second praetorship in 63. Gaius Cornelius Cethegus, too, was dangerous because he was a Senator of the same patrician clan as his colleague, and a man of formidable and (according to Cicero) murderous energy.*

This is a racy popular harangue telling an excellent tale, but it is a little disconcerting for the modern reader when Cicero – who later went on record as a sceptic about divination – once again enlarges, at considerable length, upon the signs of the divine will that had been seen. Such, however, were among the patriotic requirements of a speech delivered before the people as opposed to the more sophisticated gathering of Senators.

Cicero was speaking at extremely short notice only a very few hours after these dramatic events had occurred. The speech, as we have it, ends on a note of defiant but acute worry for his own personal safety. But such a tone may not have been so prominent in the spoken version, since it was probably introduced at the time of publication three years after the event, when the unanimous support Cicero's oratory had gained at the height of the excitement had vanished into thin air, and his enemies were in the ascendant.

Romans: your country, and the lives of every one of you, your property, your fortunes, your wives and children, this centre of your illustrious government, this most fortunate and beautiful of cities – today it has been made manifest to you that the outstanding love which the immortal gods bear you, as well as my own labours and endeavours at the risk of my life, have rescued all these blessings from fire and the sword, from the very jaws of death, and have given them back to you safe and sound.

Days on which we are preserved from danger are no less happy and bright to us than the day on which we were born. For there is a splendid certainty about the joy of being rescued from something, whereas the human condition to which we were born into this world is very far from certain – and, besides, while our births were accompanied by no feelings at all, to be rescued from peril is an exhilarating experience. And by this token, seeing that our affection and glorification have held the man who brought this city to birth to be worthy of a place in heaven, it is incumbent upon yourselves, and your descendants after you, to honour also the person who, now that Rome is founded and made great, has brought it salvation.

For under the entire city, beneath every one of its temples and shrines and habitations and walls, the flames for the holocaust were all set and prepared. But we were able to stamp them out. Swords were drawn against the state: but we blunted them and fended off their sharp points from your throats. In the Senate I have revealed all these things and brought them out into the light of day, and now, citizens, I shall briefly communicate them to yourselves. For you have not yet been told, and you are surely anxious to hear, the terrible and flagrant nature of what has been discovered, and the means by which it was investigated and detected.

First of all, when Catilina broke out of town a few days ago,[27] he left behind him at Rome the associates in his odious designs, the ferocious leaders of this horrible war. Since then I have continually been on the watch, citizens, planning how we may best be saved from these deadly clandestine intrigues. For at the time when I drove Catilina out of the city – you see I am no longer afraid that unpopularity will descend upon me for saying this; I am much more likely to incur it for leaving him alive – at the time, I say, when I wanted him to go into banishment, I believed that either the rest of the gang of conspirators would vanish with himself or those who stayed behind would be weak and impotent once he was no longer with them. But I soon saw that, instead, we still had with us in Rome a collection of men whose madness and malignancy knew no limits. And from then onwards I devoted every day

27. In fact nearly four weeks had passed since the departure of Catilina.

and every night to discovering and understanding how they spent their time and what their intentions were. For since I realized that the unbelievable enormity of their criminal design would make you incredulous of what I was going to say, I aimed at getting such a thorough grasp of the whole business that when you had seen the whole frightful scheme with your own eyes you would thereafter, at long last, take whole-hearted measures of self-preservation.

It came to my ears that Publius Lentulus had tried to corrupt the envoys of the Allobroges, in the hope of starting a war across the Alps and a Gallic insurrection; that the envoys were returning to their own people in Gaul with letters and instructions and that Titus Volturcius had been told to accompany them, and had been given a letter to Catilina.

Now, I thought, my chance had come to accomplish a very difficult purpose which I had always prayed that heaven would allow me to achieve, namely that the whole business should be shown up and exposed, not by myself alone, but by you and the Senate as well. Yesterday, then, I summoned our valiant and loyal praetors Lucius Flaccus and Gaius Pomptinus. I explained the situation and told them what they should do. They, being men whose patriotism is irreproachable, accepted my orders without the slightest hesitation or delay. And so, as it was getting to be evening, they made their way secretly to the Milvian bridge and stationed themselves within the nearest houses, dividing their forces into two detachments on either side of the Tiber and its bridge. Without arousing a breath of suspicion they had brought with them a considerable company of staunch followers, and I had added a picked unit from the country town of Reate, which I regularly employ for police duties on national business.

Very early on the following day, between three and four o'clock in the morning, the envoys of the Allobroges, accompanied by a large retinue including Volturcius, began to move across the Milvian bridge. Suddenly our men burst out upon them; and swords were drawn on both sides. Nobody had any idea what was happening except the praetors, Pomptinus and Flaccus, who intervened to bring the fighting to an end. All the letters which the company was carrying were delivered up to the praetors with their seals intact. The members of the party were taken into custody, and brought to me as dawn was breaking. I immediately sent for the worst character among all the plotters, Gabinius – as savage as any Cimbrian[28] – who as yet suspected nothing. Then Lucius Statilius was summoned, and after him Gaius Cethegus. Lentulus, on the other hand, arrived a slow last, presumably because (contrary to his usual lazy habits) he had stayed up so late writing letters.

A large number of our leading statesmen had come to see me during the morning, and when they heard what had happened they expressed the view that I should open the letters before these were taken to the Senate. That was in case nothing significant might be found in them, in which event I should have seemed to be plunging the country into a major alarm without any justification. But I replied that when our nation was in peril I could do nothing else but refer the entire matter to the principal council of state. For even, citizens, if the letters had proved not to contain the statements I had been advised to expect, I still felt convinced that in such a public emergency I need not be afraid of seeming excessively zealous. So, as you saw, I speedily convened a crowded meeting of the Senate. And meanwhile without any delay, following the advice of the Allobroges, I sent the courageous praetor Gaius Sulpicius to the house of Cethegus to collect any weapons he might discover there. He found a very large number of daggers and swords, and took them away.

I brought Volturcius into the Senate without the Gauls, and with the agreement of the members gave him a pledge of

28. C. Marius had defeated an invading German tribe, the Cimbri, at Vercellae in 101. Cicero calls this man P. Gabinius Capito 'Cimber.'

impunity on the government's behalf. I urged him to disclose fearlessly everything he knew, and before he had fully recovered from his abject panic he poured out his story. Publius Lentulus, he said, had given him messages and a letter for Catilina, urging the latter to mobilize a guard of slaves and come to Rome with his army at the earliest possible moment. The plan was to set fire to all quarters of the city – defined according to their allocation and distribution among his supporters – and to massacre an enormous number of citizens. Meanwhile Catilina himself was to be at hand, in order to intercept fugitives and effect a junction with his leading representatives in the capital.

Next the Gauls were brought into the Senate. They declared that they had been made to swear an oath, entrusted with letters from Lentulus, Cethegus and Statilius to take to their own people, and ordered by those same men, and by Lucius Crassus as well, to send cavalry into Italy as soon as they could – infantry was already in sufficient supply. Lentulus, they reported, had addressed them with a declaration, emanating from oracles of the Sibyl and assurances by soothsayers, indicating that he was the third member of the Cornelian family (after Cinna and Sulla) to whom the kingship and sovereignty of our city were destined to come. Lentulus also pronounced that this is the year preordained for the destruction of Rome and its dominion, seeing that it is the tenth year after the acquittal of the Vestal Virgins and the twentieth after the burning of the Capitol. The envoys added that there had been a difference of opinion between Cethegus and the rest of the conspirators, because Lentulus and the others had wanted to begin the carnage and conflagration during the Saturnalia,[29] whereas Cethegus thought this was too long to wait.

To cut a long story short, citizens, each man was then ordered to produce the letters he reported he had been given.

29. The Saturnalia began on 19 December and lasted several days.

Thereupon we showed Cethegus his letter; he agreed that the seal was his, and we cut the thread. The letter was written in his own hand to the Senate and people of the Allobroges, reaffirming that he would do what he had already verbally indicated to the envoys. Just before, Cethegus had been asked (in spite of the evident facts) what he had to say about the swords and daggers which had been confiscated at his home. His reply was that fine weapons had always been a fancy of his. But now when his letter was read, he suddenly seemed crushed and paralysed by guilt, and fell silent. Next, Statilius was brought in. He admitted the seal and handwriting, and his letter, too, was read. Its contents were largely similar; and he confessed. Then I showed Lentulus his own letter and inquired whether he acknowledged the seal. He nodded assent, and I commented, 'Yes, and it is a celebrated seal, too – engraved with the portrait of your eminent grandfather,[30] whose love for his country and his fellow-citizens was profound. Mute as they are, those features alone should have sufficed to deter you from your dreadful crime!'

Then Lentulus' letter to the Senate and people of the Allobroges was read out; and it was to the same effect. I offered him an opportunity to make any statement about these matters that he might wish to volunteer. At first he refused, but after a time, when the whole evidence had been gone over and recited in detail, he rose to his feet and demanded that the Gauls, and Volturcius also, should report the nature of the business which had brought them to his house. They replied briefly but resolutely, indicating through whose agency they had come to him and on how many occasions. Then they, in turn, demanded that he should confirm whether he had spoken to them about the Sibylline oracles or not. At this point, he gave a striking demonstration of what guilt does to a man. For the magnitude of his crime suddenly robbed him of

30. P. Cornelius Lentulus (consul 162) was wounded in the riot which resulted in the death of C. Gracchus (121).

his wits, and although he could have denied the allegation he caused general surprise by confessing that it was true. The detection and disclosure of his abominable design had evidently affected him so overwhelmingly that he was suddenly bereft of all the oratorical talent and experience which had always been his strength, and even of the brazenness and depravity in which he had never had an equal.

Then, all at once, Volturcius demanded that the letter which he claimed Lentulus had given him for Catilina should be produced and opened. Lentulus was terribly shaken. Nevertheless, he conceded that the seal and handwriting were his own. The letter, which was unsigned, ran as follows: 'You will know who I am from the man I am sending to you. Stand firm and understand the position into which you have brought yourself. See to whatever you need and take steps to mobilize all the help you can, even from the lowest elements.' Then Gabinius was brought in, and after defiant answers at first he concluded by denying none of the allegations that the Gauls had made.

Now, gentlemen, these letters and seals and handwritings and uniformly repeated confessions seemed to me, at least, the most convincing possible evidence and proof of these men's culpability. But even more conclusive still were their pallor, the look in their eyes, the set of their features, their silence. As they stood there stupefied, gazing fixedly upon the ground or occasionally glancing furtively at one another, their guilt was quite as manifest from their own appearance as from any one else's testimony.

Then, citizens, after the evidence had been reviewed and recited, I requested the Senate to direct that steps should be taken for the safety of the state The leading members spoke sternly and fearlessly, and the Senate unanimously adopted their proposals. Since its resolution has not yet been written out, I will tell you from memory what it was. First of all I was thanked in very generous terms because my courage, wisdom and foresight had preserved the state from the gravest of perils. Then the praetors Lucius Flaccus and Gaius Pomptinus were justly and deservedly complimented because of the assistance afforded me by their valiant and loyal endeavours. Praise was also bestowed upon the fortitude of my fellow-consul because he had eliminated the conspirators from any connexion either with himself personally or with governmental affairs.[31]

The Senate also decreed that Publius Lentulus, when he had resigned from his praetorship,[32] should be placed under arrest, and that Gaius Cethegus, Lucius Statilius and Publius Gabinius, all of whom were present, should likewise be taken into custody. The same decision was made about Lucius Cassius who had asked to be put in charge of the burning of the city, Marcus Caeparius who had been identified as the man chosen to take over Apulia and raise its shepherds in revolt, Publius Furius who was one of the colonists settled by Lucius Sulla at Faesulae, Quintus Annius Chilo who had been the constant associate of Furius in the attempt to tamper with the Allobroges, and the freedman Publius Umbrenus who was shown to have effected their original introduction to Gabinius. The Senate leniently limited its sentences to this small number of defendants, gentlemen, because in spite of the formidable character of the plot and the large number of traitors involved it was believed that the country could be saved by the punishment of only the nine worst offenders, and that the rest could be recalled to their right minds.

A thanksgiving was also decreed to the immortal gods for the exceptional favour they had bestowed upon us. The decree was in my name, and this is the first time ever since the

31. Cicero's fellow-consul C. Antonius Hybrida had been persuaded, or bribed, to terminate his association with Catilina (n.41).

32. A Roman magistrate could not be brought to trial (or executed) while in office.

foundation of the city that such an honour has been conferred on a civilian. It was framed in these terms: *because I had saved the city from the flames, the citizens from massacre and Italy from war*. If the thanksgiving in question be compared with any that has ever been decreed before, it differs from every one of them. For all the rest were voted for services to the state, but this alone was resolved because the state had actually been preserved from obliteration.

What had to be done first was done and completed. That is to say, Publius Lentulus, although on the strength of the evidence and his own confession the Senate had judged him deprived of the rights not only of a praetor but even of a Roman citizen, nevertheless resigned from that office. This was in order that he might suffer punishment as a private citizen without involving us in religious scruples: though it must be added that no such scruples had prevented the illustrious Gaius Marius from killing Gaius Glaucia while the latter still held the praetorship, even when no pronouncement had been made against him by name.

Citizens, you have in your power and custody the loathsome instigators of this most wicked and dangerous of wars. The peril within the city has been averted, and you are justified in concluding that all Catilina's troops, all his hopes and all his resources, have met with the completest failure. And indeed, gentlemen, when I was engaged in ejecting Catilina himself from the city, I already foresaw that once he was out of the way there would be no need for me to be scared of the sleepy Publius Lentulus, or the corpulent Lucius Cassius, or the unhinged and hysterical Gaius Cethegus. Out of all those men, Catilina was the only one to be afraid of – and that only as long as he remained within the city walls.

For there was nothing outside the range of his information, no one he did not know how to get at. His skill and audacity at accosting and sounding and swaying his fellow-men were extraordinary. It would be impossible to think of any criminal activity that was beyond his powers; and in everything he planned, his tongue and his hand never failed him. For each of his schemes he had his specific men chosen and told what to do. Yet, when he had assigned a task, that did not mean he thought it was completed – on the contrary, every detail was supervised, wrestled with, scrutinized and toiled over by himself in person. He possessed the capacity to endure cold, and thirst, and hunger. In all his foul intrigues he was acute, intrepid, cunning, alert and indefatigable.

Had I not managed to uproot him from his Roman plotting and propel him into the bandits' camp, I must frankly confess I should have been hard put to it to remove this burden of catastrophe from your necks. For, if I had not got him away, he would surely never have let us off until the Saturnalia! No, he would have fixed an earlier date for our doom and destruction. And it is inconceivable, that he would have allowed his seal and letters to be seized in clear proof of that terrible purpose.

As it is, as things were managed while he was out of the way, no detection of a burglary in a private house has ever been so blatant as the revelation and disclosure of this massive conspiracy against the state. And yet if Catilina had remained inside our city to this day, even with myself also here to resist and counter all his designs, it is far from an exaggeration to maintain that we should have had to fight him to the bitter and ultimate end. While his hostile presence in the city continued, we could never have released our country from that imminent menace by the peaceful, unobtrusive and noise-less methods which it has now been practicable to use.

In my planning and conduct of these matters, gentlemen, I feel conscious that the will and guidance of the immortal gods have been directly behind every single thing I have ar-ranged. This can be confidently surmised when you reflect that human initiative unaided could never have directed issues of such tremendous significance. And indeed throughout these days the gods have been so manifestly present in our midst, bringing us their succour and support, that it has almost seemed possible to see their forms before our very eyes. I say nothing of the torches that were seen by night in the western sky, and the glowing brilliance of the heavens. Nor will I speak about all the other portents which, since I became consul, have seemed by their abundance to indicate that the deities were themselves predicting what has now come to pass. But I shall tell you of one matter, citizens, which I would think it wrong to omit and pass over in silence.

Cast your minds back to the consulship of Cotta and Torquatus. In those days many objects on the Capitol were struck by lightning, the effigies of the gods were moved from their places, the statues of men of ancient times were thrown down, the brazen tablets of the laws were melted, and even the image of our founder Romulus himself was struck – that gilt figure of a baby, suckled by the she-wolf, which you remember on the Capitoline Hill. At that time the soothsayers, who had gathered together from all Etruria, prophesied the approach of slaughter and conflagration, the overthrow of the laws, civil war throughout our homeland, and the downfall of our whole city and government, unless the divinities, placated by every possible means, were persuaded to use their power to avert what amounted to the very march of destiny itself. And so, in accordance with their warnings, ceremonial games were held for ten successive days, and nothing which might appease the heavenly beings was left undone.

Moreover, the same soothsayers commanded that a larger statue of Jupiter than the one that had been here hitherto should be made and set up on a high place, facing towards the dawn, that is to say in the opposite direction to its previous orientation. They pronounced the hope that if this statue (which you now see)[33] were thus to be turned towards the

33. The Senate was meeting in the Temple of Concord, below the Capitoline Hill.

rising sun, the Forum and the Senate House, the machinations which had secretly been proceeding against the safety of this city and government would be brought out into the light and made clearly visible to the Senate and Roman people. The consuls of that time hired out the contract for the statue. But the work was so slow that it was not set up under the consuls of that year, or the year before last, or last year either – or indeed even by ourselves until this very day.

No one here present can be so blind to the truth, so obstinate and so senseless that he cannot see how the entire visible universe, and most particularly this city of Rome, is guided and governed by the will and power of the gods. For there we were, prophetically warned that massacre, incendiarism and destruction on a nation-wide scale were being actively prepared – and by Roman citizens at that. At the time, the vast range of such a criminal enterprise made some people refuse to credit its possibility. And yet you have seen that it was true – that ruffians belonging to the citizen body not only contemplated these terrible acts but even started to carry them out. And then again, in relation to these same happenings, a co-incidence, of which I shall now tell you, was so timely that the hand of Jupiter the Best and Greatest must surely have been at work. For on this very morning the conspirators and witnesses were, on my orders, being conducted through the Forum to the Temple of Concord at precisely the time when the statue of which the soothsayers spoke was being set up. And it was immediately after it had been erected, with its gaze facing towards you and the Senate, that yourselves and the Senators saw everything which had been plotted against the safety of all of us disclosed and brought out into the bright light of day.

More rigorous than ever, therefore, should be your hatred and punishment of the men who have sought to extend their detestable, death-dealing conflagration not only into your own homes but into the temples and shrines of the gods as well. Yet if I ventured to assert that the frustration of these criminals was due to myself, my claim would be intolerably excessive. For it was Jupiter by his own power who thwarted them. It was he who willed that the Capitol, and these temples, and our entire city, and every one of your own number should be brought to salvation.

Gentlemen, the guidance of the eternal gods is what has made it possible for me to persevere in my purpose and plan until I came upon this conclusive evidence. For surely – if we consider the intrigue with the Allobroges – Lentulus and the other traitors in our midst would never have been such madmen as to entrust these vital intrigues and communications to people who were both strangers and barbarians, unless the gods themselves had denuded their outrageous scheme of every shred of discretion. And think, also, of these delegates from `Gaul. It is a country imperfectly pacified, the only remaining nation which seems both capable of fighting Rome and not unwilling to do so; and in order to get the better of us they did not even have to fight but merely to hold their peace. When they abandoned all their hopes of victory over Rome, when they gave up the enormous rewards offered them unsolicited by men of patrician rank, when they sacrificed their own advantage in the interests of your preservation, can you really believe there was no divine agency behind such happenings?

A thanksgiving has been decreed at every place of worship, and do you, citizens, now celebrate these days in the company of your wives and children. Many honours have been justly and deservedly decreed to the powers of heaven on many occasions, but none more justly than this. For you have been saved from a miserable and horrible death. You have been saved without slaughter, without bloodshed, without an army, without a battle. You have won the struggle without putting off the garb of peace, with no commander but myself, who am clad in the same peaceful toga as yourselves.

For I would ask you to remember, gentlemen, all the civil wars of the past, not only those of which you have heard but the wars that you yourselves recollect and have seen. Lucius Sulla crushed Publius Sulpicius;[34] he expelled from the city Gaius Marius who was its guardian, and drove many brave men out of the land, and put others to death. Next Cnaeus Octavius, when consul, threw his colleague out of the city by force of arms.[35] The whole of this place was choked with heaps of corpses and the blood of Roman citizens. Later Cinna and Marius[36] won the upper hand, and on that occasion personages of the utmost eminence were slain, and the state was deprived of its greatest luminaries. The brutality of that victory was avenged by Sulla[37] – and there is no need for me to recall the massacre of citizens which then occurred, with calamitous results for our country. Subsequently Marcus Lepidus[38] quarrelled with the renowned and vigorous Quintus Catulus, and Lepidus also perished, though his end caused less national grief than the other deaths of that epoch.

Now, all the clashes to which I have just referred were aimed at changing the government, not obliterating it amid total anarchy. The men concerned did not propose that there should be no republic at all but a republic in which they themselves should be the chiefs. They did not want the city to

34. The tribune P. Sulpicius Rufus, who had become a supporter of Marius, was killed when Sulla marched on Rome (88).

35. The consul Cn. Octavius, an adherent of Sulla, drove out his colleague L. Cornelius Cinna but then succumbed to Cinna and Marius (87).

36. Cinna and Marius declared themselves consuls for 86 but Marius died after seventeen days of office.

37. Sulla crushed his enemies at the Colline Gate (82) and became dictator (81–79).

38. The consul M. Aemilius Lepidus tried to overthrow the Sullan constitution but was driven out by his colleague Q. Lutatius Catulus jun. (78).

burn; what they wanted was to become its leading figures. And yet all those conflicts, although in no case aimed at the actual erasure of the state, were incapable of settlement by a peaceful reconciliation. In each case there had to be a slaughter of Roman citizens. But what we are considering here and now, on the other hand, is the most appalling and savage war of all – the gravest in the whole of human history. It is the sort of war which not even a barbarian tribe has ever fought against its own people; a war in which it was ordained by Lentulus, Gabinius, Cethegus and Cassius that all who might look forward to living in a city saved from disaster would be denounced as hated foes.

Such, citizens, was the war in which I dedicated myself to ensuring that the lives of every one of you should be preserved. While your enemies were reckoning that no citizens would remain in existence except those who happened to escape the unrestricted killing, and no part of the city except what the flames might chance to spare, I have kept Rome and its citizens safe and sound.

For all this that I have done, gentlemen, I ask of you no prize for merit, no badge of honour, no monument of glory. I ask only that this day should never be forgotten. It is inside your hearts that I want you to construct and cherish my Triumphs and decorations of honour and monuments of glory and insignia of renown. Silence, absence of commemoration, even the commemoration which lesser services could have won, will leave me disappointed. Citizens, my deeds shall be perpetuated in your memories. They shall be celebrated in the talk of men. They shall wax and pass down the ages, handed on by the written word. I believe the memory of my consulship will live as long as this city survives: which means, I hope, that the term of life for both of them will be eternity. I also know that in this nation there have been two citizens, of whom one bounded your empire by no region of the earth but by the limits of the sky itself,[39] and the other brought salvation to the very centre and homeland of that same dominion.

Nevertheless, the fortune or condition associated with my own deeds is not quite comparable with the situation of commanders who have fought foreign wars. For they leave their enemies either slain or subjected; I on the other hand have to live with the persons I have defeated and overcome. And for this reason, gentlemen, if it is held right that other men should be recompensed for the deeds they have accomplished, it is your duty to ensure that my own actions should at the very least not prove, one day, to be my ruin. I for my part have ensured that the ghastly, criminal projects of this scum should leave you unharmed, and it is for you to see that their designs do not hurt me either.

And yet the plotters cannot really do me any damage now. For the support of loyal citizens counts for much, and that I have for evermore. There is also great majesty in the state, which though voiceless will always defend me. And there is a potent strength in conscience, too: any man who, in his desire to do me injury, shows that he holds this of no account, will automatically be confessing his own guilt. My disposition, Romans, is such that I shall never yield to the infamous designs of any man. Of my own accord, I shall invariably treat every scoundrel as my enemy. But if all the violence of the traitors, warded off from yourselves, is turned upon me alone, you will have to consider very seriously how much protection you are prepared to offer, on future occasions also, to those who are going to expose themselves to odium and every kind of peril in order to keep you safe.

As for myself, what greater satisfaction could life now bring? I can see ahead no loftier office, no greater renown to which I might aspire. And yet, citizens, there is one ambition

39. Pompeius had defeated Q. Sertorius in the far west and Mithridates in the far east.

that remains to me still. The things I have achieved as consul I shall continue to uphold and glorify when I return to private life, so that, if saving the state has brought me hatred, the blow will fall back on those who hate, and will make my own honour even greater. And, finally, when during future years I participate in public affairs, I shall always remember what I have accomplished; and I propose to make sure men know it was done by honourable effort and not by mere chance.

So now that night has come, gentlemen, offer worship to Jupiter here, who is the guardian of this city and of yourselves. Then go to your homes, and, although the danger is dispelled, nevertheless set guards and watchmen to defend them, as you did last night. I for my part shall ensure that you do not have to take this precaution again – and that you are able to live your lives out in everlasting peace!

THE FOURTH SPEECH
Delivered to the Senate

The conspirators who had been caught red-handed in Rome were temporarily handed over to various Senators to be held under arrest – in the absence of a prison of sufficient size – and there were alarming rumours, probably based on fact, that plans to free them were under way. Now, on 5 December, Cicero urged the Senate to delay no longer in deciding what should be done with them. According to his version, the consul elect Decimus Junius Silanus demanded their execution and Julius Caesar their detention for life instead. The orator himself declared that he was prepared to support either decision, although he made it clear that he favoured the former course. But Sallust and Appian reveal to us how, at one point, members seemed very likely to favour a suggestion that, whereas the defendants should be kept in custody for the present, a final decision should be deferred. Even Silanus rather lamely reversed his original decision, saying that he had never really meant the offenders to be executed. However, the death penalty was what was finally decided upon. Sallust totally ignored Cicero's part in this decision and (like Brutus) attributed it instead to a speech by the formidable high-principled conservative Marcus Porcius Cato. Presumably Cicero gave a sort of lead, on the lines of the written version that has come down to us but not perhaps so impressively, and Cato then spoke up in much more definite and harsh terms.

Cicero's published oration does not attempt to disguise the fact that his words were so judiciously framed as to be somewhat hesitant; and this is by no means surprising, since he was by nature far from violent, and very difficult issues were at stake. For one thing, the role of Caesar was equivocal. Both he and the millionaire Crassus had been fairly sympathetic, to say the least, with Catilina's desire for innovations, until it became clear that the conspiracy would be directed against owners of property – and in spite of all the smoke-screens thrown up by Caesar and Cicero alike, it is evident that Caesar's principal aim was not to be severe but to save the lives of the plotters. But Cicero, for his part, was justified in supposing that their imprisonment for life would be a short-lived farce; whereupon the conspiracy would soon inevitably begin again, so that execution, although it might well have unhappy repercussions later on, was really the only way to prevent a recurrence.

On the legal side everything hinged on how one interpreted the Emergency Decree (senatus consultum ultimum) which on 21 October had instructed the consuls (that is, in effect, Cicero) to take whatever steps they saw fit for the safety of the state. Did this empower the consuls, and for that matter was the Senate itself entitled, to arrange for the execution of Roman citizens? The conservatives, and at this stage (until hindsight intervened) many or most Senators, said yes; the populares, however, who stressed the sovereignty of the People, habitually said no, not without right of appeal to the Assembly. The populares looked to Caesar – who in another case earlier in the year had questioned Cicero's defence of the Senate's powers in this respect. But Caesar evidently preferred not to raise this issue in the present senatorial debate. It would have been embarrassing for him if the matter had been referred to the excited, corruptible Assembly, where to support either line simply might be damaging to his own future; and besides (even if Cicero over-stressed this urgency) any delay whatever might have resulted in the liberation of the conspirators and the outbreak of chaotic disorders. Presumably reasons of the same sort also prevented anyone from suggesting what at this distance of time would have seemed the obvious course, namely reference to the regular tribunal entrusted with cases of treason. At all events, Caesar preferred to propose a more insidious solution which, although keeping his Assembly friends and the tribunal out of it, nevertheless had the effect – a paradoxical one in the light of subsequent history – of making him seem more of a constitutionalist than Cato. This, however, was largely illusory, since his proposal of permanent detention, though not wholly unprecedented, was of almost equally doubtful legality. However, the whole legal position was obscure, though it is probable that in spite of all the distaste the Romans felt for executing their own citizens there was by this time a fairly widespread admission that times of crisis might produce summary executions under the Senate's Emergency Decree. Yet there remained a nagging uncertainty whether this grave step could really be regarded as applicable to men who were already in custody and who, it could consequently be argued (if you ignored the possibility of their escape), presented no immediate danger to the state.

So the men were executed; and in the following month Catilina was cornered and killed at Pistoria (Pistoia). But even before that culminating event, Cicero was able to see that the fears concerning his own position, which are very evident in the written version of this speech, were justified. For already before the year 63 was over, when he was laying down his office as consul, the tribune Quintus Metellus Nepos forbade him to deliver the usual valedictory address on the grounds that a man who had put citizens to death unheard ought not to be allowed to speak. The tribune was a partisan of Pompeius, who during these excitements had been far away carrying out military

*conquests of unprecedented magnitude in the east. He had disposed of
the war against Mithridates, with which he had been entrusted by
the advocacy of Cicero. But his hopes of coming home in time to
crush the Catilinarian conspiracy in person had been disappointed,
and he found Cicero's naïvely evident belief that its suppression was
a greater triumph than his own massive victories both ridiculous and
highly irritating.*

*This proved one of the rocks on which Cicero's new policy, out-
lined in these speeches, almost immediately foundered. That policy
was a Harmony of the Orders (Senate and Knights) based on widespread support throughout Italy, for the conspiracy had opened
Cicero's eyes to the importance of loyal opinion throughout the
peninsula. But it was a fallacy to suppose that this unity, the precarious product of an emergency, would be strong enough to kill
factional interests. And the offence caused to Pompeius by Cicero's
boastfulness (and indeed by his success) was fatal: although, when
Pompeius returned to Rome, Cicero, in accordance with his usual
persevering admiration of the man, did his not very tactful best to
achieve a reconciliation.*

Senators, I see your heads and eyes all turned in my direction.
I see you not only feel anxiety concerning the perils which
menace yourselves and our country, but also, even if those be
averted, that you are worried about the personal risks to myself. Your goodwill brings me happy reassurance amid my
troubles, and solace in my grief. But in heaven's name set it
aside! Forget my safety! Think, instead, of your own selves
and your children. As for me, if the condition of occupying
the consulship is that I should suffer the deepest anguish and
sorrow and torment, I shall endure these things intrepidly
and even cheerfully, if only the authority and security of
yourselves and the Roman people are safeguarded by my
labours.

I am that consul, gentlemen, to whom neither the Forum
which is the seat of all justice, nor the Campus Martius which is

hallowed by the auspices of consular elections,[40] nor the Senate which is the mighty protection of all nations, nor my own home which is usually a man's refuge, nor even my bed which for others is a place of rest, nor this seat of honour the curule chair, has ever been free from plots and mortal hazards. There are many things that I have not told you about. I have had much to endure. I have been obliged to give way many times;[41] and numerous, also, have been the situations which have caused you alarm, and which I have laboured greatly to put right. But if the immortal gods have desired that this should be the outcome of my consulship, that I should rescue you and the people of Rome from a miserable death, your wives and children and the Vestal Virgins from savage persecution, our temples and shrines and this fairest homeland of us all from flaming ruin, and every corner of Italy from war and devastation, then I am ready to bear all that fate has in store for me. For if Publius Lentulus felt convinced by the soothsayers that his name was destined for the annihilation of the Roman state, why should I not rejoice because of destiny's clear edict that this consulship of mine has been set aside for its salvation?

On this account, members of the Senate, look to your own welfare, take thought for our homeland, preserve yourselves and your wives and your children and your property, defend the renown and security of Rome. Cease to trouble about my safety, or to be concerned about me at all. For I am entitled to hope that all the gods who have this city in their care will give me such recompense as I may deserve. Besides, if disaster befall me, I shall die tranquil and fully prepared. For to the brave there is no disgrace in death. To a man who has occupied

---

40. Before a consular election could be held the auspices had to be declared favourable.

41. In order to secure the neutrality of his fellow-consul C. Antonius Hybrida, Cicero had traded to him his right to become the governor of Macedonia.

the consulship it cannot be untimely; to a man of wisdom there is nothing tragic about it.

And yet I am not so hard of heart that I can remain unmoved by the grief of my affectionate, beloved brother,[42] who is with us today, or by the tears of all those you see around me here. And my feelings, I confess, are ever and again carried back to my home: to my terrified wife, and my daughter prostrated with fear, to my little son whom I feel that the state must be said to have taken in its own embrace as a hostage for my consulship, and to my son-in-law whom I see standing outside this chamber and awaiting the outcome of the day. All these thoughts deeply touch my heart. My family could well perish along with us, at one and the same time, in the total destruction of our country. But what I pray instead is that, even if I myself may come to a violent end, each and every one of them shall still remain safe, amid the general safety of you all.

Attend, then, Senators, to the security of the state. Gaze well at all the storms which menace its very existence, unless you are able to forestall them. This is not just a repetition of Tiberius Gracchus facing the ordeal of your stern verdict because he aimed to become tribune a second time,[43] nor of Gaius Gracchus because he had incited the land-reformers to revolt, nor of Lucius Saturninus because he had murdered Gaius Memmius.[44] No, the men whom we have under arrest today are those who stayed on in Rome to burn the entire city down, to assassinate you all – to welcome Catilina! Their

42. Cicero refers to his brother Q. Tullius Cicero (praetor elect), his wife Terentia, his daughter Tullia (aged about thirteen), his son Marcus (about two), and Tullia's first husband C. Calpurnius Piso Frugi, who was not yet a member of the Senate but stood before the open doors of the Temple of Concord where the meeting was being held.

43. It was illegal to hold the office of tribune for two consecutive years.

44. C. Memmius was murdered when he was standing for the consulship of 99 as a rival of Saturninus' ally C. Servilius Glaucia.

letters, seals and handwriting are in our hands; and so are confessions from every one of them. Attempts have been made to undermine the Allobroges, and stir up the slaves. And Catilina is called in! That is the plot they have entered upon, so that after the universal slaughter there will be not a living person left even to mourn the name of Rome and grieve over the downfall of our once mighty empire.

All this has been proved by witnesses. The criminals have admitted the whole thing, and you, by a number of resolutions, have already given your verdict. In the first place, you expressed gratitude to myself in superlative terms, and declared that it was my courage and energy which enabled the machinations of these traitors to be revealed. Secondly, you compelled Publius Lentulus to resign from his praetorship. You also ordered that he and the others upon whom you had pronounced judgement should be taken into custody. And above all you decreed a thanksgiving in my name, an honour which no man acting in a civil capacity has ever been awarded before. And then yesterday, too, you allocated substantial rewards to the envoys of the Allobroges and to Titus Volturcius. All these things show that you very clearly indicated your condemnation of the men concerned, who were specifically, by name, placed under arrest.

And yet I now propose to refer the whole question to you Senators, just as if it still remained entirely open. I do so because I want you to pronounce your sentence on what has been done and declare your judgement as to what the punishment shall be.

I will first offer certain observations which seem to me appropriate for a consul. Very early on, I began to detect that a large-scale movement of a totally insane character was under way within our midst, and that perils of an unprecedented nature were seething and boiling up. All the same, it did not occur to me that conspiracy was being plotted on such a vast and utterly destructive scale, and plotted by Roman citizens at that. But now that things have come to the present point, whatever the outcome of our debate, whatever the inclinations of your own personal feelings, it is imperative that you should make up your minds – and do so before tonight. You are now in a position to appreciate the full magnitude of the pernicious design which has been disclosed to you. If you suppose that only a few people are involved in this enterprise, you are badly wrong. The evil has spread more widely than you think: it has not only extended throughout all Italy but has even crossed the Alps,[45] and has continued to creep stealthily further on, and has already pervaded many of our provinces. It cannot be suppressed by delay and procrastination. Whatever the punishments you decide to decree, that decision must be taken with the utmost speed.

I see that up to now there are two proposals. One was made by Decimus Silanus,[46] who moves that the men who have attempted to destroy our community should be put to death. The other is the proposal of Gaius Caesar, who sets aside the death penalty but welcomes the full rigour of all the other punishments.

Each of these two gentlemen, in accordance with his own lofty rank and the grave issues involved, desires that the greatest severity should be shown. Silanus believes that the people who have sought to take the lives of ourselves and every other Roman, who have endeavoured to abolish the Republic and blot out its very name, should not for a single moment be permitted to live and enjoy the air we all breathe. He also recalls that, in dealing with vicious Roman citizens, the government has often made use of this kind of punishment before. Caesar, on the other hand, takes the view that death

45. According to Sallust there were Catilinarians in Spain and Mauretania.
46. Dec. Junius Silanus, as consul designate for 62, gave his opinion first.

has been appointed by the gods not as a punishment at all, but as an inevitable natural happening, or a relief from toil and trouble; so that wise men have never been reluctant to meet their deaths, and brave men have often died willingly enough. Whereas imprisonment, he says, including imprisonment for life, was unmistakably devised as the special penalty for atrocious crimes. He moves, therefore, that the defendants should be imprisoned, and distributed among the municipalities for incarceration.

That proposal seems to me unfair if you intend to order the towns to accept the prisoners, and difficult to implement if you limit yourselves to the mere expression of a wish. Still, let it be so resolved, should that be your pleasure. If so, I shall assume the necessary responsibility, in the hope of finding people in the townships who feel they are in honour bound not to refuse a request which, after all, you will be only making in order to preserve us all. Caesar adds a further proposal that, if any of the prisoners break out, the places in charge of them should be severely penalized. He commands that formidable guards shall be set, in keeping with the crime which these malefactors have committed. He also ordains that neither the Senate nor the Assembly shall have the power to annul the penalty imposed on any of the convicted men. And that means that he even takes away their hope: which is the only comfort people have in dire affliction. He further pronounces that their property shall be confiscated. That is to say, he leaves the wretched creatures nothing but their lives. If he had taken those as well, he would, simultaneously and by a single stroke, have relieved them of severe mental and physical suffering, and of all the retribution they will be undergoing for their offences. It was to scare criminals here on earth that men of ancient times held that punishments for living evil-doers are paralleled by similar penalties which they will still continue to suffer after they are dead; because our ancestors realized, evidently, that if the terror of these posthumous sanctions were removed the threat of death itself would hold no fears any longer.

Senators, I can see which of these courses is of advantage to myself. Gaius Caesar has been a supporter of the national policy which is regarded as democratic;[47] so if his proposition is the one you decide to accept I shall have less reason to fear popular disfavour, seeing that he is its initiator and advocate. If, on the other hand, you adopt the other motion, a great deal of trouble is likely to lie in store for me. Nevertheless, the national interest must outweigh any considerations of my personal danger.

Well, we have, then, from Caesar a proposal which is in keeping with his own lofty distinction and the renown of his ancestors, and must clearly be regarded as a pledge of his everlasting goodwill towards our country. It is also a vivid indication of the contrast between the light-weight pronouncements of mere demagogues and a truly democratic mentality devoted to the welfare of the state. I see that some of the men who like to be considered supporters of popular causes are not here today, and I appreciate that this is because they want to avoid voting on a capital charge concerning Roman citizens. But Caesar on the other hand, the day before yesterday, backed both the decision to arrest Roman citizens and the decree that there should be a thanksgiving in my name. And yesterday, too, he favoured the resolution that substantial rewards should be conferred upon the witnesses. When a man has voted a guard for the defendants, a congratulatory tribute to the investigator, and a reward for the witnesses, no one can entertain the smallest doubts about the views he holds concerning the rights and wrongs and implications of this whole affair.

47. The *populares* ('democrats') and *optimates* were shifting groups not to be regarded as actual political parties; roughly speaking, the former favoured doing business through the Assembly (people), the latter through the Senate (p. 33).

However, Caesar is conscious that there is a Sempronian law[48] which safeguards the lives of Roman citizens in cases where the Assembly has voted no measure against them. But he must also know that a man who is a public enemy cannot possibly be regarded as a citizen at all; and he undoubtedly recalls that the very proposer of the Sempronian law himself paid the supreme penalty to the state without any order coming from the Assembly. He does not surely believe that Publius Lentulus can still be seen as the people's friend. Lentulus spends his money wildly, it is true, but he is also the man whose ruthless and ferocious plans have aimed at nothing less than the extermination of the Roman people and the obliteration of our very city. That is why Caesar, though himself a humane and lenient man, shows no reluctance to consign this individual to everlasting darkness and imprisonment, and lays it down for all future time that no one shall be able to make a boast of lightening his punishment by the offer of some gesture which might have a democratic look but would bring ruin upon Rome. Caesar even adds that their property should be confiscated, thus supplementing all their tortures of mind and body by destitution and beggary as well.

Well, if that is your decision, you will be providing me, when I address the people, with an associate whom they like and approve. If on the other hand you prefer to adopt the motion of Silanus, I shall find no difficulty in defending myself and yourselves against the reproach of cruelty. Indeed, I shall maintain that his proposal shows much the greater clemency of the two. There can, I know, gentlemen, where the punishment of such a terrible crime is concerned, be no question of cruelty entering into the matter at all. Nevertheless, I cannot help being influenced by feelings of mercy. For, whereas I hope from the bottom of my heart to be granted a happy life with yourselves, in a country restored to the blessings of

48. The *Lex Sempronia* of C. Gracchus (123) provided that no Roman citizen should be put to death without the consent of the Assembly.

safety, I have an equally heartfelt conviction that, for all the vehemence I may seem to be showing on this issue, there is not the slightest element of cruelty in my attitude. I am the mildest of men, and my intentions are wholly lenient and humane.

And yet I also have a vision of this city, the light of the world and the stronghold of every nation, suddenly plunged into all-engulfing flames. I see, in my mind's eye, our country reduced to a graveyard. I see the corpses of unburied citizens lying in miserable heaps; and I see the countenance of Cethegus gloating in maniac fashion over the dead bodies of you all. I picture Publius Lentulus fulfilling the destiny of his confessed ambitions and reigning as our lord, with Gabinius as his purple-clad henchman and Catilina on the spot with his army. I shudder at the wails of mothers, the panic flight of girls and boys, the rape of Vestal Virgins.

And then, because these would be horrible events inviting all our pity, I find myself determined after all to be rigorous and unbending towards the men who have schemed to bring such things to pass. Just imagine some father of a family whose children were killed by a slave, his wife murdered, his home burnt down. If such a man failed to punish that slave in the most relentless manner, would he seem to you kindly and merciful, or would he not rather, surely, appear so hard-hearted as to be positively inhuman? A person who felt no inclination to relieve his own grief and torment by inflicting grief and torment on the criminal would, as I see it, be as unfeeling as if he were made of iron. Exactly the same applies to the abominable creatures who have plotted to assassinate ourselves and our wives and children, who have determined to reduce all our homes to rubble and indeed to wipe out this very nation which is the common home of every one of us, and who aimed by these acts to set up, upon the ruined fragments of this city and the ashes of our burnt-out empire, the tribe of the Allobrogian Gauls. By the analogy which I have indicated, if we act severely, we shall be considered merciful. But if there is the least sign of laxity on our part, we shall be accused of extreme hard-heartedness concerning a matter which involves nothing less than the utter annihilation of our country and all its citizens.

I did not hear anyone say the courageous and patriotic Lucius Caesar was showing cruelty the day before yesterday when he declared that his own sister's husband deserved to be executed.[49] He said so in the man's own presence and hearing – with the added remark that his own grandfather had been executed by a consul, and that his uncle, a mere boy who was acting as the emissary of his own father, had also been thrown into prison and put to death.[50] And yet what had they done which could be compared with the present appalling offences? What plan for the complete destruction of our whole political system had they ever formed?

At that time people were busy spreading around large bribes, and there was party strife. So the distinguished grandfather of this Lentulus took up arms, went in pursuit of Gaius Gracchus, and even sustained a severe wound on that occasion, all in order that our country should come to no harm. But his grandson, on the other hand, seeks to plunge it into total anarchy; and for this purpose he mobilizes Gaulish tribesmen, whips up slaves, beckons Catilina in, hands us Senators to Cethegus to be massacred, passes the rest of the citizen body to Gabinius for slaughter, assigns the city of Rome to Cassius for burning, and gives over the whole of Italy to be the victim of Catilina's lootings and ravages. Am I really to suppose, members of the Senate, that you are scared

49. The conspirator P. Cornelius Lentulus Sura was the husband of Julia, sister of L. Julius Caesar.

50. L. Julius Caesar was the son of Fulvia, the daughter of M. Fulvius Flaccus whom L. Opimius had killed (with his son) as an adherent of C. Gracchus (121).

of criticism for acting too harshly against these atrocious, unspeakable crimes? Surely, when such desperate enemies are concerned, we are much less likely to seem cruel to our fellow-citizens if we administer stern punishment than if we err on the side of laxity.

But I have to admit, Senators, that certain reports are reaching my ears. Some people, it is being said, are nervous that when you have made your decisions today I shall not have the necessary physical backing to bring them into effect. But do not worry, gentlemen. For everything has been foreseen and prepared and arranged – by myself with all the care and thoroughness of which I am capable, and, far more significant, by the Roman people, determined as it is to maintain its full authority and safeguard the possessions of the whole community. Everyone, of every order, class and age, is assembled here today at this one spot. The Forum is crowded with people, the temples round about are packed tight, all the approaches to this shrine and this place are crammed. Since the very beginnings of the city there was never before a crisis in which all Romans have been so thoroughly of one accord.

The only exceptions are the men who see they have to die: and so they have preferred to perish in a universal slaughter rather than by themselves. These persons I treat as a special case. I willingly set them apart. For indeed I do not even think they should be classed merely as bad citizens. They should be regarded, instead, as the most deadly of enemies.

But as for the rest of the population, heaven alone could measure the size of the multitude, and its enthusiasm, and its determination, and the courage with which it is united in defence of the security and greatness of Rome! Let me speak first of the knights. Although they yield the primacy in rank and counsel to yourselves, in patriotic feeling they are your equals. The long period of their disagreement with your order[51] came to an end when this day and this emergency reunited them with yourselves in harmonious association. And if we can make this union, achieved during my consulship, into a permanent feature of our system, I declare to you that from now onwards each and every part of Roman public life will remain wholly free of internal frictions and disturbances.

I see also that the same eagerness to protect our country has brought together the excellent tribunes of the treasury,[52] and that the entire body of clerks,[53] who happened to have flocked to the treasury today in considerable numbers, have switched their attention from the allotment of posts, which they had come to hear, to the exhibition of concern for the safety of us all. Indeed, an enormous crowd of freeborn men, from the very humblest upwards, is assembled in this place. For no single class of citizens has a monopoly of the emotion that looks upon these temples, our whole city of Rome, the freedom that we enjoy, this light of day itself, and our country's own soil which belongs to us all, as the most beloved and precious and delightful of blessings.

And the keenness of the freedmen is equally remarkable. They are men who through their own endeavours have won a place in our community and very properly consider this to be their home. They present a marked contrast to those others – including some of the highest birth – who were born in our country and yet have treated it as no homeland at all, but an enemy city. There is no need for me to say more about these

51. The principal issue between Senators and knights related to the membership of judges' panels in criminal trials.

52. The tribunes of the treasury (originally in charge of the collection of war-tax) were now a class similar to but less wealthy than the knights. Between 70 and 46 they were included in judges' panels. Perhaps their title also describes an official post. See p. 28.

53. On 5 December the clerks (including respected financial officials) drew lots for the magistracies to which they were to be attached for the forthcoming year.

classes and persons whose private fortunes, patriotic feelings and enjoyment of liberty (the most desirable thing of all) have stirred them to defend the common cause. But it should also be added that every single slave too, provided the conditions of his slavery are tolerable, is horrified at the audacity of these Roman citizens who enter upon plots. Each one of them prays that our present way of life will survive, and contributes to the general salvation whatever goodwill he dares and can.

A rumour is going about concerning a pimp of Lentulus[54] who circulates around the shops and hopes to corrupt the minds of poor and simple men by bribery. In case any of you are disturbed by such stories, I can tell you that this plan was, indeed, set in motion and attempted. But nobody proved sufficiently impoverished or evilly disposed to want to throw away the security of his own work-place and job and livelihood, his own place of rest and his bed, in a word the whole tranquil course of his existence. On the contrary, an enormous majority of the workers in the shops, in fact I may say this entire class, are thoroughly devoted to peace. For all their chattels and their labours and their profits depend upon a steady flow of customers – and they will only come in peaceful conditions. Now, since this income diminishes even when shops are closed, what do you imagine would happen if they had been gutted by fire-raisers?

And so, Senators, you have no lack of support from the people of Rome. But it is for you, on the other hand, to ensure that you do not seem to be failing *them*. For in the first place you have a consul who, not on his own behalf but yours, has only by the barest margin escaped from many perils and intrigues, and from the very jaws of death. Secondly, all the orders are united, in heart and spirit and voice, for the preservation of the state. Beset by the torches and weapons of a devilish conspiracy, the country to which we all belong holds

54. This agent was apparently attempting to free Lentulus.

out its hands to you in supplication. She entrusts her safety to your care. She entrusts the lives of every citizen, the citadel and Capitol of Rome, the altars of her household deities, the sacred undying fire of Vesta,[55] the temples and shrines of every one of the gods, the walls and habitations of our city. Indeed, the survival not only of yourselves but of your wives and children, of your properties and homes and hearths, hangs upon the decisions you will make today.

You have a leader who is thinking of you and not of himself – an opportunity which does not always occur. Every class and every man is on your side; for the first time in the history of Roman politics we see today a united and unanimous people. Consider all the toil which went to the foundation of our empire, all the valour which was devoted to establishing our freedom, all the favour of the gods which increased and multiplied our fortunes. And then consider how one single night very nearly destroyed every one of these things! Today we must ensure that throughout all time to come no Roman citizen shall be able to bring about such a disaster or even contemplate the possibility of its perpetration. Believe me, I have not spoken in these terms in the hope of arousing your emotions. Indeed, your enthusiasm often outruns my own. I have spoken because the voice of the consul ought to be the chief voice in the state, and I do not want it to fail in the performance of a consul's proper task.

And now, before I ask you for your votes, I want to say a brief word about myself. I am all too well aware that the number of conspirators is only equalled by the mass of enemies I have made for myself. Yet I estimate them to be worthless and impotent and abject, one and all. Even if, one day, aroused by some raving ruffian, they should rise to a position of power superior even to your own authority and that of the

55. A perpetually burning fire in the round temple of Vesta near the Forum symbolized the perpetuity of the state.

state, even then, Senators, I shall never regret these deeds and counsels for which I have been responsible. Perhaps I am in grave danger of death at their hands. Yet death comes to everybody, and while I have lived I have through your resolutions received compliments which no one has ever received before. Others have earned thanksgivings for being of service to the state, but the present honour has been decreed to me, and me alone, for bringing about its salvation.

We must admit the illustriousness of Scipio, because his was the strategy and valour which forced Hannibal to leave Italy and return to Africa.[56] Great renown is also due to the second Africanus, who destroyed the two cities which were our most dangerous enemies, Carthage and Numantia. A noble reputation likewise belongs to Paullus, whose triumphal chariot was graced by the once mighty and noble monarch Perseus. Everlasting honour attends the name of Marius, who twice freed Italy from siege and the dread of servitude. And all these are outranked by Pompeius, whose deeds and talents are bounded only by the farthest confines of the earth and the course of the sun itself. And yet, amid all these celebrities, there will assuredly be left some room for my glory as well: unless, maybe, it is more distinguished to open up overseas provinces to which we may journey, than to ensure that those who have done the journey shall have a home to which after their conquests they can return.

However, in one respect, I must admit that success abroad is better than victory in civil war. For foreign enemies are either vanquished and enslaved or enrolled as friends and bound by obligations of gratitude. Consider, on the other hand, those among our own citizens, who, smitten by some mania, have turned into enemies of their own country. When you have defeated *their* attempts to overthrow the state, coercion by

56. P. Cornelius Scipio Africanus the elder made Hannibal evacuate Italy (203). Other references are repeated from the speech *On the Command of Cn. Pompeius*.

force and reconciliation by kindness remain equally impracticable. I have, in consequence, to face the prospect of an unending war against these god-forsaken criminals. To preserve me and mine from their menaces, I place all my reliance upon the support of yourselves and every loyal citizen, and upon the thought of all the perils we have shared – perils of which the memory will abide for ever, not only among this community of ours which has been rescued from destruction, but on the lips and in the hearts of all the nations of the world. And assuredly it could never be possible to find a force strong enough to break and shatter your union with the knights, and this total unanimity among the entire body of patriotic Roman citizens.

My claims to a military command, to an army, to a provincial governorship – I have renounced them all. I have declined the opportunity of a Triumph and other honours, in order to devote myself to the protection of this city and yourselves. I have lost the chance to enlist numerous provincials as my clients and hosts (and am compelled instead to depend upon my influence here at Rome for the laborious task of securing and maintaining supporters). As a substitute for these advantages, and as a recompense for my unparalleled devotion to your interests and for the vigilance which you see me dedicating to the salvation of our country, I ask nothing of yourselves except that you cherish the memory of this time and of my whole consulship. For as long as that memory remains implanted in your hearts, I shall feel securely encompassed by the strongest of protective walls.

But if, on the other hand, the violence of wicked men defeats all my hopes and is crowned with success, I commend to you my little son. He will have enough protection, without a doubt, not only for his continued existence but for his whole career, if you will just remember that his father was the man who, at his own risk, and his alone, preserved the entire Roman world. Carefully and courageously then, as you have already begun, you must vote the necessary measures to secure the survival of your own selves and the people of Rome, your wives and children, your altars and firesides, your shrines and temples, the houses and dwellings of this entire city, your dominion and your freedom, this whole land of Italy, and the very existence of our country. For you have a consul who will carry out everything you decide without hesitating for a moment. As long as he lives, as long as he is able of his own power to guarantee enforcement, he will uphold every resolution that it ever becomes your pleasure to decree.

CHAPTER THREE

IN DEFENCE OF
THE POET AULUS LICINIUS ARCHIAS

*The Greco-Syrian poet, Archias, whom Cicero now defended in 62
B.C., was a friend and protégé of the cultured Lucius Licinius
Lucullus, and was therefore an automatic target for prosecution from
the friends of Pompeius, whose relations with Lucullus had become
extremely strained when the former superseded the latter in the
circumstances described in the speech* About the Command of
Cnaeus Pompeius. *Lucullus called Pompeius a carrion bird who
had come to feast on another's kill; Pompeius named Lucullus a
tragedy general whose successes were merely stage effects. Lucullus
had come home in 64, and now Pompeius was on his way back. The
indictment of Archias was a minor incident in the skirmishing
between the noble oligarchy who backed Lucullus and the forces of
innovation who were hopeful rather than frightened after the immense eastern victories of Pompeius.*

*·This was one of the recurrent occasions in Cicero's life when
disappointment at Pompeius momentarily got the better of his usual
policy of supporting him (p. 129). He also realized that the military
prestige of these oriental triumphs (though it was he himself who had
got Pompeius appointed to accomplish them) was a threat to the
Republican, senatorial form of government to which Cicero remained unvaryingly devoted.*

*The case he had to defend was somewhat obscure, but legally quite
strong. A law of the tribune Gaius Papius (64 B.C.) had expelled all
non-citizens from Rome. The law had been intended to clear the city
not of poets but of its huge gangs of thugs. Yet if Archias could be
proved an alien he would have to leave the city, and this would be
a successful pinprick in the campaign against Lucullus and the conservatives. Archias had claimed the Roman franchise as a citizen of*

Heraclea in Lucania. The prosecution then asserted that there was no good evidence either of his Heraclean or of his Roman citizenship; but Cicero argues to the contrary. The court almost certainly decided in his favour.

But his speech, said Lord Brougham, 'of which not more than one-sixth is to the purpose, could not have been delivered in a British court of justice'. Its most remarkable and famous feature is a long, irrelevant and moving digression on the glories of Greek culture and literature, and of the civilized life which they alone made possible. This is perhaps the finest eulogy of the literary life in the whole of ancient literature. It presents a contrast with Cicero's distaste for most contemporary Greeks – which is significant to our estimate of the Romans' schizophrenic attitude towards their Hellenic heritage and subjects.

It must also be remembered, since Archias was a poet, that although Cicero's verse was laughed at by Juvenal, he began as a young man to acquire a reputation for being the best poet as well as the best orator at Rome. Surviving fragments hardly enable us to form an opinion, and Archias' poetry has not come down to us either, since some epigrams in the Greek anthology bearing his name are unlikely to be his work at all. In praising his poems, Cicero, in deference to Roman practicality, had pointed out how they contributed to the glory of Rome; and he hoped that this speech would inspire Archias to write a panegyric on his consulship. Alas, a letter from Cicero to Atticus in the following summer shows that this complimentary composition never materialized.

Whatever benefit, gentlemen, can be extracted from any or all of my qualifications, I feel in duty bound to place it at the disposal of Aulus Licinius.[1] I appreciate the limitations of my natural ability. But I cannot deny that my experience as a public speaker has been considerable; and I admit I have

1. Cicero deliberately describes his client here as Aulus Licinius (without the addition of Archias) since that is his name as a Roman citizen.

never at any time felt a disinclination to study the theoretical background of the art. Upon all my efforts, then, the best I can achieve, Archias has a pre-eminent, overriding claim. For as far as I can cast my mind back into times gone by, as far as I can recollect the earliest years of my boyhood, the picture of the past that takes shape reveals that it was he who first inspired my determination to embark on these studies, and who started me upon their methodical pursuit. And so if this voice of mine, trained by his encouragement and instruction, has on occasion been of service to others, my capacity to come to their assistance – and even to save some of them from destruction – is derived from him: and it is he, therefore, who must receive from me all the help and salvation it lies within my power to provide.

To hear such words from my lips may cause a certain surprise, seeing that his own talents have found expression in spheres far removed from my own study and practice of oratory. But in fact I myself have never concentrated exclusively on this one activity. And besides, all branches of culture are closely related and linked together with one another. A further point, however, which some may equally find surprising, is that in a formal inquiry and official court of justice, at a hearing conducted by a carefully chosen Roman praetor and judges of the highest principles in front of a crowded audience, I have planned that my speech shall assume a form out of keeping with forensic tradition and style. But this deviation from the usual custom happens to be particularly appropriate to my client, yet will not, I hope, cause any inconvenience to yourselves; and so I urge you to allow me this indulgence. The fact is that I am speaking on behalf of an excellent poet, who is also a man of great learning. And I am speaking before listeners of strong literary tastes, judges thoroughly well versed in the humanities, and a praetor of exceptional calibre. What I therefore ask is that you should permit me to enlarge with rather more freedom than usual on cultural and literary matters. The studious seclusion of Archias' life has kept him unacquainted with the hazards of the courts, and it is because of the special nature of his talents that I want to frame my defence in these somewhat novel and unfamiliar terms. If I can but feel that you will have the kindness to concede me this request, I for my part undertake to convince you that Aulus Licinius should not be excluded from the list of Roman citizens; and indeed that he should certainly be made a Roman citizen here and now – if it were not the case that he is one already.

As soon as Archias had grown out of his boyhood and the studies which form a boy's usual liberal training, he began to devote himself to becoming a writer. He came from a good family at Antioch. At that time, it was a city of extensive population and wealth, overflowing with fine scholars and scholarly activities, and it was there that he first succeeded, very rapidly, in showing gifts of an exceptional nature. Later on, when he visited various parts of Asia and toured round the whole of Greece, his arrival in a place would arouse the keenest interest. His talents had by now won him a high reputation, and the excitement aroused by the news of an imminent visit by Archias reached remarkable heights. Nevertheless, even this excited expectation was eclipsed by the admiring enthusiasm with which he was actually received.

Southern Italy was in those days full of Greek culture and learning, and in Latium too such studies were pursued with greater keenness than could be found in the same towns today; while here at Rome also, where the internal situation was peaceful at the time, these pursuits were by no means neglected. Accordingly, Archias was granted citizenship and other honours by Tarentum and Rhegium and Neapolis, and all who were able to recognize a brilliant mind were glad to make his acquaintance and offer him hospitality.

We, too, became aware of his considerable fame, although

we had so far never seen him; but soon he made his way to Rome. That was during the consulships of Marius and Catulus,[2] so that the consuls he had the good fortune to find in office included one man who could provide a splendid theme for his pen, and a colleague who was able to supply him not only, again, with notable exploits but also with an appreciative ear. As soon as Archias arrived, while he was still very young,[3] the Luculli welcomed him to their house – and it is a tribute to his literary genius, and indeed to his whole personality, that the home which was first opened to him in his very youthful years is also the one he most constantly frequents now that he is an older man.

In those early days, Archias also enjoyed the most affectionate relations with the famous Metellus Numidicus and his son Pius. He used to read out his poems to Marcus Aemilius Scaurus. He associated with Quintus Catulus senior and junior. His friendship was cultivated by Lucius Crassus. He was also on very intimate terms not only with the Luculli but with Drusus and the Octavii and the whole family of Hortensius. He was held in the greatest honour; so much so, indeed, that the roll of his admirers was by no means limited to men who really wanted to learn and listen, but also came to include the sort of people who found it desirable to pretend they had a taste for such things.

Next, after a certain lapse of time, he went to Sicily with Marcus Lucullus, and then, after returning from that province in the company of that gentleman, he proceeded to Heraclea. This was a town which possessed the fullest treaty rights with Rome, and Archias expressed a desire to become a citizen of the place. His own personal qualities were quite sufficient recommendation in themselves, but he also had the support

2. Q. Lutatius Catulus sen. (consul 102) was associated with Marius in the destruction of the Cimbri at Vercellae (101).

3. Cicero speaks of the garb of manhood (*toga praetexta*, worn at 17) as if Archias was a Roman boy.

of Lucullus' authority and influence; and his wish was granted by the Heraclean people. In consequence of this, he also received the citizenship of Rome, according to the law of Silvanus and Carbo which granted the franchise to all who have been admitted as citizens of federated towns on the condition that, when the law was passed, the persons concerned were domiciled in Italy.[4] They were also required to report to a praetor within sixty days. Archias had long been resident at Rome, and reported to the praetor Quintus Metellus who was one of his close friends.

If the question of his Roman enfranchisement, and the legal position in this respect, are the only issues we have to bear in mind, I have nothing more to say; and I can close my case. For I am convinced, Gratius,[5] that you would not be able to disprove a single one of these facts. You will not, surely, attempt to deny that he was enrolled at Heraclea at the time of which I am speaking? If this should be your intention, Marcus Lucullus, whose authority and conscience and honour are beyond question, is here to say that he not only believes this happened but also knows it did, that he did not hear of the enrolment from someone else but saw it being done with his own eyes – and indeed, that he was not merely among those present but took the initiative in person. Envoys are also on the spot from Heraclea itself. They are a very distinguished group of men, who have come to Rome specially to attend this case. They are commissioned by their city, they bring with them its official testimonial, and they are prepared to confirm that Archias was, in fact, made a citizen of their town. On this point you have asked for the public archives of Heraclea to be produced; but we all know that they were destroyed when the local record office was burnt during the Italian war.[6] It is ridiculous to ignore proofs

4. This is the *Lex Plautia Papiria* (89).
5. Gratius, otherwise unknown, was the prosecutor.
6. Italian war: Social (Marsian) War (90–88).

which are available, yet to demand evidence which we cannot possibly obtain; to be deliberately silent about things that men are actually in a position to remember, but to clamour for documentary record. You have the word of a great and scrupulous gentleman. You have the sworn affidavit of an irreproachably honest town council. There can be no tampering with things like that. Yet you brush them aside and call for documents! And you do this although you admit in the same breath that the possibility that such records might be forged is seen by experience to be considerable.

Or do you propose to deny that Archias lived at Rome? Surely not! Years before he ever became a Roman citizen he had established Rome as his residence, and the place where all his worldly possessions were concentrated. Or did he omit to report? No, he reported as he should have. Indeed, out of all the registrations sought from the board of praetors at that time, his was actually the only application which was accompanied by truly valid supporting evidence.

There were allegations that the citizen-lists of Appius had not been very carefully kept. Indeed, the authenticity of all such compilations had been cast into doubt first by the unreliability of Gabinius,[7] before he was condemned by the court, and then by the discredit brought upon him by his conviction. Nevertheless the conscientious and law-abiding Metellus Pius exhibited such scruples with regard to these lists that he went to the praetor Lucius Lentulus and a board of judges, and indicated to them that he was extremely disturbed at having to erase even one single name. And yet when you consider the documents which relate to the present case, you will see that there is not the slightest question of any erasure in respect of the name of Aulus Licinius.

These facts regarding his position at Rome are very far from suggesting any doubts about his previous enfranchisement at

7. P. Gabinius Capito was condemned for extortion after his governorship of Achaia.

Heraclea. Besides, as to that, Heraclea was by no means the only town where he became a citizen. It has, as a matter of fact, been not uncommon for the Greek communities of Italy to bestow their citizenship for no particular reason at all, even on individuals whose qualifications were extremely slender or non-existent. So how can you venture to suggest that the people of Rhegium, Locri, Neapolis or Tarentum, when they were perfectly prepared to make a habit of bestowing such honours even upon mere actors, would have refused it to this man of really brilliant and outstanding gifts?

All the other persons whose Roman status has been questioned contrived to insinuate their names into the citizen-lists of their municipalities not merely after the dates of their alleged enrolment but even after the passing of the Papian law.[8] But my client, on the other hand, does not even think it necessary to cite the lists on which his name was inscribed, because there has never been a time during all this period at which he has not looked upon himself as belonging to Heraclea. You say you miss his name on the census-rolls. But is it really such a deadly secret that at the time of the last census he was with the army, on the staff of the eminent Lucius Lucullus, and on the immediately preceding occasion he was likewise with Lucullus, during the latter's quaestorship in Asia? The census before that, when Julius and Crassus were censors – the first after his enfranchisement – is irrelevant since on that occasion no registration of any part of the population was in fact conducted at all.

In any case, however, it has to be recognized that census-lists are no real proof of Roman citizenship, but merely indicate that the men whose names appear on them claimed it at that particular time. It may therefore be helpful for me to add that during the years in question my client, so far from not being one of our citizens even in his own eyes (as you

8. The *Lex Papia* made all non-citizens liable to eviction from Rome (64).

pretended), made his will on a number of occasions according to Roman law, received legacies left him by Roman citizens, and was recommended to the treasury by the proconsul Lucius Lucullus, as a Roman, so that a reward might be given him for his services.

As regards your contrary assertions, the burden of proving them rests with you and no one but you. For no judgements he has passed on himself, and no judgements passed on him by his friends, will be of the smallest assistance towards the refutation of his claim.

You will no doubt be asking me, Gratius, why I feel such an affection for this man. The answer is that he provides my mind with refreshment after this din of the courts; he soothes my ears to rest when they are wearied by angry disputes. How could I find material, do you suppose, for the speeches I make every day on such a variety of subjects, unless I steeped my mind in learning? How could I endure the constant strains if I could not distract myself from them by this means? Yes, I confess I am devoted to the study of literature. If people have buried themselves in books, if they have used nothing they have read for the benefit of their fellow-men, if they have never displayed the fruits of such reading before the public eye, well, let them by all means be ashamed of the occupation. But why, gentlemen, should I feel any shame? Seeing that not once throughout all these years have I allowed myself to be prevented from helping any man in the hour of his need because I wanted a rest, or because I was eager to pursue my own pleasures, or even because I needed a sleep!

I cannot therefore, I submit, be justly rebuked or censured if the time which others spend in advancing their own personal affairs, taking holidays and attending Games, indulging in pleasures of various kinds or even enjoying mental relaxation and bodily recreation, the time they spend on protracted parties and gambling and playing ball, proves in my case to have been taken up with returning over and over again to these literary pursuits. And I have all the more right to engage in such studies because they improve my capacity as a speaker; and this, for what it is worth, has unfailingly remained at the disposal of my friends whenever prosecutions have placed them in danger. Even if some may regard my ability as nothing very great, at least I realize the source from which the best part of it has come. For unless I had convinced myself from my earliest years, on the basis of lessons derived from all I had read, that nothing in life is really worth having except moral decency and reputable behaviour, and that for their sake all physical tortures and all perils of death and banishment must be held of little account, I should never have been able to speak up for the safety of you all in so many arduous clashes, or to endure these attacks which dissolute rogues launch against me every day. The whole of literature, philosophy and history is full of examples which teach this lesson – but which would have been plunged in utter darkness if the written word had not been available to illuminate them. Just think of the number of vividly drawn pictures of valiant men of the past that Greek and Latin writers have preserved for our benefit: not for mere inspection only, but for imitation as well. Throughout my public activities I have never ceased to keep these great figures before my eyes, and have modelled myself heart and soul on the contemplation of their excellence.

It might be objected that those great men, whose noble deeds have been handed down in the literary record, were not themselves by any means thoroughly well versed in the learning which I praise so highly. Certainly, it would be difficult to make a categorical assertion that they were. Nevertheless, I am quite clear what my answer to such a point should be. I agree that there have been many people whose exceptional inborn qualities, expressed in almost godlike endowments of mind and character without the support of any cultural qualifications at all, have enabled them by their own unaided endeavours to reach the heights of self-management and moral excellence. Indeed, I would go further, and express the view that the number of virtuous and admirable men produced by character without learning exceeds those who are the products of learning without character. Nevertheless I do also maintain that, when noble and elevated natural gifts are supplemented and shaped by the influence of theoretical knowledge, the result is then something truly remarkable and unique. Such a personality could be seen by our fathers in the superhuman figure of the younger Scipio Africanus. Such, too, were those paragons of moderation and self-control Gaius Laelius and Lucius Furius;[9] such was the courageous and venerable Marcus Cato, the most erudite man of his day. They would certainly never have spent their time on literary studies if these had not helped them to understand what a better life could be, and how to bring that ideal into effect for themselves.

And yet let us leave aside for a moment any practical advantage that literary studies may bring. For even if their aim were pure enjoyment and nothing else, you would still, I am sure, feel obliged to agree that no other activity of the mind could possibly have such a broadening and enlightening effect. For there is no other occupation upon earth which is so appropriate to every time and every age and every place. Reading stimulates the young and diverts the old, increases one's satisfaction when things are going well, and when they are going badly provides refuge and solace. It is a delight in the home; it can be fitted in with public life; throughout the night, on journeys, in the country, it is a companion which never lets me down.

And indeed even if we ourselves were not capable of any inclination or taste for these pursuits, we ought all the same to

9. C. Laelius (Minor) Sapiens and L. Furius Philus were prominent members of the circle of Scipio Aemilianus (Africanus junior).

feel admiration when we see such gifts exemplified in others No one can have been so boorish and insensitive that he remained unaffected when Roscius[10] recently died. Although he was an old man at the time of his death, we had a feeling that such a superb and attractive artist ought somehow to have been exempted from our common fate. And if such a man's mere physical comportment on the stage was enough to win the hearts of us all, surely we cannot be left indifferent by genius of a purely intellectual kind, with all its enigmatic motions and scintillations.

Many is the time, gentlemen, that I have listened to this Archias – for I am going to presume on your indulgence, since I see that the unconventional shape of my speech has succeeded in gaining your attention – many is the time I have listened to him improvising quantities of admirable verses about topics of the day without having written down one single letter before he spoke. Many times also I have heard him respond to demands for an encore by repeating the same subject-matter in an entirely new set of words and phrases. And as for his written works, the products of meticulous care and cogitation, I have seen them accorded a degree of appreciation in no way inferior to the reverence felt for writers of ancient times. Should I not love and admire such a man, and deem it my duty to defend him by every means in my power?

We have it on eminent and learned authority that, whereas other arts need to be based upon study and rules and principles, poets depend entirely on their own inborn gifts and are stimulated by some internal force, a sort of divine spark, within the depths of their own souls. Our great Ennius[11] was therefore right to call poets holy, because they seem to bring

10. Q. Roscius Gallus was the outstanding comic actor of the Roman stage and also played tragic parts.
11. Ennius of Rudiae, 'the father of Roman poetry' (d. 169).

to us some special gift and endowment which the gods have accorded them as a passport for this world. Even the most barbarous of races has never treated the name of poet with disrespect. How imperative therefore it is that you yourselves, with all your noble culture, should regard it as holy indeed! The very rocks and deserts echo the poet's song. Many is the time when ferocious beasts have been enchanted and arrested in their tracks as these strains come to their ears. Shall we, then, who have been nurtured on everything that is fine, remain unmoved at a poet's voice?

The people of Colophon declare that Homer came from their city, the Chians assert he belongs to them, the men of Salamis lay a rival claim, while the people of Smyrna are so sure he is theirs that they have even allotted him a shrine within their town; and a great many other communities, too, have joined in this competitive struggle to be regarded as Homer's birth-place. These people, in fact, are eager for the possession of a man who has long been dead and who, even when he lived, was a foreigner. It is because of his poetic genius that they feel this powerful urge. Are we, on the contrary, to reject a poet who is still alive, and who is indeed ours by law, and ours by his own inclination as well?

This would be particularly misguided in the case of Archias, since he has for many years past devoted all his expert skill and talent to celebrating the glorious renown of Rome. When he was a young man he wrote about the Cimbrian war, and he even succeeded in gaining the approval of Gaius Marius himself, although that great man did not have a reputation for appreciating this kind of activity. But no one is, in fact, so uninterested in the Muses that he does not want his own deeds to be glorified and perpetuated in verse. There is a story that the renowned Athenian Themistocles was asked which actor or singer he liked the best. His favourite, he replied, was whichever one praised his exploits the most highly! And that, for example, was the reason why Gaius

Marius was attached to Lucius Plotius,[12] whose gifts he saw to be well fitted for the commemoration of the deeds that he himself had accomplished.

Archias has also dealt with the entire war against Mithridates, a vast and complicated war consisting of many varied operations on land and sea. This work sheds lustre on the valiant and magnificent Lucius Lucullus, but in so doing it contributes to the splendour of Rome as well. For it was Romans whom Lucullus led to open up Pontus, protected though it was by the resources of its king and by its own geographical position. It was Romans who under the same general, with a force of only moderate size, put the numberless hordes of Armenians to flight. It was Romans, still under the direction of Lucullus, who gained the glory for rescuing and preserving the friendly city of Cyzicus from all the onslaughts of the king and the ravening jaws of warfare. To Rome, too, comes eternal honour for that amazing naval battle at Tenedos in which Lucullus slew the enemy's admirals and crushed their fleet.[13] Ours are the trophies, ours the monuments, ours the triumphs. Those who dedicate their powers to the literary celebration of such events are increasing the fame of the people of Rome itself.

Our noble Ennius was held in affection by the elder Africanus, and the tomb of the Scipios is said to have contained a marble statue of the poet. And yet his compliments to Africanus surely illuminate not only that hero himself but the entire commonwealth of Rome. Ennius also extolled to the skies the Cato whose great-grandson is with us today; and bright is the brilliance shed by those panegyrics upon the renown of our country in general. In the same way, again, when compliments are paid to the names of Maximus,

12. L. Plotius Gallus was said to be the first man to teach Latin rhetoric at Rome (c. 95–93).

13. L. Licinius Lucullus defeated Mithridates VI of Pontus off Tenedos in 73.

Marcellus and Fulvius,[14] it is all of us Romans, and not just themselves, to whom distinction is added by such eulogies. That is why the writer from Rudiae who uttered these praises was admitted by our ancestors to the citizenship of Rome.

The man whom we are now considering possesses the franchise of Heraclea. Many other Greek townships, too, have competed to make him a citizen of their own communities. He has also received a similar gift, by due legal process from Rome itself. How on earth can we deprive him of this manifest entitlement?

Archias is a Greek poet. But it would be entirely wrong to suppose that Greek poetry ranks lower than Latin in value. For Greek literature is read in almost every country in the world, whereas Latin is understood only within its own boundaries which, as you must admit, are restricted. Our deeds, it is true, extend to all the regions of the earth. But the effect of this should be to inspire us with the determination that every country where the strong arm of Rome has carried its weapons should also be given an opportunity to learn of our illustrious achievements. For literary commemoration is a most potent factor in enhancing a country's prestige. And to those who hazard their lives for the sake of glory, such literature is a vigorous incentive, stimulating them to risk fearful perils and perform noble endeavours.

We are told that Alexander the Great took around with him a great number of authors engaged in writing about his achievements. And yet, as he stood beside the tomb of Achilles at Sigeum, he uttered these words: 'Fortunate youth, who found Homer to proclaim your valour!' He was right; for, if the *Iliad* had never existed, the tomb where Achilles' body was buried would have buried his memory as well. And

14. Q. Fabius Maximus, M. Claudius Marcellus (captor of Syracuse, 211) and Q. Fulvius Flaccus (captor of Capua in the same year) were all eulogized in the *Annals* of Ennius.

then again Pompeius known as Magnus, outstanding alike for his bravery and good fortune, conferred Roman citizenship upon Theophanes of Mitylene,[15] the historian of his deeds, before his whole assembled army. Now, our gallant men, countryfolk and soldiers though they were, felt influenced by the splendid tale Theophanes had told. And so, feeling that part of the grandeur belonged also to themselves, they declared their approval with a mighty shout.

If the law did not happen to have made Archias a Roman citizen already, he would find it the easiest thing in the world, as I am certain you cannot deny, to win the franchise from one of our generals in this selfsame way. Surely Sulla, who dispensed citizenship so freely to Spaniards and Gauls, would never have refused such a request from Archias. Once, at a public meeting, some bad poet from out of the crowd handed Sulla an epigram the man had written about him, with every other line longer than it ought to be. Sulla, who was conducting an auction, immediately ordered a reward to be paid the scribbler from its proceeds – on the condition that he never wrote anything again! Here then was a personage who felt that even the worst of poets should be rewarded for his industry; so how could he have failed to help a writer with the talent and style and fluency of Archias? Or, again, if Quintus Metellus Pius had been approached, the personal influence of Archias, not to speak of the intervention of the Luculli, would unmistakably have been successful, especially as Metellus was his intimate friend and had, besides, conferred the franchise on numerous other people as well. Moreover, Metellus was eager to have his own actions recorded; he even gave a hearing to certain poets who came from Corduba, for all the ponderous, exotic flavour of their language.

For there is no concealing the fact, and it had better be

15. Theophanes wrote an account of the campaigns of Pompeius in the east.

accepted and openly admitted: we all like to be praised! The better the man the greater his desire for celebrity. The philosophers who bid us despise ambition do not forget to affix their names to their own books! On the very writings in which they deplore publicity and self-advertisement, they publicize and advertise themselves. And then again that heroic commander Decimus Brutus, when he erected temples and monuments, adorned their forecourts with verses written by his friend Accius.[16] Another outstanding example is Fulvius,[17] who took Ennius with him on his campaign against the Aetolians, and when it was over forthwith dedicated the spoils of war to the Muses. In a city, then, where even generals scarcely lay down their weapons before offering honours to poetry and the Muses' shrine, it would indeed be unbecoming for judges, who wear the garb of peace, to act in a fashion repugnant to the honour of those divinities and the well-being of the poetical profession.

To incline you to my way of thinking, gentlemen, I will place myself in your hands and confess to you my own passion to be famous. This is a passion which may seem exaggerated; but I am sure it is not dishonourable. The fact is that the measures which I took during my consulship, with your collaboration, to ensure the salvation of this city and the empire and the lives of all its citizens and everything that our country stands for, have been chosen by Archias as the subject of a poem. He has already started upon its composition, and when he read out to me what he had written, I judged the project a very worthwhile and attractive one, and singled him out as just the man for the task.

16. Dec. Junius Brutus Gallaicus celebrated a Triumph in 136 for the conquest of Lusitania and Gallaecia (Galicia). L. Accius of Pisaurum (d. *c.* 85) was regarded as the leading tragic poet.

17. M. Fulvius Nobilior defeated the Aetolians during his consulship of 189.

A person with right ideas hopes for no reward whatever for any toils and perils he may have to undergo – except only praise, and the good opinion of his fellows. Take those things away, gentlemen, and in the brief and transient span of this life I cannot see what stimulus remains to encourage our arduous labours. If the human spirit felt no anticipations of posterity, if the range of its imagination were bounded by the limits that circumscribe human existence, we should never be prepared to tire ourselves out with all these exertions, suffer torments of sleepless anxiety, face ceaseless confrontations in which our very lives are at stake. It does appear, however, that men of true nobility contain within themselves a force which day and night applies the prick of ambition to their hearts, and never allows us to stop struggling to ensure that the memory of our names shall not perish with our deaths, but shall survive them for all time to come.

For how could we, who undergo the toils and hazards of public life, be spiritless enough to feel satisfied with the idea that, after we have spent not one single moment of our lives in peace and tranquillity, all this effort will go for nothing at the very moment when we die? Many distinguished men have taken great pains to leave their statues and representations behind them. But those are likenesses only of the body, and not of the spirit at all, and so have not we all the more reason to feel enthusiastic about bequeathing a similar image of our intellectual and moral personalities as well, to be moulded and elaborated by the very finest talents available?

As for myself, even at the actual time when I was busiest with great matters, I felt I was also diffusing and disseminating a knowledge of those very same deeds throughout the entire earth to be remembered for ever. Perhaps, when I am dead, I shall no longer be able to perceive whether their memory does, in fact, remain. Or possibly, as certain philosophers have argued, some part of my being will still be conscious that this is happening. But however that may be, at least I derive satisfaction here and now from the thought and the hope that what I have done will not be forgotten.

So I call upon you, judges, to pronounce in favour of my client. He is a man whose honourable character you see confirmed by the high rank of his friends and the unbroken durations of their friendships with him. You can appreciate his gifts from the extent to which they have been in demand from leading men who are extremely gifted themselves. Moreover, the justice of his cause is demonstrated by the sanction of the law, the authority of his municipality, the testimony offered by Lucullus, and archives going back to Metellus.

To you and your generals and the deeds of the Roman people Archias has always done honour. To those recent internal perils which threatened myself and yourselves he proposes to offer an undying testimonial of praise. He belongs, moreover, to a profession which has universally and at all times been declared and believed to possess a sacred character. If then, gentlemen, such great powers warrant the applause of mankind – and truly they deserve the commendation of the gods themselves! – I entreat you to take him under your protection. Let it not be said that a severe judgement of yours has done harm to such a man. Let it be seen instead that your humane decision has brought him relief.

I have made the statement of my case as brief and simple as usual; and I have the feeling that it has gained your approbation. I hope my digression from the custom of the courts and the bar, in order to tell you something about my client's talent and about literary studies in general, has been to your taste. To the chairman of this tribunal[18] – I venture to express the conviction – it has proved acceptable enough.

18. According to tradition the chairman of the panel was Cicero's brother Quintus (praetor).

CHAPTER FOUR

IN DEFENCE OF
MARCUS CAELIUS RUFUS

*Fears that Pompeius was not concerned to maintain the old oligarchic,
senatorial system of government proved justified, since in 60 he
formed the dictatorial First Triumvirate with Caesar and Crassus.
Cicero was invited to join it, and to his credit eventually refused to
do so. When, therefore, the tribune Publius Clodius Pulcher, who was
now Cicero's bitterest enemy (having been alienated by the orator's
sharp demolition of his alibi when he was accused of sacrilegious
violation of the secret rites of the Bona Dea),[1] proposed a law sending
him into exile for his execution of the Catilinarian leaders, the
Triumvirs did nothing to save him from this fate. Nor, to his bitter
distress, did the senatorial leaders, whom he had wrongly believed to
be his supporters for ever after the Catilina affair. Cicero's subsequent sixteen months of exile were the most miserable period of his
life.*

*Recalled when Pompeius began to find Clodius unbearable, Cicero
resumed his legal practice, and discovered an opportunity to attack his
enemy's great family when Clodius' second sister Clodia, a famous
immoral beauty for whom the poet Catullus had a hopeless passion,
attacked her former lover Marcus Caelius Rufus. This clever young
politician was charged by a prosecutor with whose family he had a
feud – and this rather than Clodia may have been the beginning of
the whole case – with a shocking array of offences, including the
murder of one or more Alexandrian envoys and the attempted poisoning of his estranged mistress herself. Although some of the charges
may well have had more substance than Cicero admits, his brilliant
and amusing advocacy evidently got Caelius off (56 B.C.).*

But this speech is interesting above all for the startling insight it

1. See pp. 224, 245, 250, 252, 260, 267.

offers into the private and social lives of the smartest people in Rome during the first century B.C. – *lives evoked lushly (though euphemistically) in the banqueting scenes of a thousand films. It is curious to see Cicero, who was usually inclined to take a more puritanical line, obliged to adopt a genial 'boys will be boys' attitude in speaking of his client's early life, which had combined violent dissipation with active support of Catilina. The speech is graceful, humorous and light of touch, written in a vivid, dramatic, elliptical and sometimes almost epistolary style.*

If, gentlemen, there should happen to be anyone present who is unaware of our laws and courts and customs, I am sure he would wonder what the special gravity of this case might be, seeing that it is the one and only trial to be held at a time of festivities and public games,[2] when all legal business is on vacation. He would undoubtedly conclude that the defendant must be guilty of so serious a crime that unless it is tackled the entire structure of the state will collapse!

Let us suppose he was next told of the law[3] which prescribes that in the event of criminal, traitorous Roman citizens taking up arms to obstruct the Senate, attacking the men in charge of the government, and trying to destroy the government itself, it is obligatory to hold an investigation on any and every day. He would not object to the law. But he would want to know what sort of charge was involved in the present action. And then, just imagine him being told that no real crime, no outrage, no act of violence was before the court at all, but that a talented, energetic, popular man is being accused by the son[4] of a person against whom this defendant is himself about to

2. The speech was delivered on 4 April, the opening day of the Ludi Megalenses.

3. The trial was being conducted under the *Lex Lutatia de vi* (78). There was also a later *Lex Plautia* of wider scope.

4. This prosecutor is L. Sempronius Atratinus, seventeen-year-old son of L. Calpurnius Bestia who was twice prosecuted by Caelius.

bring an indictment (for the second time); and, furthermore, that the current action is financed by a whore.[5] The conclusion of this observer would surely be that the prosecutor's filial dutifulness is excusable, that woman's malicious passions ought to be kept under control, and that you, members of the bench, are overworked, since even on public holidays you do not get time off.

And in fact, gentlemen, if you care to note the circumstances carefully and form an accurate estimate of the case as a whole, you will inevitably come to the conclusion that none of those concerned would ever have lent themselves to this prosecution if they had been given any choice; nor, having taken it on, would they have had the slightest hope of success were they not pushed by the insupportable tantrums and savage malevolence of a third party. I am prepared to forgive Atratinus, who is a civilized and excellent young man and a friend of mine. He can plead as his excuse either filial feeling, or coercion, or his tender age. If he wanted to bring the charge, ascribe it to filial duty; if he was obeying orders, it was coercion; and if he saw prospects for himself in the case, I put this down to boyish inexperience. The other counsel for the prosecution, on the other hand, are entitled to no such indulgence, and deserve to be vigorously opposed.

The defence of the young Marcus Caelius can appropriately be introduced, in my opinion, by replying to the slanders which the other side has produced in order to blacken his reputation and damage and ruin his good name. His father has been brought up against him in various ways, either on the grounds that the old gentleman lives in squalor or because my client is said to be a bad son. With regard to the personal situation of Marcus Caelius senior, men who belong to the

5. This and other sneers concerning female influence are all directed against Clodia.

older generation, and know him personally, appreciate that he is perfectly able to act as his own silent witness without any justifications from myself. And as for those who are less well acquainted with him since his age has so long prevented him from joining us in the Forum, they can rest assured that the dignity proper to a Roman knight – which can be something very considerable – has always been a strong feature of the elder Caelius, and the same is definitely still felt to be the case today, not only by his own circle but by all who for any reason may have come to know him. To be the son of a Roman knight should never have been used as a smear, either by the prosecutors, or before these examiners, or in the hearing of myself as defending counsel.[6]

To turn to your point about his attitude to his father, that is, indeed, a matter on which we can form our own opinion, but the best judge is really the parent himself. Our view you will learn from witnesses on oath; and as to what the parents feel, that is sufficiently proclaimed by his mother's sobs and indescribable distress, his father's dismal mourning clothes, and all the misery and grief you see because of this trial.

With regard to your further insinuation that the young man is not thought highly of by his own fellow-townsmen, the people of the Praetuttian region[7] have never awarded higher honours even to anyone right in their very midst than those they conferred on Caelius – though he was not in the place at all. For they enrolled the young man, absent though he was, in their highest council, and thus granted him, quite without any request on his part, a distinction which many who solicited similar honours had sought from them in vain. Furthermore, they have sent a deputation, including eminent fellow-Senators of mine and Roman knights as well, to be present at the

6. The panel of judges partly consisted of knights, and Cicero was the son of a knight and the supporter of their Order.

7. According to this reading Caelius came from Interamnia Praetuttiorum (Teramo) in Picenum.

trial; and these delegates have brought with them a most imposing and eloquent testimonial.

I fancy I have now placed my arguments for the defence on a firm foundation: because nothing could be firmer than a case founded upon the convictions of my client's own townsmen. For I can certainly see that you would not feel that a young man like this brought you a very satisfactory recommendation if he had incurred the disapproval either of a town of such distinction and importance or, indeed, of a man with the qualities of Caelius' father. If I may turn for a moment to my own personal position, it is from just that sort of background that I, too, first issued forth to begin to make my reputation, before the days when my forensic labours here and my professional career in general, with the approval and backing of my friends, gradually flowed into a broader course and won public recognition.

Now let us consider the criticisms directed against the morals of Caelius, and all the prosecution's attacks on this subject. These are not, in fact, actual charges at all, but mere slanders and defamations; and none of them will distress Caelius enough to make him wish he had been born ugly! For disagreeable remarks of such a character are commonly directed against every good-looking young man. But defamation is one thing, prosecution another. Prosecution needs specific grounds of sufficient strength to define the facts, leave their mark on the defendant, supply convincing demonstrations, and back them up by evidence. Abuse, on the other hand, has no purpose except to be insulting. If its character is crude, it is called invective; and if it is amusing it passes as wit.

That this part of the prosecution was allotted to Atratinus caused me both surprise and annoyance. For such a vein was appropriate neither to his personality nor to his youthful years, and, as you no doubt noted, this estimable young man's own scruples meant he was far from comfortable with language of the kind. I should have felt much happier if this abusive role had been left to the more mature members of the group; for then, in contradicting the vituperation, I would have been able to speak in more outspoken, forcible and natural terms. But towards you, Atratinus, I shall show greater leniency. For one thing, the fact that you yourself have a sense of propriety makes me feel inclined to handle you gently. And besides, I am not at all eager to undo the services I performed for yourself and your father on an earlier occasion.[8]

However, I do want to give you some advice. First, so that everyone can see what you are really like, I venture to suggest that you ought to keep clear of intemperate language just as carefully as you avoid intemperate behaviour. Secondly, never say against someone else things that you would blush to hear fabricated against yourself. For that road lies open to all the world. For instance, anyone can make as vicious an attack as he pleases upon somebody of your own age and handsome looks – and even if there is not the slightest cause for any suspicion he can make his criticisms sound quite plausible. However, the blame for the role you have assumed cannot really be attributed to yourself at all; it must go to the men who chose you for the part. To you, on the other hand, to your own feeling for what is right, belongs credit, since it was easy for all of us to see the reluctance with which you spoke. And a compliment to your ability is also due, because of your admirable and elegant speech.

All the same, my answer to everything that you said will be brief. In so far as the youthful life of Marcus Caelius might have given reason for suspicion, I must tell you that it was protected by two things: his own decency, and his father's careful training. Moreover, the elder Caelius, as soon as he had given his son the toga of manhood, immediately placed

8. Cicero defended Atratinus' father Bestia on 11 February, and had perhaps been the boy's teacher of public speaking.

him under my own personal care. That is all I will say, because I am not at this juncture going to speak about myself. I shall be satisfied to leave the matter to your judgement. The situation is that the young Marcus Caelius, during his early youth, was never seen by anyone except in the company of his father or myself or in the highly respectable household of Marcus Crassus. He spent those years receiving an excellent education.

Caelius has been accused of being a friend of Catilina. But he has a right to dissociate himself completely from any such smear. True, at the time when Catilina, along with myself, was a candidate for the consulship, Caelius was still very young. And I admit many worthy young men were fond of that degraded brute. Still, if Caelius had at that time ever attached himself to Catilina or detached himself from me, then it would have been proper enough to criticize him for forming such an association. But the actual circumstances of the case completely rule out any suggestion of the sort. Afterwards, certainly – as you point out – we know and we saw that he was, in fact, one of Catilina's political supporters. That is a thing which nobody denies. At the moment, however, I am defending that earlier stage of his youth which by its very nature is vulnerable and is easily imperilled by other people's wilful passions. Well, in those days, while I was praetor, Caelius was continually in my own company. Catilina, who was at that time governor of Africa, was not even one of his acquaintances. Then came the year when Catilina was prosecuted for extortion;[9] Caelius was still with myself, and did not even attend the court to help him. In the next year I stood for the consulship. Catilina was also a candidate, but Caelius never joined him, and never left my side.

It was not until he had been going to the Forum for all that time, without incurring the slightest suspicion or disrepute, that he became a follower of Catilina, who was then making

9. Catilina, prosecuted by P. Clodius, was acquitted (summer 65).

his second attempt to become consul. Very well; but surely one must not expect that a youth's early years can go on being sheltered indefinitely! When I was young we used to spend one year 'keeping our arms in our togas', and doing physical training on the Campus Martius, and if we started our military service straightaway we had a similar probationary period in our army life at camp. Now, at that age, unless a young man had the necessary strength of mind, sexual restraint, good home training and also, one must add, natural decency to look after himself, however carefully he was watched over by his friends he could not avoid giving grounds for scandal, and justifiable scandal at that. But when someone had spent the earliest years of his youth living a clean and chaste life, then later on, after he had finally grown up and become a man among men, aspersions on his reputation and his morals were generally felt to be out of place.

Yes, after he had served several years' apprenticeship in the Forum, Caelius did become an adherent of Catilina. So did many other people of every rank and age. For as I am sure you will recall, Catilina had many excellent qualities, not indeed maturely developed, but at least sketched out roughly in outline. It is true that he got a large number of deplorable individuals to flock round him. But he also put up a show of affection towards men guided by the loftiest principles. There was a good deal about him that exercised a corrupting effect on other people; and yet he also undeniably possessed a gift for stimulating his associates into vigorous activity. Catilina was at one and the same time a furnace of inordinate sensual passions, and a serious student of military affairs. I do not believe that the world has ever seen such a portent of divergent, contrary, contradictory tastes and appetites.

At one stage in his life, no one on earth had a greater capacity for ingratiating himself with his superiors – and, equally, for making close friends with people lower down the scale. Nobody, at a certain period, held sounder political views; and yet he became the most loathsome enemy his country ever possessed. His disgusting pleasures were as exceptional as his unflagging endurance. Where else could you ever find such insatiable greed – or such open-handed generosity? Gentlemen, paradoxical features abounded in that man. He had the gift of making many friends, and in order to keep them there was no service that he would not perform. He was ready to share his possessions with everyone, to help needy friends with money, influence, physical exertion and even reckless crime. No one knew better than he did how to adapt and guide his ways to suit an occasion, bending and manipulating them this way and that. He was perfectly capable of living austerely with the austere and gaily with the self-indulgent, gravely with the old, genially with the young, audaciously with criminals and extravagantly with debauchees. And so this complex and many-sided character, at a time when he had attracted evil scoundrels from every quarter, still held the allegiance of many good, respectable men by a sort of fictitious mimicry of virtue. Indeed, even that frightful impulse to overthrow our whole system could never have come from him unless all these vices had been united with qualities of efficiency and toughness.

For these reasons, gentlemen, you should discard the prosecution's entire line of argument. Let no blame attach to Caelius because he associated with Catilina. For that is something which he has in common with many other people, including persons who are beyond reproach. Indeed, I declare that I myself was once nearly deceived by him.[10] I took him for a patriotic citizen attached to our national leaders, and for a faithful and reliable friend. I did not believe his misdeeds before I saw them; until I had actually caught him in the act I had no suspicion they even existed. If Caelius, too, was one of his numerous friends, he would, I agree, be right to feel

10. In letters to Atticus, Cicero mentions that in 65 he was thinking of speaking in Catilina's defence.

annoyed that he had made such a mistake, just as I sometimes regret my own misconception about the man. But the fact should certainly not give my client the slightest cause to fear that the friendship might be used as the basis for an indictment in court.

After you had dropped offensive hints about this relationship, you got down to the job of creating prejudice concerning the conspiracy. For you let it be supposed, though admittedly in a tentative and casual fashion, that because Caelius was a friend of Catilina he must have been a fellow-conspirator as well. However, at this point the charge was so unconvincing that my eloquent young friend's speech scarcely held together. For surely Caelius was not such a lunatic! Did his character and habits, or his position and resources, really impose upon him such an overwhelming disability as all that? At the time when suspicion was going around, no one ever heard the name of Caelius even being mentioned.

But there is no need for me to enlarge on this subject – for the facts are indisputable. Still, I must add just one further point. If Caelius had really been a party to the conspiracy, or even if he had been anything other than violently hostile to such an abominable act, he would never under any circumstances have tried to promote his youthful career by charging someone else with complicity in the same crime![11]

And now that I have reached this juncture I am inclined to think that the suggestions of corrupt electoral practices and clubs and agents distributing bribes deserve just the same sort of answer. For if Caelius had stained his reputation with the unlimited bribery to which you refer, he would never have been such an idiot as to charge a different person with precisely the same offence, thus involving someone else in suspected

11. In March 59 Caelius had prosecuted, and Cicero unsuccessfully defended, C. Antonius Hybrida, probably for treasonable conduct in Macedonia and collusion with Catilina, with a subsidiary charge of extortion.

guilt for a criminal activity in which he wanted to keep a free hand for himself! Nor, if he imagined that he himself was going to have to face even a single prosecution for bribery, would he have been likely to have brought an identical charge against another individual not only once, but actually on a second occasion as well. I admit that in this matter he has been acting indiscreetly and against my wishes. All the same, his determination, even if directed, it would seem, against an innocent man, clearly shows not the slightest trace of apprehension on his own account.

He is also accused of being in debt. His expenses are criticized, his account-books demanded for inspection. But to these points I shall give you a very succinct reply. A young man who is still subject to his father's authority does not keep accounts at all. Nor has Caelius ever borrowed money. He is only blamed for expenditure of a single kind – the rent of his house, which you claim is thirty thousand sesterces a year. But I can see what you are driving at. For Publius Clodius' block of houses, in which Caelius rents an apartment for, I believe, ten thousand, is up for sale. And so, consequently, what you have done is to give a fictitious figure, as a favour to Clodius and in order to help his deal.

You reproached Caelius for living apart from his father. But surely there is nothing wrong with that at his age. In a case with political implications he had just gained a success which, although admittedly unwelcome to myself, brought him considerable prestige. He had also reached the time of life when he could stand for public offices. That was the stage at which he moved out of his father's house – with his father's approval, and indeed actually upon his advice. For the elder Caelius lives too far from the Forum, and in order to be able to visit our homes more easily, and receive visits from his own friends, his son leased a house on the Palatine, at a moderate rent.

In this context I should like to repeat what the eminent Marcus Crassus recently said when he was expressing regret at the arrival of King Ptolemy[12] of Egypt.

Would that in Pelion's forest the vessel had not[13] . . .

But you will I am sure allow me to go on with the same quotation.

For then never would a lady bereft of her wits . . .

have given us all this trouble, namely

Medea, sick in her spirit, wounded by cruel love.

And that, gentlemen, hints at what I am going to demonstrate when I come to the appropriate point in my speech: namely that all this young man's trouble, or rather all the gossip about him, has been caused by his change of residence – and by this Medea of the Palatine.

Confident of your sound judgement, gentlemen, I am not worried by the various fictions which I gather from the speeches for the prosecution are being concocted to bolster up their case. One of these fabrications related to a Senator who was going to testify he had been assaulted by Caelius during the election of priests. If he comes forward I shall ask him, first why he took no legal action straight away, and secondly – granted that he chose to complain informally rather than to bring a formal charge – why he was produced by yourselves instead of stepping forward of his own accord; and why, in addition, he preferred to make his protest so very much later rather than at the time. If he can supply shrewd and pointed answers to these questions, then I will conclude by

12. Ptolemy XII Auletes, after buying recognition as king of Egypt in 59, was expelled in the following year and sought help in Rome.

13. The quotation, from Ennius' *Medea*, is used by Crassus in reference to the arrival of a delegation led by Dio of Alexandria to present a counterblast to Ptolemy's plea.

inquiring where this Senator originated. If it turns out that the spring from which he emanates and bursts forth into our midst is himself and himself only, I may well be impressed, as I always am, by such a display of independent initiative. But if, on the other hand he proves merely to be a minor tributary rivulet, drawn off from the main source of your prosecuting organization, my reaction will be one of particular pleasure – because this means that in spite of all your influence and resources no more than one single Senator has been found willing to do you a favour!

Nor am I in the least scared of that other category of witnesses, who may be described as the Gentlemen of the Night. For it was indicated that certain persons will be ready to declare that their wives, while on their way home from a dinner-party, were criminally assaulted by Caelius. What high-principled characters these must be to volunteer such an assertion on oath, when they are obliged to admit that they never made the slightest attempt to obtain satisfaction for these grave wrongs by asking for a settlement out of court, or even for an informal meeting!

Now, gentlemen, you are in a position to foresee the entire nature of the prosecution's line; and when the onslaught is launched it will be your duty to beat it back. For the people who are really eager for the destruction of Marcus Caelius are not these counsel at all. Ostensibly, the attack is launched by them. But the shafts are supplied by a hidden hand.

I am not just saying this to bring opprobrium upon the prosecutors. They are perfectly entitled to feel proud of the job they have undertaken. They are doing their duty, they are defending their friends, they are behaving as men of courage should. Injured, they resent it; angered, they let themselves go; challenged, they fight. But granted that men of spirit may have reason to assail Marcus Caelius, you yourselves are in duty bound to pay less attention to other people's resentments than to your own honour as a panel of judges.

Besides, look at the crowds of people of every class and occupation and kind with whom the Forum is always packed. Out of all this number there are sure to be quantities of individuals prepared, for the sake of profit, to offer their services and exert themselves and undertake to give evidence. If creatures of this type should happen to have intruded into the present trial, I ask you, gentlemen, to use your good sense to treat their greedy aspirations as totally irrelevant. If you do, you will demonstrate that you have simultaneously had regard for the preservation of my client, your own feelings of conscience, and the welfare of the entire citizen body, at a time when all these are menaced by dangerous and formidable personages.

I, on my side, have no intention of troubling you with witnesses. The facts of the case are unalterable, and I do not propose to suggest that they hinge on witnesses' evidence, which can so easily and readily be manipulated and twisted and distorted. I prefer to use the rational method: I shall rebut these charges by proofs that are clearer than the light of day. Fact will be answered by fact, reason by reason, proposition by proposition.

I am therefore entirely content that Marcus Crassus should have spoken so fully, so earnestly and so eloquently about the sections of the case relating to the disturbances at Neapolis, the assault on the Alexandrians at Puteoli, and the property of Palla.[14] I wish he had also dealt with Dio's murder.[15] And yet what more could you possibly expect to hear from anyone about that particular matter, when the actual perpetrator of the deed is either wholly unafraid of retribution or even willing to admit what he has done? – since he is, after all, a king. Besides, the man who was said to have been his agent and

14. Nothing is known for certain of these incidents.

15. The envoy Dio was murdered in Italy on Ptolemy's instructions. P. Asicius was successfully defended by Cicero.

confidant in the murder, Publius Asicius, has been brought to trial and acquitted.

Here, then, is a crime which the guilty party does not deny; and the person who claimed he had nothing to do with it has got off. So why should any charge under this heading worry my client, who has never been under suspicion or indeed even the slightest shadow of complicity? The suggestion has been made that Asicius was only acquitted because of collusion between prosecution and defence. That point, however, can very easily be contradicted, and most easily of all by myself who was his defending counsel. But in any case Caelius – although incidentally he has a strong belief in Asicius' innocence – argues that, whatever the situation in that respect may be, the position of Asicius has no connexion whatever with his own.

And that is not his view only; it is also the opinion of Titus and Gaius Coponius. These two very civilized and cultured young men, possessing all the advantages of an excellent education in the arts, were more profoundly distressed than anybody else by the death of Dio, to whom they were attached by ties of hospitality and by a shared devotion to learning and the humanities. Dio, as you were told, was staying with Titus Coponius, who had got to know him at Alexandria. What he and his eminent brother think about Marcus Caelius you will hear from their own lips if they are produced as witnesses.

So let us set this whole business aside, and finally come to the real facts behind the case.

I saw you were paying very careful attention to the points my friend Lucius Herennius made. What particularly attracted your notice, no doubt, was his talented manner and a special quality in his style. But I was also afraid at times that the substance of his speech, so tellingly planned to create a damning effect, would exercise an imperceptible and insidious influence on your judgement of the case. He said a lot about extravagance, lust, youthful vices and immoral behaviour. Herennius is usually a mild enough man, and indeed an attractive representative of the urbane and well-bred manners which are now in fashion. Yet here in court, on the other hand, you could not have imagined a sterner kind of uncle and moralist and tutor. He reprimanded Marcus Caelius in terms which no father has ever dreamt of using towards his own son. He went on at great length about the evils of wild and intemperate living. In short, gentlemen, I began to excuse you for listening so intently, because the grim and glum manner of his speech was beginning to cause even me to tremble.

The first part of his speech, however, did not trouble me very much. This contained his allegation that Caelius was intimate with my friend Bestia – that he used to dine at Bestia's home, visited him on many occasions, and supported his candidature for the praetorship. These assertions do not bother me because they are manifestly false. For Herennius also mentioned other people who had dined with Bestia; and they are not here – or if they are here it is merely because they have been forced to tell the same story.

Nor am I in the least worried by Herennius' suggestion that Caelius was one of his fellow-members of the Luperci.[16] The original Wolf-men were a kind of primitive brotherhood, of a pastoral and rustic character, who in the days before civilization and law formed bands together in the woods. And indeed its members are still, apparently, savage enough not only to lay information against their own brethren but actually, when they are doing so, to boast about the fraternal relationship – anxious, it would seem, to ensure that people should be aware of the bond! But enough about that. I will pass on to allegations which gave me greater concern.

Herennius' attack on dissipation was lengthy; and it was

16. The Luperci were an ancient fraternity who ran round the bounds of the Palatine wearing goat-skins and striking women with strips of the same material to promote fertility.

delivered in a quieter tone of voice. It also aimed at logical argument rather than mere abuse, which was one reason why it received such close attention. His fellow-prosecutor, my friend Publius Clodius,[17] was very different, for he flung himself about with extreme vigour and abandon, and expressed everything in the most fiery and acid terms, and at the top of his voice. I was impressed by all this eloquence. But I was by no means alarmed; for I had been to a good many trials in which Clodius ended up on the losing side. So it is you, Herennius, whom I will first answer, if I may. I will reply to your question whether it is right and proper for me to defend a man who has not always refused invitations to dinner-parties, who has ventured to go for walks in parks, who has not abstained totally from the use of perfume, and who has been known to pay visits to Baiae.[18]

There are people I have seen and heard of in our community who have taken more than a little sip of that kind of life, who have gone beyond just giving it the proverbial touch with their finger-tips, and who have indeed devoted their entire youth to debauchery: but then they have turned over a new leaf and become respected and eminent citizens. For everyone agrees young men may be allowed a certain amount of indulgence. Indeed, nature herself is generous in supplying them with sexual appetites – and if their outbreaks do not ruin anyone's life or destroy anyone's home these are usually regarded as reasonable and tolerable. But it seemed to me that you were using the excesses common to young men in order to stir up prejudice against Caelius in particular; and that the silent concentration with which your speech was heard owed much to the fact that, although its criticisms were directed against a single individual, what we were thinking about was the widespread diffusion of these faults.

17. This is evidently not the P. Clodius Pulcher who was Cicero's enemy.

18. Baiae was a fashionable resort on the Bay of Naples.

It is easy, gentlemen, to attack immorality. Daylight would rapidly fail me if I tried to bring out every aspect of the topic: seduction, adultery, lechery, waste of money – the list is endless. Even if we are not censuring any particular person but are merely considering the general theme of such vices, the subject in itself offers scope for a weighty and extended diatribe. But sensible men like yourselves, gentlemen, must not allow yourselves to be distracted in such a way from the actual person of the defendant himself. Your own high principles of strictness and responsibility empower you to administer a sting of very great severity. What the prosecutor has done is to direct this sting against a universal situation, against the sins and wickedness of the age. It would therefore be wrong for you to turn it instead against one single defendant, who has been subjected to a prejudicial attack inspired by no personal fault of his own but by failings that are found in a great many people.

Consequently, Herennius, I shall not aspire to give the sort of reply to your strictures that their form would seem to have demanded. If I had done so, I could have begged for the indulgence to which a young man is entitled, and asked that he should be pardoned on those grounds. But, as I say, I shall not adopt that course. For I am taking no refuge in excuses about his youth; I renounce such a right, although it is one which anybody would be entitled to claim. All I ask instead is that, whatever general prejudice our generation may feel against young men's debts and excesses and dissipations – and I know this feeling is a powerful one – the transgressions of the others, and juvenile shortcomings in general, and the evils of the times, should not be produced as reasons why Caelius should be condemned.

Yet at the same time, while insisting on this request, I have not the slightest objection to replying most meticulously to the specific accusations which are brought against him.

Two of these charges, one relating to gold and the other to poison, concern one and the same individual. The gold is supposed to have been taken from Clodia, the poison to have been acquired so that Clodia should drink it. All the other matters raised are not really accusations in any proper sense of the word, but only slanders, more appropriate to some vulgar shouting-match than to a national court of justice. Declarations that Caelius is adulterous, immoral and a briber's tout are not charges at all but just plain insults. Slurs of such a kind have not the smallest foundation or basis. They are nothing but mere vituperation, uttered at random by a prosecutor who has let his temper get the better of him and holds forth without a trace of supporting evidence. But as for the two other charges, I can see clearly enough what the foundation is for *them* – there is someone in the background, a source, a definite individual from whom they stem.

Here is the first story: Caelius needed gold, took it from Clodia, took it without witnesses, kept it as long as he wanted to. A demonstration, you will tell me, that the two of them were remarkably intimate! The second story goes like this: he proposed to kill her, he procured poison, bribed collaborators, made the necessary arrangements, fixed a place, conveyed the poison there. Evidence, this time, of a violent rupture and overwhelming hatred!

Gentlemen, the whole of the case revolves round Clodia. She is a woman of noble birth; but she also has a notorious reputation. My observations about this lady will be limited to what is necessary to refute the charge. You, Cnaeus Domitius,[19] in your wisdom, must appreciate that she is the one and only person with whom we really have to concern ourselves at all. If she denies she lent Caelius gold, if she puts forward no claim that he tried to poison her, we are, I fear, guilty of disagreeable behaviour for using the name of a married Roman lady in a manner far removed from what is due to

19. The praetor Cn. Domitius Calvinus was chairman of the tribunal.

such a lady's virtue. Yet since the elimination of this woman from the case will also mean the elimination of every single charge with which Caelius is faced, we who act as his counsel are left with no alternative; if someone attacks Clodius we are obliged to show they are wrong. Indeed, my refutation would be framed in considerably more forcible terms if I did not feel inhibited by the fact that the woman's husband – sorry, I mean brother,[20] I always make that slip – is my personal enemy. Since that is the situation, however, my language will be as moderate as I can make it, and I will go no farther than my conscience and the nature of the action render unavoidable. And indeed I never imagined I should have to engage in quarrels with women, much less with a woman who has always been widely regarded as having no enemies since she so readily offers intimacy in all directions.

However, there it is; and I shall begin by asking her a question. Does she prefer me to deal with her according to the stern, severe tradition of ancient times, or in a light-hearted, mild and civilized fashion instead?

If in the bleak old manner and style, then I must call up from the dead one of those personages with heavy beards – not the modern sort of neat little beard which she is so keen on, but the bristling kind that we see on antique statues and busts – to reprimand the woman and speak to her in my place (which has the advantage of directing her fury away from myself). So let me conjure up, then, some member of her own family. And why not the venerable Appius Claudius the Blind[21] –

20. This is an implied allegation of Clodia's incest with her brother P. Clodius Pulcher. He was rumoured to have incestuous relations with his other sisters also.

21. Ap. Claudius Caecus (censor 312, consul 307, 296) built the first Roman aqueduct and the first portion of the Via Appia and tore up the proposed peace with Pyrrhus (280). Clodius and Claudius are the same name, the former being the less aristocratic version, since P. Clodius Pulcher had to resign from the patriciate to become a tribune.

who will suffer less than anybody else because he will not be able to see her?

If he returned to the scene, I imagine this is how he would treat her and what he would say. 'Woman, what business have you with Caelius, who is little more than a boy, and is none of yours? Why have you formed such a close friendship with him that you lend him gold, or such a deep enmity that you are afraid of poison? Did you not know, from what you have seen, that your father, and from what you have heard that your uncle, your grandfather, your great-grandfather, your great-great-grandfather, and your great-great-great-grandfather were all consuls? And did you not recall that you had lately been married to Quintus Metellus,[22] a notable, courageous and patriotic man who only had to set foot out of doors to outshine almost all his fellow-citizens in merit, glory and rank? When your marriage had transferred you from one illustrious house to another, what induced you to form so intimate a link with Caelius? Was he, by any chance, a blood-relative, or a marriage connexion, or a close friend of your husband? He was none of these things. What other reason, then, could there be except sheer uncontrollable lust?

'If the statues of the menfolk of our house did not stir your better feelings, were you not aware of promptings from my female descendant, the celebrated Quinta Claudia,[23] to rival her glorious achievement which added to the renown of our House? Did you derive no inspiration from the noble Vestal Virgin Claudia,[24] who during her father's Triumph gripped him tight and did not suffer him to be dragged down out of his chariot by a hostile tribune of the people? Why did you

22. Clodia was suspected of murdering her husband Q. Caecilius Metellus Celer (59).

23. Claudia Quinta pulled free the image of Cybele, brought from Pessinus, when it was grounded at the mouth of the Tiber (205–4).

24. The Vestal Claudia was the daughter of Ap. Claudius Pulcher (consul 143) who celebrated a Triumph over the Alpine Salassi.

let the vices of your brother[25] influence you more than the virtues of your father and your ancestors – virtues that have reappeared again and again ever since my own time, not only among the men of our family but among the women as well? Did I tear up that bargain with Pyrrhus merely in order that you should drive some disgusting sexual bargain every day? Did I bring water to Rome only that you should have something to wash yourself with after your impure copulations? Was the sole purpose of my Road that you should parade up and down it escorted by a crowd of other women's husbands?'

But I wonder why I introduced this personage at all: for his austere methods might seem to raise a dangerous possibility of the selfsame Appius suddenly turning round and using that famous censor's strictness on my client as well! However, that is a point which I shall be seeing to later on. And when I do, gentlemen, I am quite certain I shall be able to defend Marcus Caelius' way of life even to the sternest of judges.

As for you, on the other hand, woman, for now I am speaking to you directly and not through some stage personage, if you will condescend to justify your goings on, your declarations, your fabrications, your intrigues, your allegations, it is also your responsibility to explain and account in full for this intimacy, this familiarity, this whole relationship. The prosecutors are making play with orgies, cohabitations, adulteries, trips to Baiae, beach parties, dinner parties, drinking parties, musical parties, concert parties, boating parties – and they indicate that everything they are talking about is said with your approval. And since you have been misguided and headstrong enough to want all these incidents brought up in the Forum and in court, either you must disprove them and demonstrate that they are false, or, if you cannot do so, you will have admitted that neither your charge nor your evidence has the slightest claim to be believed because you yourself are

25. The reference is to Cicero's enemy P. Clodius Pulcher.

discredited by direct personal involvement in every one of them.

You may, on the other hand, prefer me to adopt a more polished manner. If so, this is how I shall deal with you. I propose to dismiss that harsh, almost rustic old gentleman, and instead to take one of these modern young men. Indeed, I shall take your own youngest brother. His taste in that kind of thing is unerring. Besides, he loves you very much, and when he was a little boy suffered, I presume, from nerves and baseless night terrors since he always went to bed with you, his elder sister. Well, imagine him saying to you, 'Sister, what on earth is all the disturbance about? Why are you behaving in this lunatic fashion?

Why do you make such an outcry, why such a fuss about nothing?[26]

'Very well then,' he will continue, 'and so the boy who lived next door to you caught your eye. His fine complexion, his upstanding figure, his fine features and his eyes bowled you over. You wanted to see a lot of him. Sometimes you found yourself in his company in a garden. You are a great lady, and he is a youth who has a stingy and parsimonious father; and so you intend to use your riches to keep him in your grasp.

'But this you are unable to achieve. He spurns you and casts you off, your presents fail to impress him. Well, try somewhere else then. You have got your park beside the Tiber, carefully sited on the spot where all the young men come to bathe. From there you can pick up a lover any day. So why bother this man – who evidently does not care for you?'

And now it is your turn to hear from me, Caelius. To suit the occasion, I am going to assume the authority and sternness of a father. But I wonder which particular father I ought to play – the rough and ill-tempered one of Caecilius:

26. The quotation is from a comic dramatist, possibly Caecilius Statius (d. 168).

For now at last my spirit is afire, and my heart is heaped full of anger!

Or that other parent who cried:

O unhappy rascal!

The hearts of all these fathers are made of iron.

What am I to say? What am I to hope for? Whatever you do, your shameful deeds make all my wishes vain.

What an intolerable lot they are! That is the sort of father who would say,'Why on earth have you settled so close to that prostitute? When you saw through her enticements, why ever did you not run away?'

Why have you got to know a strange woman? Scatter and squander – do as you please for all I care. If you lose all your money it is not I who will be the sufferer. I have enough to keep me comfortable for what remains of my life.[27]

To this gloomy, blunt old man Caelius could plead that he was not, in fact, ever diverted from the straight path by any serious infatuation whatever. How could he prove this? Because there was no extravagance, no waste, no borrowing to pay his debts. There were reports, it is true, that such things occurred. But what a problem it is for anyone to escape such rumours in a city so full of malicious gossip as ours! Does it surprise you that this woman's neighbour gained a bad reputation, when her very own brother was unable to avoid unpleasant comments?

Well then, let us take a mild and kindly father instead. There was the old gentleman who declared:

My son has broken a door, it shall be repaired. He has torn your clothes, they shall be mended.[28]

27. The quotation is from the *Adelphi* of Terence (d. 159) (ll. 120–21).
28. ibid.

And indeed the case of Caelius, too, is a very easy one. On each and every charge he would find it the simplest matter to defend himself. As regards that woman, I am not at the moment criticizing her at all. But just imagine, for the purposes of argument, someone who bears not the slightest resemblance to her. Imagine a person who offered herself to every man, who quite publicly had a calendar of different lovers for every day, whose gardens, home and house at Baiae were thrown wide open to every sort of lecherous riff-raff, who kept young men and helped them to endure their fathers' meanness by paying them herself. Imagine a widow living unconventionally, a shameless widow giving rise to scandal, a wealthy widow behaving riotously, a lascivious widow carrying on like a common harlot. If any man had been a little free in his attitude towards a woman like that, surely it would be unreasonable to regard him as having committed any real misconduct.

'So this,' it will be objected, 'is Cicero's educational method! So now we know how you propose young men should be brought up. But was this boy commended and entrusted to your care by his father merely in order that he should occupy his youthful years in vicious and libidinous behaviour, while you yourself actually excuse that sort of life and those pursuits?' But, gentlemen, was there ever a man on this earth whose will-power, high-mindedness and self-control were sufficient to make him reject all pleasures whatsoever and devote his whole life to physical exercise and intellectual exertion; a man who was not attracted by relaxation or recreation or the pursuits of his contemporaries or making love or going to parties; who believed that nothing in all the world was worth striving for unless it was directed towards honour and glory? If a person with these qualities ever existed, then I for one should regard his endowment and apparatus of virtues as something truly superhuman.

Of such a kind, it seems to me, were those famous Camilli,

Fabricii and Curii,[29] and all the heroes who raised our state to greatness from small beginnings. Nowadays, virtues of this calibre no longer form part of our moral system. They are scarcely even to be found in books; even the records which told of that old-fashioned sternness are no more to be seen. And that is not only true of us Romans, who have put this design for living into practice more conscientiously than we have followed it in theory. Among learned Greeks also, whose speeches and writings (though unmatched by actions) attained such grandeur and brilliance, precepts of quite another sort have become fashionable in the changed Greece of today. For one idea, nowadays, is that the truly wise man does everything for the sake of pleasure; and learned scholars have not been repelled by this shameful assertion. Others have supposed that virtue and pleasure should be combined, thus uniting by verbal dexterity two things which are, in fact, wholly incompatible. And the result is that the philosophers who have tried to demonstrate that the only straight road to glory is the road of laborious effort are left almost alone and stranded in their lecture-rooms.[30]

And indeed nature herself spontaneously generates many enticements which can at times lull virtue into somnolence and cause her eyes to droop. Nature has offered the young many slippery paths on which they can hardly set foot or start to move without falling or losing their balance. She has lavished upon them a great variety of pleasant things – things, moreover, which are calculated to charm not only these early years but the subsequent times of fuller maturity as well. So if you should happen to find someone who despises the sight of beautiful objects, who derives no pleasure from scent

29. M. Furius Camillus captured Veii (396), C. Fabricius Luscinus was the hero of the war with Pyrrhus, Man. Curius Dentatus (d. 270) defeated Samnites, Sabines and Pyrrhus.

30. Cicero refers in turn to the Epicureans, Academics (and Peripatetics), and Stoics.

or touch or taste, who shuts out all sweet sounds from his ears, such a man I perhaps, and a few others, will hold to be the favourite of the gods; but most people will account him the victim of their wrath.

So we have to abandon this forsaken, untrodden byway, obstructed so thickly by foliage and undergrowth. Let youth be permitted its fun, and tender years a measure of liberty. Allow a certain amount of amusement! Do not always give preference to logical, unbending reason. Grant that it should sometimes be overborne by the desires and pleasures of the heart, provided that in so doing the following rule and limitation be observed. A young man must be scrupulous of his own good name and not do violence to that of others. He must not squander his inheritance or become crippled by the interest on his debts. He must not destroy people's homes and reputations. He must not corrupt the uncorrupted, or blemish the virtuous, or bring scandal upon those of good repute. He must refrain from violent intimidation and stay clear of conspiracy and crime. Finally, after he has indulged his taste for entertainments and spent time on love affairs and the trivial passions of youth, he must, eventually, turn back and attend instead to his home, and the business of the Forum, and public life. For he will then have shown that satiety has caused him to discard, and experience to spurn, the things which reason had not hitherto enabled him to see in their true light.

Both in our own times, gentlemen, and within the memory of our fathers and forefathers, there have been many great men and distinguished citizens who, once their youthful desires had simmered down, behaved in their maturity with exemplary correctness. I prefer not to indicate any of them by their names – these you may remember for yourselves – because I do not want to associate the renown of any brave and eminent citizen with even the slightest of defects. Were it my intention to do so, I could indicate many important, illustrious personages who were notorious during their younger days for excessive wildness, unrestrained dissipation, enormous debts, extravagance and debauchery, but whose faults were later so completely covered over by a host of virtues that anyone who felt so inclined could excuse those earlier manifestations on the score of youth.

But in Marcus Caelius – for my readiness, relying on your good judgement, to concede certain points gives me all the greater confidence in telling you the many creditable things about him – in Marcus Caelius you will find no loose living, no extravagance, no debts, no addiction to parties and low haunts, none of that vice of over-eating and over-drinking which does not diminish but grows with age. Love-making too, the taste for sexual adventures, which does not usually trouble people of reasonably strong character – for such loves are quick to bloom and fade – has never ensnared him in its toils.

You have heard Caelius pleading for himself.[31] In a previous case you also heard him as a prosecutor.[32] Now, what I am going to say is said to defend him, and not for the sake of boasting on my own account, but I am sure that with your appreciation of such things you noticed his oratorical style and skill, his fluency of thought and expression. And you saw how these qualities mirrored his own natural gifts. Such talents, even when there is no effort behind them, often make an impression by their own unaided power. But Caelius, unless my affection misled me, added to these natural qualifications a sound theoretical knowledge based on the liberal arts and perfected by unremitting attention and strenuous work.

I would have you know, gentlemen, that the dissipated tastes for which Caelius is blamed, and the occupations which I am discussing now, are by no means easily to be found in one and the same man. For a mind given up to sensuality and

31. Caelius opened his own defence. He had been taught by Cicero.
32. The reference is to Caelius' prosecution of C. Antonius Hybrida.

impeded by love, passion, craving, and in many cases excessive wealth (or sometimes the lack of it), cannot possibly undertake the sort of thing that we others contrive to perform in the way of making speeches. They cannot manage the physical effort, and the intellectual exertion is beyond them as well. Can you think of any other reason why, when high rewards exist for eloquence, when public speaking gives the speaker such great satisfaction and brings him so much favour and influence and honour, the people who adopt this occupation are and always have been so few? The reason is that every pleasure has to be renounced, all relaxations, liaisons, amusements and social gatherings refused – even conversation with one's friends virtually has to be given up. That, rather than any lack of natural talents or boyhood training, is why the labours required by this career scare men off and deter them from its pursuit.

So if Caelius had immersed himself in the kind of life which has been imputed against him, then how on earth could he, at such a very early age, actually have brought to trial a man so senior that he had held the consulship? If he shrank from hard work and was plunged into self-indulgence, however could he appear on this battle-ground day after day, pursuing campaigns against enemies, summoning them into the dock, exposing himself to criminal proceedings, and before the eyes of the whole Roman people maintaining these many months past a struggle on which his whole reputation and future have been staked?

Surely that notorious neighbourhood on the Palatine[33] gives us a whiff of what the true facts are. Popular rumour clearly has something to tell us – and so does Baiae. Yes, Baiae does not simply tell us a tale, but rings with the report that there is one woman so deeply sunk in her vicious depravities that she no longer even bothers to seek privacy and darkness and the

33. Caelius lived near Clodia on the Palatine (p. 175).

usual veil of discretion to cover her lusts. On the contrary, she actually exults in displaying the most foully lecherous goings on amid the widest publicity and in the glaring light of day.

All the same, if anyone thinks young men ought to be forbidden affairs even with prostitutes, he is certainly very austere (that I would not deny), but he is out of touch with our present permissive age. Indeed, he is also not in harmony with the customs of our ancestors, and the allowances which even in those times people were quite accustomed to make. For name any epoch when this was not invariably the case. When was such behaviour ever censured or forbidden? When was the permitted thing not permitted?

I will just propound a general theme, without mentioning any particular woman by name – that much I will leave open. If a woman who has no husband throws open her home to every debauchee and publicly leads the life of a whore; if she makes a habit of being entertained by men who are total strangers; if she pursues this mode of existence in the city, in her own gardens, among all the crowds at Baiae; if, in fact, she behaves in such a way that not only her general demeanour but also her dress and associates, her hot eyes and uninhibited language, her embraces and kisses, her beach parties and water parties and dinner parties, all show that she is not only a prostitute but a lewd and depraved prostitute at that; if a young man should happen to be found in the company of such a woman, then surely, Lucius Herennius, you would agree that this was not so much adultery as just plain sex – not an outrage to chastity, but mere satisfaction of appetite.

I am forgetting the injuries you have done me, Clodia. I am brushing aside the memory of what I suffered. Your cruel actions to my family while I was away I am deliberately not taking into account. And do not, please, suppose that what I have been saying was directed against yourself. However, since the prosecutors claim that you are the source of this charge and prepared to give evidence in its support, I am obliged to address to you one single question in your own person. What I ask you is this – if ever there *did* exist a woman of the type I have just described, bearing no resemblance to yourself, with the life and habits of a harlot, would you consider it very scandalous or wicked that a young man should have had some relationship with her?

If this woman is not recognizable as you – and that is what I shall be much happier to believe – then the basis for the prosecution against Caelius falls to the ground. But if, on the other hand, my opponents insist on identifying the hypothetical person with yourself, and if *that* does not frighten you, then I fail to see why any suggestion about what Caelius is supposed to have done need scare us either! So it is entirely up to you to show us the direction and method our defence should follow. If you have the least shred of decency, you are bound to agree that Marcus Caelius has not behaved viciously at all. If you do not concede this, then you have no decent feelings whatever; and that very fact will provide my client with an impregnable justification – and will justify any others who may find themselves in the same boat.

And now I have brought my speech clear of the shallows and away beyond the reefs; and the rest of the course does not seem to present any difficulty. Two charges are brought against Caelius. Both allege very serious crimes. But both are again concerned with one and the same woman. He is accused of taking some gold away from Clodia, and of having prepared poison for Clodia's murder. According to your story, he took the gold to give it to the slaves of Lucius Lucceius,[34] so that they should kill Dio of Alexandria, who was staying with Lucceius at the time. It is a dreadful thing to assert that a man plotted to take the life of an envoy, and dreadful also

34. L. Lucceius, a wealthy Senator, unsuccessfully prosecuted Catilina for murder (64). Later he became a historian.

to claim that he instigated slaves to assassinate their master's guest – a scheme both audacious and horrible.

But in regard to this accusation, it is necessary for me to ask, first of all, whether Caelius is supposed to have informed Clodia of the purpose for which he needed the gold, or not. If he did not tell her this, why did she give it to him? If, on the other hand, he did tell her, then she, too, involved herself in the crime as his accomplice. Did you, woman, have the nerve to fetch this gold from your chest, to denude of its adornments that statue of Venus[35] which carries the trophies of your other lovers, knowing full well the ghastly crime for which the gold was intended – the assassination of an envoy, an indelible stain of guilt upon the virtuous and honourable Lucius Lucceius?

No, to that abominable deed your generous heart would surely not have lent itself. Such a project would never have obtained the cooperation of that open house of yours, the complicity of your hospitable Venus. And Herennius Balbus fully appreciated this. For he maintained that Clodia was indeed kept in the dark, and that the explanation Caelius made to her was that he wanted the gold to pay for some Games. But if he was as close a friend of Clodia as you maintain (since you emphasize his fornications at such length), then surely he must have told her of the purpose for which he wanted the money. If, on the other hand, he was *not* so close a friend, then she never gave it him. Either, then, Caelius told you the truth, you unspeakable woman, and you knowingly let him have the gold for a criminal purpose: or he did not bring himself to tell you, in which case you can never have given it to him at all!

And so there is evidently no need for me to refute this indictment with the infinite number of arguments that would be available for the purpose. I need merely say that the

35. Cicero pretends Clodia had a statue of Venus which she adorns with mementos of her lovers.

character of Marcus Caelius is wholly incompatible with such a loathsome action; and that, besides, a sensible and intelligent person like him could not have failed to realize the error of entrusting an atrocity of this magnitude to unknown slaves belonging to another master. I am also at liberty, in pursuance of my own practice and that of other counsel, to ask the prosecutor the familiar questions: where did the encounter between Caelius and the slaves of Lucceius take place, how did he get into contact with them? If directly, this was very rash; if through a third party, could we have his name? I could go on and ransack every possible cranny where a suspicion might lurk. But the result would still inevitably be that no motive, no location, no opportunity, no accomplice, no prospect of carrying out or hiding the evil deed would come to light. Nor would any trace of a plausible sequence of events, or any clue indicating that the whole appalling crime was anything but a figment of the imagination.

Points of that kind are an orator's stock in trade. And besides, not because of any gifts of my own but because I have some practice and experience in speaking, the elaboration of such inquiries as part of the general argument might well have done my case some good, since they would have the appearance of evidence that I myself had taken the trouble to work up. Nevertheless, for the sake of brevity, I allow them all to go unsaid. For instead, gentlemen, I am able to produce a personage whom you will be only too willing to admit as your partner in the bond of a solemn oath. I refer to Lucius Lucceius: a man of complete integrity, the most impressive of all possible witnesses. If Caelius had really perpetrated the suggested offence against his reputation and his position, Lucceius would assuredly have heard of it and would have utterly refused to let such a thing pass, or indeed take place at all. For how could so civilized a man, with his outstanding scholarship and culture and learning, have disregarded the danger threatening someone to whom he was so devoted because they shared all these interests in common? Even if Lucceius had learnt that such an outrage was planned against someone quite unknown to him, he would still have viewed it with horror. How, then, could he have turned a blind eye when the victim was actually going to be his own guest? Even if the murderers had been strangers, he would still have been appalled. So how could he conceivably have paid no attention when they were his own slaves? Had the act been perpetrated somewhere out in the country, or in a public place, he would unmistakably have denounced such an abomination. Was it in the least likely, therefore, that he would accept the situation calmly when the crime was devised inside the city itself and, indeed, even within his very own home? If the proposed victim had been some unknown rustic, it would have been unthinkable for him to let the plot go ahead. Would he, then, have thought it proper to say absolutely nothing about it when its victim was a man who completely shared his own erudite tastes?

But I need not detain you any longer on this point, gentlemen, since he himself has given evidence on oath. Mark well the solemn tone of his deposition, and note carefully every word of what he says.

[THE EVIDENCE OF LUCIUS LUCCEIUS IS READ]

Surely that is all you can have been waiting for – short of expecting that the case and Truth themselves will somehow take shape and speak and plead in their own persons! And indeed here, in this evidence of Lucceius, in this supreme justification of an innocent man, is precisely the plea which the case itself, were it able to talk, would have uttered from its own mouth – the voice of incarnate Truth.

The indictment is supported by not the slightest ground for suspicion. Proofs of the alleged facts just do not exist. The dealings which are supposed to have taken place have left not a trace of what was said or where or when. No witness has been named; and nor has any accomplice.

The whole accusation emanates from a house that is malevolent, disreputable, merciless, crime-stained and vicious. Whereas the family alleged to have been involved in this shocking deed is notable for its lofty standards, honourable principles, dutifulness and sense of responsibility; and that is the home from which you just heard a sworn affidavit. The question under dispute, therefore, is easy to settle. You are invited to say whether you do not agree that the parties who confront one another are, on the one side, an unstable, evil-tempered nymphomaniac, who has completely fabricated the charge, and, on the other, a man of responsibility, wisdom and self-restraint whose evidence has shown the utmost conscientiousness and accuracy.

There remains the accusation of poisoning. I am unable to discover how this originated; nor can I work out what it was supposed to lead to. For what motive could Caelius possibly have possessed for wanting to poison this woman? So that he should not have to give back the gold? But did she ever ask for it back? To avert the charge of Dio's assassination?[36] But did anyone really believe he was guilty of this? Indeed, if Caelius had not himself launched a prosecution, would anyone ever have connected his name with it at all? You actually heard Lucius Herennius say that, if Caelius had not brought a second action against his friend Bestia after the latter had been acquitted in the earlier case, he for his part would never have uttered a word against Caelius. But, to go back to the attempt on Clodia's life, no one could be expected to believe that such a ghastly act should have been undertaken

36. The suggestion which Cicero seeks to refute is that Caelius wanted to poison Clodia in order to remove a witness to his complicity in the murder of Dio.

without any motive at all! And that, you must inevitably conclude, is why the accusation involving the terrible crime of Dio's murder was fabricated: in order to invent such a motive for doing away with Clodia, since she allegedly knew he was guilty of the murder. [37]

And finally, whom is Caelius supposed to have employed to carry out the poisoning? Who acted as his assistant and partner and accomplice? Into whose hands did he hazard this shocking deed – and, in the process, his own self and his very life? To this woman's slaves? That is what has been claimed. But do you suppose that this man (whom you evidently credit with a brain even if your unfriendly language belittles all his remaining qualities) was stupid enough to entrust his entire fate to someone else's slaves?

And, I ask, what type of slaves? For this point, too, is of considerable importance. If they belonged to Clodia, would not Caelius have known they were not living at all the ordinary life of a slave, but were enjoying a far more relaxed, undisciplined, familiar relationship with their mistress? For in a household of that sort, gentlemen, under a woman who behaves like a prostitute, where everything that happens is quite unfit to be published abroad, where abnormal lusts and excesses and unheard-of perversions and vices of every kind are rife, it is perfectly obvious and universally known that slaves are slaves no longer. For everything is delegated to them and put in their charge, they become her associates in all her loose living, they share her secrets, and they make a good bit every day from her extravagant expenditure. Was Caelius unaware of all these things? If he was as intimate with the woman as you say he was, then he must, surely, have realized she treated those slaves as her intimates too. The alternative supposition is that he was *not* so friendly with her as

37. Cicero is saying that Caelius' involvement in Dio's murder was invented to make his alleged attempt on Clodia sound more plausible.

you allege. But, that being so, how could he have had such a close connexion with her slaves?

And now with regard to the actual poison – what theory is concocted about that? Where was it obtained from, how was it prepared, how and to whom and where was it handed over? Well, their answer is that Caelius had it at his home and tried it out on a slave who had been procured for this specific purpose; and that the very rapid death of the slave proved that the poison was effective.

Why, I would ask the immortal Gods, when an individual has committed an outrageous wrong, do you sometimes close your eyes to what has been done, or at least put off punishment until a future date?

I personally participated in the scene which caused me as profound a feeling of sorrow as anything else in my life, when Quintus Metellus was torn from the bosom and embrace of our nation. He had always regarded himself as dedicated to the service of Rome; but while he was still in the prime of life, enjoying excellent health and full bodily vigour, only two days after he had been seen at the height of his powers in the Senate, the law courts, and all the political affairs of our city, his life was snatched away from our midst, to the most grievous loss of every loyal citizen and the entire commonwealth of Rome. At that moment, when death was already approaching and his mind in all other respects had begun to fail, he devoted his last thoughts to his country, and fixing his gaze upon myself as I wept, he endeavoured in broken, dying words to warn me of the grim storm that hung over my head, and the tempest that menaced the state.[38] Then, striking again and again upon the wall which separated his home from the house where Quintus Catulus had lived, he repeatedly called

38. The impending disasters were Cicero's banishment and the tribunate of P. Clodius Pulcher (58).

POLITICAL SPEECHES OF CICERO

on the name of Catulus, and often on my name also, and
again and again cried out the name of Rome itself – for he
was lamenting not so much his own imminent death as the
unhappy fact that our homeland, and particularly I myself,
would henceforward lack his protection.

Now, he being a man of consular rank and the person that
he was, if that deed of sinful violence had not suddenly
bereft us of his help, just imagine how he would have opposed
his own deranged cousin Clodius,[39] whose earlier ravings and
thunderings had caused Metellus, when consul, to declare in
the hearing of the Senate that he himself would kill the man
with his own hand. Now, shall the woman who comes from
such a house have the audacity to start discussions about the
speeds with which poisons take effect? Ought that dwelling
not, rather, to inspire her heart with terror, in case it shrieks
forth the tale of her guilt? Will she not recoil in dread from
the walls which know her secret, and shudder at the memory
of that fatal, miserable night?

But I returned to the indictment – though my mention of
that noble and valiant man has choked my utterance with
tears and shrouded my mind in grief.

It is still not explained where the poison came from and how
it was prepared. The story is that it was given to Publius
Licinius here, a decent and respectable young man who is a
friend of Caelius, and that an arrangement was made with
the slaves that they should proceed to the Senian Baths, where
Lentulus would join them and hand over the box of poison.
Here I must first ask, what was the point of arranging that the
poison should be taken there? Why did the slaves instead not
go to meet Caelius at his own home? If Caelius and Clodia
were still so close and intimate, the appearance of one of that
woman's slaves at Caelius' house would not have aroused any
suspicion. But if, on the contrary, their relations were now

39. The cousin of Q. Caecilius Metellus Celer was P. Clodius Pulcher,
whose mother was the sister of Celer's father.

strained, if their friendship had been broken off, if there had
been a rupture, then

That is the source of those tears[40]

– and the whole tale of fictitious crimes and charges is explained. The prosecutor's version, on the other hand, is this.
After the slaves had disclosed Caelius' whole villainous plot
to their mistress, that clever woman, he says, directed them to
promise Caelius their complete cooperation. However, in
order to catch Licinius in the act of handing over the poison,
she also gave instructions that the Senian Baths should be fixed
as a meeting-place. For she intended, the story continues, to
send certain friends, who would lurk on the premises of the
baths out of sight, and then suddenly, when Licinius had put
in an appearance and was handing over the poison, spring out
from their hiding-place and seize hold of him.

But all this, gentlemen, is extremely easy to refute. For why
had she particularly fixed upon public baths, where I cannot
see how men wearing outdoor dress could find any hiding-
place whatever? If they were in the entrance court of the
baths they would have been visible; and if they proposed
to stow themselves away inside, this would have been most inconvenient in their shoes and street clothes, and they might
very well not even have been admitted – unless, of course,
that influential female had gained the friendship of the bath
attendant by her customary penny deal.[41]

I was eagerly waiting, I can tell you, to hear the names of
these fine witnesses who were actually supposed to have seen,
there and then, that the poison was in Licinius' hands. But so
far no names have been mentioned. However, they must
evidently be highly reputable individuals. For one thing they

40. This famous tag is from the *Andria* of Terence (l. 126).

41. This is a complicated pun involving the admission fee to the
baths, the cheap rate for which Clodia allegedly sold her favours, and
the nickname 'penny Clytaemnestra' which she was given by Caelius.

are intimate friends of this remarkable lady. And besides, they acquiesced in the role of being packed away in the baths, which she could never have induced them to do, however influential she might be, unless they had been quite exceptionally respectable and worthy characters!

But there is no need for me to enlarge on their worthiness because you can learn for yourselves how resourceful and painstaking they were. 'They hid out of sight in the baths.' Just the men to see everything and be perfect witnesses! And in due course they burst out – by mistake. What splendid self-control! For what the story pretends is that after Licinius had arrived, and while he was holding the box in his hand and was just in the process of handing it over but had not yet actually done so, then suddenly these superb nameless witnesses darted forth: whereupon Licinius, who had already held out his hand to give the box to the slaves, drew it back at this unexpected onslaught and took to his heels.

All the same, Truth has a power of its own. Against all the ingenuity, artfulness and cunning of human beings, against all imaginable falsifications and intrigues, it is perfectly capable of defending itself unaided. Take this little drama, for instance – the effort of a poetess who has many such works to her credit. How badly off the play is for plot, how completely lost for an ending! For the men who had hidden themselves in the baths must have been pretty numerous if they were to seize Licinius and provide a good supply of eye-witnesses of what took place. But in that case how on earth did all those fellows allow Licinius to get away? Why was it harder to grab him when he stepped back, and refrained from parting with the box, than it would have been if he had relinquished it? For it was precisely in order to arrest Licinius that they had been stationed there, with the intention of catching him in the act either when he had the poison in his hands or when he had passed it on. That was the woman's whole idea, and that was the job of the men who had been asked to help.

Why you maintain that they leapt out by mistake and pre-maturely, I cannot understand. For surely that was exactly what, according to the story, they had been asked to do. They had allegedly been posted there with the specific pur-pose of ensuring that the poison, the plot and the whole crime should be palpably exposed. And how could they possibly have chosen a better time to jump out than when Licinius had arrived and was still holding the box of poison in his hand? For if the lady's friends had suddenly broken out of their hiding-place and grasped hold of Licinius *after* he had transmitted the poison to the slaves, he would have been able to protest his innocence and deny utterly that the box had ever come from him. And how, in that case, could they ever have refuted such a statement? Were they to say they had seen him handing it over? In that case they would have aroused suspicions that they themselves were the people who had produced the poison. And they would also have been pretending to have seen something they could not possibly see from the place where they were hidden. Instead, therefore, the stowaways revealed themselves at the exact moment when Licinius had arrived, and was getting out the box, and holding out his hand, and passing on the poison.

Well, that is not the sort of finale a real play has. It is more the ending of a song-and-dance show[42] – the type of produc-tion where nobody has been able to think of a suitable ending and so someone escapes from someone else, and the clappers sound,[43] and it's the curtain.

For why, I ask you, when Licinius was tripping, stumbling, backing, struggling to get away, did the gang of this female

42. The reference is to the mimes, which contained many improba-bilities, were acted by prostitutes, and sometimes included poisoning scenes.

43. Clappers fastened to the shoes were used to mark time and prompt the man who, according to a practice which was the reverse of modern procedure, lowered the curtain at the beginning of a performance and raised it at the end.

boss let him slip through their hands? Why ever did they not seize him tight and get a confession and exploit the abundance of available witnesses, and the general outcry raised by the incident, to drive home his guilt on this very serious charge? With their numbers and physical strength and preparedness, surely they cannot have been nervous about their capacity to overpower one single weak and terrified individual!

It is impossible to find any sign of factual arguments or justifiable suspicions that might make the accusation sound plausible; and the drama comes to no sort of a convincing conclusion. So in default of rational argumentations, or cogent inferences, or indications capable of throwing any light on the situation, the case falls back entirely upon the witnesses. And these I now await, gentlemen, without even the slightest degree of alarm, and indeed with a certain hope of amusement. For one thing, I am excited at the prospect of seeing these smart young men who are a wealthy noblewoman's intimate friends but managed to transform themselves into her intrepid warriors, stationed by their commandress in a fortified ambush within the baths. I want to ask them how or where they hid themselves, and whether it was a bath-tub, or perhaps a Wooden Horse, which harboured and covered all these invincible fighters battling in the interests of their lady. I intend also to compel them to answer one question: why did so large a number of men, of this calibre, not succeed either in grabbing hold of this single, feeble person (whom you see) while he still stood there, or why did they not at least overtake him as he ran away?

If these characters do appear in the witness box, I cannot for the life of me see how they will ever disentangle themselves from all those difficulties. Granted that they may be humorous and amusing enough fellows at a party, and fluent on occasion in their cups, a court-room and a dining-room are not at all the same thing. The benches here and the couches there have little in common. To face judges is one thing and to face people over a drink is quite another: there is a big difference between the light of lamps and the light of day. If, then, they do decide to come forward, all their refined poses and fooleries will be sharply jolted out of them. So I suggest that they should listen to what I am now going to say. They must turn their energies into quite another direction. By all means let them find some other way of ingratiating themselves and showing off. Let them bask as much as they want to in their lady's favour, and display those charming manners of theirs. Let them perform any feat of competitive extravagance they like. Let them cleave inseparably to her side and grovel before her feet, and be her obedient servants in every way. But they must spare the life and career of an innocent man.

The prosecutors inform us that the slaves to whom the poison was allegedly being handed have been made free men, with the approval of the woman's aristocratic and illustrious relatives. At last then we have discovered something which she is supposed to have done with the agreement and sanction of those gallant kinsmen of hers.[44] But I am eager to know what is behind this act of liberation. For either it means that the freed slaves were helping her to concoct the charge against Caelius, or the intention was to prevent them from having to undergo a legal examination,[45] or it was an abundantly merited reward paid to the sharers of her secrets. But your relations agreed, we are told. How could they have failed to, when the information you placed before them consisted, according to your own account, not of facts which you had learnt from others but of things you had discovered for yourself?

44. Women could not officially free slaves in their own right.
45. Once freed, the slaves could no longer be compelled to give evidence under torture.

And, incidentally, can we really be surprised if the imaginary box has given rise to an extremely indecent story?[46] It all tallies very well with the behaviour of a woman of this type. The anecdote has been listened to and has gone the rounds. You have already identified the incident I am wanting (or rather not wanting!) to tell you about. However, even if the tale is true, Caelius was certainly not responsible; for what had it got to do with him? The thing was done by some other young man whose sense of propriety, perhaps, was less highly developed than his wit. But even if the story is an invention, it is at any rate quite an amusing one, though somewhat improper. And it would never have been so widely accepted in general opinion and conversation if it were not for the fact that every sort of pornographic rumour fits in perfectly with that lady's reputation.

I have now stated my case, gentlemen, and my task is done. Please appreciate that the responsibility you bear is an important one, and that the matter entrusted to your decision has grave implications. The action you are investigating relates to violence. Now, the law concerning violence[47] has to do with the administration, the dignity and the condition of our country and the welfare of all its citizens. It is the law which Quintus Catulus brought into force during a period of armed civil strife, when the government was in an almost desperate situation. It is the law which, after the conflagration that had blazed during my consulship, extinguished the last smoking embers of the conspiracy. But can *this* also be the selfsame law under which the youthful life of Caelius is placed in hazard – not in the least because he needs to be

46. Unfortunately this funny story has not survived and so the whole passage, referring apparently to a trick played on Clodia, is inexplicable.

47. This otherwise unknown *Lex Lutatia* was evidently passed during the disturbances caused by Catulus' fellow-consul M. Aemilius Lepidus (78).

punished for the sake of our national interests, but merely for the satisfaction of a woman's filthy purposes and degraded whims?

In this context the prosecution chooses to remind us of the conviction of Marcus Camurtius and Gaius Caesernius.[48] But that is preposterous. Or should I call it not merely preposterous but outrageously impudent? Do you really have the audacity to come from that woman and mention the names of Camurtius and Caesernius? Do you have the nerve to resuscitate the memory of that very serious offence, after the lapse of time has not, indeed, relegated it to oblivion but has at all events pushed it out of sight? For what was the charge which led to the condemnation of those two individuals? Surely it was because of that sexual outrage which was their means of taking vengeance upon the woman's resentful spite. I suppose it was just in order to drag in Vettius' name, as well as that old story about the bronze, that the trial of Camurtius and Caesernius was brought up again.

Yet those individuals, although they certainly could not be proceeded against under the law on violence, were nevertheless so deeply implicated in the crime concerned that it is really impossible to think of any law at all which was not capable of somehow holding them in its meshes. But why on earth should Marcus Caelius be summoned before this court? No indictment of the slightest relevance to its activities is preferred against him, and indeed not even the sort of accusation which, although outside the actual scope of the law on violence, might still be sufficiently relevant to entitle you, its judges, to pronounce your censure.

48. These unknown cases (the one concerned with sexual outrage being related, by what appears to be a marginal gloss, to the name of the unknown Vettius mentioned just afterwards) seem to have been cited as precedents for applying the law or laws on violence to offences against morality.

The early years of Marcus Caelius, then, were dedicated to training, and to the studies which prepare youths for legal practice, public life, offices of state, public recognition, and elevated rank. He made friends with older men of the type who could serve him as models of industry and sobriety;[49] and the pursuits he shared with his contemporaries indicated that he was following the same honourable course which the best and noblest of our citizens had taken before him. When in the course of time he reached years of adult strength, he proceeded to Africa in attendance upon the governor, who was the high-principled, ever conscientious Quintus Pompeius.[50] Caelius' father had business and property there, and, besides, the young man was able to gain the sort of experience in provincial administration which our forefathers rightly thought appropriate to that stage in a career. When he left Africa he was very highly thought of by Pompeius, as you will hear from the latter's testimonial.

Next, following a traditional practice and the precedent of other youths who had subsequently risen to eminent positions, Caelius decided to make his endeavours known in Rome by a spectacular prosecution. I should have preferred his ambition for renown to have led him in some other direction; but the time for expressing regrets about that is past. Anyway, he brought a charge against Gaius Antonius, my colleague in the consulship, whose misfortune it was that the memory of an important service to our country[51] proved of no avail to him, whereas the suspicion of an intended misdemeanour succeeded in damaging his reputation.

Thereafter Caelius rivalled each and every one of his con-

49. Cicero is referring to Caelius' association with himself and M. Licinius Crassus.

50. Q. Pompeius Rufus was praetor in 63 and governor of Africa in 61.

51. Cicero exaggerates the services of C. Antonius Hybrida in suppressing his former associate Catilina, since Antonius took no part in the final battle of Pistoia on the plea of gout (January 62).

temporaries in his assiduous dedication to the Forum, to legal
cases, and to defences of his friends in the courts. He rivalled
them also in the high opinion his collaborators held of him.
Whatever successes go to men who are alert and sober and
hard-working, the industry and application of Caelius won
them all.

At what one might describe as a critical juncture, however
(for I am going to be quite frank with you, gentlemen, relying
on your sympathy and good sense), his youthful reputation
encountered a temporary set-back. This was caused by his
recent acquaintance with this woman, by the unfortunate
proximity of their residences, and by his inexperience in
those forms of self-indulgence which, after a somewhat prolonged repression and restraint in early years, often suddenly
break forth thereafter and burst out on a formidable scale.
But from this life, or rather from this theme for gossip (because the reality was nothing like as bad as people said), at all
events from this kind of thing whatever it was, he disentangled
and emancipated himself completely. Indeed, he is now so far
removed from the disrepute of being an intimate friend of the
female in question that he even has to defend himself against
her malignant hatred. And to put a stop to all the talk about
dissipation and idleness that had meanwhile arisen – this was
done completely against my wishes and in the face of my
strong opposition, but it was done all the same – he prosecuted one of my friends, Bestia, for bribery. The defendant
was acquitted, but Caelius returned to the attack and accused
him again.

He refuses to pay attention to what any of us say; and his
violence goes beyond what I should have desired. But I am
not discussing his good judgement, which is, after all, a
quality not to be expected of his years. What I do want to
stress, on the other hand, is his drive, and his keenness to win,
and his burning ambition to do well. In men who have
reached our time of life these passions ought to have become

somewhat less ardent than they were, but in youths, as in plants, they give promise of what future ripeness and the rewards of industry are going to bring. Very clever young men, in their pursuit of glory, always need the rein more than the spur; the intellectual exuberance of early years requires pruning more than grafting. So if anyone feels that Caelius has shown too much energy or spirit or obstinacy in taking on or pursuing disputes, and if minor grounds for criticism, such as the shade of purple he wears, or his crowds of friends, or the flamboyant glamour of his personality, are felt to give offence, you will find that in due course such things will settle down. Age, and events, and the passage of time, will mellow them all.

I appeal to you, then, gentlemen, to preserve for our country a good, loyal and patriotic citizen. I can vouch for his possession of these noble qualities; and I can assure our country upon oath that, if I myself have served it well, he, too, will never cease to follow the same political ideas. This I am able to promise, both because I can rely upon the friendship that exists between the two of us, and because he has also spontaneously bound himself by the most rigorous guarantees. For it is impossible that a man who has brought a personage of consular rank into the dock on the charge of breaking the laws of the state should himself be a disorderly citizen. It is inconceivable that a man who refuses to accept another man's acquittal for bribery should ever dream of offering anyone a bribe himself. Our country, gentlemen, has in its hands two actions brought by Marcus Caelius. They can be considered as hostages against dangerous behaviour; but they should also be welcomed as pledges of good intentions.

This, judges, is the city where a few days ago an accusation was brought against Sextus Cloelius[52] and failed. Yet for two

52. Sex. Cloelius (or, according to another statement by Cicero, Clodius himself) burnt the shrine of the Nymphs in the Campus Mar-

years past you have seen that individual helping to stir up sedition and even acting as its principal instigator. He is a person without property or credit, without hope or home or resources. His lips, his tongue, his hands, everything about him is corrupt. Those were the hands with which he burnt a sacred temple, the archives of the Roman people and the records of the state. He wrecked the monument of Catulus.[53] He demolished my own house,[54] and set fire to my brother's. On the Palatine, before the eyes of the entire city, he incited slaves to massacre and incendiarism. After such a creature has been acquitted here in Rome itself, and acquitted through feminine influence, I implore you not to allow Marcus Caelius to be sacrificed to her wanton temper. Never let it be said that this same woman, in collusion with the brother who is also her husband, has been able first to preserve a thieving rogue and then to destroy a fine young man as well.

And when you have considered the position of the youthful Caelius, I urge you to keep also before your eyes this unhappy old gentleman who is his father. Caelius is his only son and his support; on the future of Caelius depends all his peace of mind. The one thing he most dreads is that his son should be in trouble. Submissive to your authority, he kneels, figuratively, before you, appealing to your hearts and emotions, and pleading for your compassion. Bid him rise! Think of your own parents. Think of *your* children and how fond you are of them. Feel for him with the sympathy of sons or fathers, and bring comfort to his grief. Heaven forbid that

tius, where records were kept. Recent research has demonstrated that the name of Clodius' principal henchman was Sex. Cloelius and not Sex. Clodius as was supposed.

53. Q. Lutatius Catulus sen. built the Porticus Catuli on the Palatine to commemorate the battle of Vercellae (101).

54. During Cicero's exile Clodius' gangsters destroyed the Porticus Catuli and Cicero's own house, and then burnt down Q. Cicero's residence (November 57).

this venerable figure, already in the course of nature approaching the last days of his life, should desire death to come to him even more rapidly, because of a wound dealt him not by fate but by yourselves. And do not, I beg you, be the whirlwind or sudden tempest which shall strike down, in his early prime, this youth whose splendid qualities have planted such sturdy roots. Save the son for his father – and the father for his son! You must not give people the chance to say that you disdained an aged citizen whose hopes are nearly at an end; and that, instead of helping a young man full of promise, you actually preferred to crush and destroy him instead. If you restore Caelius to me, and to his own people, and to our country, you will find in him a person pledged and dedicated and bound fast to yourselves and to your children after you. And it is you above all, judges, who will reap the abundant and lasting fruits of his exertions and endeavours.

CHAPTER FIVE

IN DEFENCE OF
TITUS ANNIUS MILO

In 56 the First Triumvirate, which had begun to show signs of strain, was patched up at the Conference of Luca (Lucca). Cicero submitted to the renewed autocracy, and was much criticized for this by conservatives. Caesar hastened back to Gaul, which he was in the process of conquering. Pompeius (whom Cicero vainly hoped to seduce from the alliance) sought to control Rome through its ood-supply and an army in Spain; and Crassus wanted to win glory in the east. Instead he was killed by the Parthians (53), and a direct confrontation between Pompeius and Caesar consequently developed.

Meanwhile Pompeius found that the government of Rome was being rapidly reduced to anarchy by the appalling excesses of gang warfare – which he was not so quick to put down as he might have been, since he saw it might lead people to invite him to assume even larger powers. The principal gang-leader was Publius Clodius Pulcher, the brother of Clodia whom Cicero had attacked in his defence of Caelius, a revolutionary who – although at different times favoured both by Caesar and Pompeius – attached himself to no party, exercised influence over the proletariat as provider of largess, and possessed considerable control over the urban voting machine. A rival hooligan was Titus Annius Milo, a violent nobleman of Samnite origin who, as Clodius' enemy, enjoyed the support of Cicero and the traditional conservative elements.

In the winter of 53 the skirmishing and disturbances between the two toughs revived (after a period of comparative calm) with increased bitterness, when Milo was standing for the consulship and Clodius for the praetorship. On 18 January, each with his followers and thugs, they encountered one another on the Appian

Way – probably by accident, a likelihood to which Cicero does not even refer – and in the scuffle that followed Clodius was killed.

His supporters cremated his body in the Senate House itself, which was severely damaged by the fire. Rioting raged unchecked, and all turned to Pompeius. He was authorized to save the state and raise troops, and was then, on the proposal of extreme conservatives, appointed sole consul – a significant step towards monarchy. He passed new laws concerning violence and bribery which shortened trials and made corruption almost impossible, and on 4 April Milo was brought to trial before the newly established court entrusted with cases of violence. After a chaotic start, soldiers were brought in, and Cicero was intimidated by the violent hostility of his audience into delivering a speech less imposing than the one which is here published – though it cannot have been entirely negligible, since it was complete enough to be taken down by shorthand writers. Milo was convicted (by a vote of 38 to 13), and subsequently condemned in three other courts, and went into exile at Massilia (Marseilles), his property being sold to pay his debts. When Cicero sent him a copy of the revised speech, he remarked that he was glad the orator had not delivered it, since otherwise he would not have been enjoying the excellent Massilian mullets. But four years later he could not resist the temptation of returning to Italy, to foment disorders against Caesar, and he was captured and executed at Cosa.

An account by the first century A.D. commentator Quintus Asconius Pedianus gives a different picture of the fight on the Appian Way, from which it looks very much as though, even if the encounter was perhaps accidental, Milo deliberately ordered his formidable companions to kill Clodius. But although Cicero's speech is not exactly convincing – indeed it is probably riddled with lies – it was regarded by some ancient critics as his masterpiece. The story of the fatal incident, in particular, is an exciting one, superbly told. But the oration has another and sadder distinction, for it casts a lurid light upon the savage chaos and vendetta which signalized these last moribund years of the Republic, and helped to make it inevitable that

*this once mighty institution should come to an end and be replaced by
an autocracy.*

For a speaker, who is beginning the defence of an extremely
courageous man, to exhibit fear is a disgraceful thing, I must
admit. And the fact, judges, that my client Titus Annius himself shows more concern for our country's salvation than for
his own makes it particularly unbecoming that I am unable to
muster the same intrepid spirit when I speak on his behalf.
However, the unfamiliar aspect of this unfamiliar tribunal
exercises an alarming effect on me. Wherever my eyes turn,
they look in vain for the customary sights of the Forum and
the traditional procedure of the courts. The usual circle of
listeners is missing; the habitual crowds are nowhere to be
seen. Instead you can see military guards, stationed in front of
all the temples. They are posted there, it is true, in order to
protect us from violence, but all the same they cannot fail to
have an inhibiting effect on oratory. This ring of guards is, I
repeat, both protective and necessary, and yet the very freedom from fear which they are there to guarantee has something frightening about it.

If I believed these precautions to be aimed against Milo,
gentlemen, I should bow to necessity and conclude that amid
all this weapon-power there was no place for an advocate at
all. But on this point the wisdom of the sage and fair-minded
Cnaeus Pompeius has relieved and reassured me. For once he
has committed a man to a court to be tried, he would certainly
not regard it as compatible with his sense of justice to place
that same man at the mercy of troops bristling with arms. And
it would also, surely, be inconsistent with his sound judgement to add official incitement to the violence of a wild and
excited mob. In other words, what all these weapons and
centurions and cohorts surely promise is not danger but a
safeguard. They are meant to encourage us to be not only
calm but determined as well; as I speak in defence of Milo they

assure me physical security, but they also guarantee an un-interrupted hearing.

All the other Roman citizens in this audience are sympathetic. From any and every point overlooking the Forum you can see crowds gazing this way, and there is not a single soul among them who does not applaud the sterling qualities of Milo. And every one of these persons feels the same conviction: that not only Milo's future but his own, and the future of his children and his entire country, everything he possesses in the whole world, is at stake in this court today.

The people who are against us, on the other hand, the people who bear us ill-will, are those whom the hysteria of Publius Clodius has fed with loot and incendiarism and every sort of national calamity. They are the same crowd who at yesterday's mass-gathering were whipped up to dictate to you the verdict you are supposed to give today. And if their racket reaches your ears, it should, I hope, warn you of the necessity of cherishing as a fellow-citizen the man who has always spurned individuals of that type, however loud they shout, because his one preoccupation is with the safety of you all.

So give me your attention, gentlemen. If you feel any nervousness, dismiss it from your minds. For here is the greatest opportunity you have ever had to declare your attitude towards a fine and gallant gentleman, a citizen of proven loyalty. You who are members of our country's most distinguished Orders have often expressed your appreciation of goodness and bravery by looks and words, but this is your unequalled chance to clothe those sentiments in actual votes and deeds. For here and now a vital decision is yours and yours alone to give. We, for our part, have never failed in devotion to your authority, and now it is for you to decide whether we must continue to pine away in miserable hardship or whether instead, by your staunch, courageous and wise support, our prolonged persecution by these ruffians can at long last come to an end, so that we may begin to live again.

For the situation in which my client and myself find ourselves is in the highest degree painful and anxious and distressing. When he and I originally took up politics, we nourished the ambition that honourable rewards might come our way. But what has happened? Instead we suffer from incessant, tormenting fears of terrible penalties. I always realized Milo would be buffeted by storms and tempests of every other kind, that is to say of the kind encountered on the troubled waters of popular meetings. There was very good reason for this, since he has invariably backed the patriotic cause against disloyalty in all its forms. But in a trial, conducted in a court of law, where the most eminent members of all the Orders in the state pronounce their judgements, I never imagined for a moment that the enemies of Milo could entertain the smallest hope that such men might lend themselves to damaging his splendid reputation – much less that they would actually be willing to ruin him utterly.

And yet I do not propose to defend Titus Annius, gentlemen, by exploiting the success that he made of his tribuneship, or by dwelling on all the noble actions he performed at that time in the interests of our country. Far be it from me, I repeat, to ask that you should condone anything he may now have done on the grounds of his many outstanding services to the state. On the contrary, what I propose to do instead is to make you see, with your own eyes, that it was Clodius who subjected Milo to a treacherous attack. And if, again, the death of Publius Clodius has in fact proved your salvation, it is by no means my purpose to allow you to ascribe this to Milo's valour – when the credit should rather go to the good fortune of Rome itself. However, if I can make it as clear as day (as I shall) that it was Clodius who laid this plot, then, gentlemen, and then only, I shall have one favour to ask of you most earnestly. It is this. Even if all else be taken from us, do not, I beg and beseech you, deprive us of this inalienable right: the right to defend our own lives when they are threatened by the brutal weapons of our foes.

But before I start dealing explicitly with the events you have come here to investigate, I feel it incumbent upon me to refute certain persistent allegations which have been spread by hostile individuals speaking in the Senate, as well as by scoundrels holding forth at public meetings – and just now they have been repeated by the prosecuting counsel as well. When I have dealt with this point, you will be in a position to examine, without any further risk of misapprehension, the issue which is before you. What these people are maintaining is that a person who has killed someone and confesses to the deed has by that very act lost all right to look upon the light of day and live. But the people who say this are evidently not very intelligent, if you consider the place in which they have chosen to develop this argument. For that place is actually the self-same city where the very first defendant in any capital trial was the valiant Marcus Horatius. And he was the man who, even in those days before the state was liberated from despotism, won his own liberation at the hands of the Assembly of the Roman people which absolved him from the charge of murder – in spite of his own voluntary admission that he had killed his sister with his own hands.[1]

Surely everyone must realize that any investigation into a murder offers two alternatives: either the deed is categorically denied, or it is admitted with the defence that it was justified and right. When a seditious tribune of the people, Gaius Carbo, asked Publius Africanus at an open meeting what he

---

1. According to the legend Marcus Horatius, after his two brothers had fallen in the fight in which they killed the three Curiatii of Alba, slew his sister Horatia because she displayed grief at the death of one of the Albans, who was her betrothed.

thought about the death of Tiberius Gracchus,[2] you will not, I am sure, accuse the great man of mental aberration for his reply that, in his opinion, the killing was deserved. And if, again, it was automatically wrong to put Roman citizens guilty of criminal acts to death, then the famous Servilius Ahala, and Publius Nasica, and Lucius Opimius, and Gaius Marius,[3] and the Senate during my own consulship, would all have to be regarded as having acted sinfully. But the true conclusion, gentlemen, is that of the myth, handed down to us by the most eminent of writers, which tells of the man who slew his mother to avenge his father.[4] The votes of the human judges were divided; yet he was absolved by a verdict pronounced by the voice of divinity itself, speaking through the wisest among all the goddesses. Besides, the Twelve Tables themselves ordained that a thief by night may be killed under any circumstances – and that he may be killed also by day if he attempts to defend himself with a weapon. That being so, it is impossible to argue that every act of homicide must necessarily deserve punishment, since in certain circumstances the laws themselves place a sword in our hands to inflict death upon our fellow-men.

There are, in fact, many occasions on which homicide is justifiable. In particular, when violence is needed in order to repel violence, such an act is not merely justified but unavoidable. Once upon a time a soldier in the army of Gaius Marius was indecently assaulted by a military tribune who was

2. The reference is to an inquiry made of P. Cornelius Scipio Aemilianus by C. Papirius Carbo after the murder of Ti. Sempronius Gracchus (133).

3. C. Servilius Ahala killed Sp. Maelius (439), P. Cornelius Nasica Serapio led the attack on Ti. Sempronius Gracchus (133), and L. Opimius on C. Sempronius Gracchus (121); C. Marius was regarded as responsible for the deaths of L. Appuleius Saturninus and C. Servilius Glaucia (100).

4. Aeschylus and Latin tragedians told of the slaying of Clytaemnestra by her son Orestes to avenge his father Agamemnon.

a relative of the general. But the victim of the assault slew his seducer because he was an honourable young man who believed that resistance, whatever the perils involved, was preferable to shameful compliance; and the great commander acquitted him and let him go free. And so, equally, to end the life of a man who is a bandit and a brigand can never be a sin. For what, if it were, would be the point of the bodyguards we take around with us, the swords we carry? We should obviously not be allowed to have them if they were never intended for use.

And indeed, gentlemen, there exists a law, not written down anywhere but inborn in our hearts; a law which comes to us not by training or custom or reading but by derivation and absorption and adoption from nature itself; a law which has come to us not from theory but from practice, not by instruction but by natural intuition. I refer to the law which lays it down that, if our lives are endangered by plots or violence or armed robbers or enemies, any and every method of protecting ourselves is morally right. When weapons reduce them to silence, the laws no longer expect one to await their pronouncements. For people who decide to wait for these will have to wait for justice, too – and meanwhile they must suffer injustice first. Indeed, even the wisdom of the law itself, by a sort of tacit implication, permits self-defence, because it does not actually forbid men to kill; what it does, instead, is to forbid the bearing of a weapon with the intention to kill. When, therefore, an inquiry passes beyond the mere question of the weapon and starts to consider the motive, a man who has used arms in self-defence is not regarded as having carried them with a homicidal aim. So, for the purpose of the present trial, let us regard that principle as established. For if you bear in mind that the slaying of a man who waylays another may on occasion be justifiable – and you can scarcely do otherwise – I am certain I shall be able to convince you that my case for the defence should prevail.

The next point is one which Milo's enemies repeatedly stress. The fatal skirmish which resulted in the death of Publius Clodius, they emphasize, has been defined by the Senate as an act contrary to the interests of the state. And yet the Senate really approved of the deed. It showed that it did so, both by votes it had registered on earlier occasions, and by other clear manifestations of sympathy as well. Think of all the times I have pleaded this very same cause in the Senate and received its approbation in unanimous, unconcealed, out-spoken terms. Even at its most crowded meetings there have never been more than four or at most five members who failed to support Milo's policy. This was openly admitted by that tribune[5] (half-roasted by the conflagration in the Senate House) whose dead–alive harangues, day after day, malignantly attacked what he called my 'supremacy', declaring that the Senate's resolutions did not reflect its own opinions at all, but merely echoed mine. Supremacy, as a matter of fact, is not the right word for what is really just a modest influence for the good, based on a considerable record of public service – or it could be described as a measure of popularity among right-minded people because of all the efforts I have made to help them in the courts. However, call it supremacy if you will, provided you concede that I use it to save loyal citizens from the frenzied attacks of scum.

I am not saying there is anything unfair about the court conducting this trial. All the same, the Senate has never on any previous occasion regarded the establishment of such a commission as a necessity. For laws and courts covering murder and violence already existed – and the grief and lamentation aroused in the Senate by the news of Clodius' death were not

5. T. Munatius Plancus Bursa is described, perhaps accurately, as having sustained burns in the fire in the Senate House caused by the supporters of the dead Clodius who cremated him there (19 January). He was one of the extremely few men ever prosecuted by Cicero (for violence).

so overwhelmingly large as to necessitate the institution of an altogether novel tribunal. Since the Senate had not been allowed to appoint the judges who tried Clodius for immorality and sacrilege,[6] it seems very strange that this same body should have thought it imperative to set up a brand-new investigating commission to report on the circumstances of his death. For, if that needed to be done, why was the Senate itself perfectly prepared, on its own account and without any such special machinery, to pronounce that the burning of the Senate House, and the attack on the house of Marcus Aemilius Lepidus,[7] and the bloodshed which is the subject of the present case, were all acts that contravened the interests of the nation? And they were quite right to do so, because in a free country any and every violence used by one citizen against another cannot fail to be contrary to the welfare of our country. Even self-defence against violence, which I was upholding just now, is very far from being actually desirable. Nevertheless, sometimes it is necessary. Take, for example, those occasions on which Tiberius Gracchus and Gaius Gracchus were killed, and the armed action of Saturninus was put down. Their repression could not fail to convulse the Republic; though it was to safeguard the Republic that it had to be carried out.

That is why, bearing in mind that a death was the outcome of that skirmish on the Appian Way, I refrained from voting in favour of the proposition that the man who had caused it in self-defence acted against the interests of the state. Instead, conscious that violence and treacherous attack were involved, I voted my disapproval of the whole affair, leaving, however, the question of guilt to be decided by a court of law. And if

6. Clodius was accused of bursting into the rites of the Bona Dea in woman's clothes in order to prosecute his affair with Caesar's wife Pompeia (December 62). The religious violation could be classified as *incestum*. Much to Cicero's disappointment he was acquitted.

7. After Clodius' death his gangs attacked the house of M. Aemilius Lepidus the Interrex (appointed to conduct the elections), the future triumvir.

that demented tribune had allowed the Senate to do as it had wished, we should never have been obliged to have this freshly created court. For what the Senate had wanted was that the action, while accorded a special degree of priority, should be tried by existing laws. But the motion was brought forward in two parts, on someone or other's proposal[8] (there is no need for me to expose the deplorable errors of each and every individual!). The first part denounced the deed, and the proposal to which I have just referred became the second part; but it failed to come to anything because bribery managed to get it stopped by a veto.

You may, perhaps, suggest that Cnaeus Pompeius' bill made it clear what opinion he himself held regarding not only the facts of the case but the distribution of blame as well, since the terms of his measure referred explicitly to the fight on the Appian Way 'in which Publius Clodius was killed'. But the point of his measure, in fact, was that there must be an investigation. Now the inquiry had no need to consider whether the act had been committed or not, because there is no disagreement about this. By whom was it committed? That too is obvious. In other words, Cnaeus Pompeius fully appreciated that avowal of the deed by no means excludes the possibility of justification. Had he not realized that a man who confessed to such action might reasonably be acquitted, he would never, once he had heard the confession, have ordered an inquiry to be held at all, and would not, therefore, have given you the choice of recording upon your tablets, instead of C for condemn,[9] the welcome A for absolve. As I see it, Cnaeus Pompeius has definitely refrained from making any sort of pronouncement in Milo's disfavour. What he has done

8. Q. Fufius Calenus. Any Senator could demand the division of a composite motion. The 'demented tribune' was T. Munatius Plancus Bursa.

9. A (*absolvo*) and C (*condemno*) were marked on either side of the voting tablets of the judges, who erased one of the letters.

instead is to point out what you yourselves ought to look for when you come to your decision. For by ensuring that the result of the confession should not be a penalty but a chance to plead justification, he has indicated his conviction that it is not the actual fact of the death that needs investigating at all; the subject of the examination must instead be the circumstances in which that death occurred. And as to his reasons for this step, which he took entirely upon his own initiative – whether he meant it as a tribute to the virtues of Publius Clodius or a concession to a critical situation – he himself will no doubt shortly be explaining to us what his intentions were.

The noble Marcus Drusus,[10] who was tribune of the people, champion and in those difficult times virtually patron of the Senate – and he was also the uncle of the valiant Marcus Cato who is sitting on our bench today – succumbed to murder in his own house. And yet no motion of any kind bearing upon his death was proposed before the Assembly of the people; no special inquiry was decreed by the Senate. Our fathers have also told us of the great grief into which the city was plunged when Publius Africanus the younger,[11] resting quietly at his home, was fatally struck down during the night. There was universal sorrow and burning indignation that the man whom everyone wanted to become immortal, if such a thing be possible, should not even have been permitted to last out the natural term of his mortal life. Well, was there any special commission to look into the death of Africanus? There was not. And why? Because there is no distinction, as a crime, between the murder of the great and the murder of the humblest citizen in the land. In life, it is true, the positions of the highest and lowest are very different. But as to their death,

10. M. Livius Drusus was killed after proposing a law to extend the franchise to Italians (91).

11. It was suspected that P. Cornelius Scipio Aemilianus was the victim of assassination owing to his resistance to the Gracchan land commission (129).

when this is feloniously brought about, the same penalties and laws have to apply universally. A man who kills his father is just as much a parricide when the victim is a nonentity as when he has held office as a consul.

And, that being so, the death of Publius Clodius does not assume any the graver significance because he was killed among the monuments of his ancestors. For that is what the other side keep on repeating. They seem to imagine that the famous Appius Claudius Caecus had built his Appian Way[12] not for public use at all, but as a place where his descendants might prey on their fellows with impunity. That, I can only suppose, must be why Publius Clodius was able to murder a very distinguished knight, Marcus Papirius,[13] without the crime apparently calling for any punishment whatever. For the murderer was an aristocrat, surrounded by his own family memorials; and the man he was disposing of was merely a Roman knight. And now, on this occasion, what sagas are being woven round the name of this same Appian Way, with its Claudian origins! When its stones were drenched in the blood of an innocent, honourable man, this aspect was not even mentioned. But now that the blood is of a robber and a traitor, the talk about it never stops.

Nor need we restrict ourselves to instances from the past. For this very Publius Clodius himself posted a slave in the temple of Castor to assassinate Cnaeus Pompeius. The slave was caught, and the dagger was wrenched from his hand, and he confessed. From then onwards Pompeius kept away from the Forum and the Senate and the public gaze altogether. Evidently he did not consider his rights under the laws and courts to be sufficient protection: the shelter of his own door

12. The Appian Way was built by Ap. Claudius Caecus (censor 312) and lined with tombs of the Claudii.

13. M. Papirius and others were trying to prevent the escape (from Pompeius' custody) of Tigranes I, whom Clodius was hoping to restore to the kingdom of Armenia (58).

and walls seemed preferable. Yet on that occasion, again, no new law was proposed, no novel court of inquiry set in motion. But surely no previous occasion, or personage, or emergency, had ever pointed so imperatively to the need for such a step! The conspirator was stationed right inside the Forum; he was actually within the forecourt of the Senate House itself. Moreover, the proposed victim of his ambush was the personage on whose life the whole future of the country depended – and the criminal design was entered upon at such a grave hour of national crisis that if Pompeius had fallen, and even if he had been the one and only man to fall, this country of ours and all the nations of the world would have collapsed in ruin. For you will not, I imagine, wish to suggest that the failure of the plot exonerates it from punishment. Such a proposition would signify that the laws take no cognizance of intentions, and are only interested in results. The fact that the assassination did not come off gave us less cause to grieve, it is true, but surely did not diminish in any way the need to punish the attempt.

And many is the time that I too, gentlemen, have narrowly managed to escape from Publius Clodius' weapons and gory hands. If, by my own good fortune and that of Rome itself, I had not succeeded in dodging them, I am perfectly sure that no one would have proposed a special investigation into my death!

But how ridiculous of me to presume to compare Drusus, Africanus, Pompeius and myself with Publius Clodius. The actions against them were, I suppose, not beyond our endurance; but obviously no one could be expected to bear with equanimity the death of a man of Clodius' calibre! See how the Senate grieves for him! The knights have broken hearts, the whole country is in a state of collapse, deepest mourning shrouds every town, the colonial settlements are plunged in abject misery. For how could the entire population be anything but inconsolable at the loss of this citizen who was so noteworthy for his kindly and benevolent and gentle personality?

No, members of the bench: that was certainly *not* why Pompeius decided upon the establishment of a special commission. The fact of the matter rather was that his lofty wisdom, a wisdom which is not as other men's, appreciated a number of considerations. That Clodius had been his enemy, that Milo was his friend, he was perfectly well aware. Yet, if he associated himself with the universal rejoicing at Clodius' death, he was afraid that the authenticity of his recent reconciliation with Clodius might take on a dubious appearance. And, among the many other factors that he bore in mind, one predominated over all the rest: he was absolutely certain that, however severe the terms of his own proposal, your decision would still be impartial.

With this in view, the judges he selected were the brightest luminaries of the most excellent Orders in the state. The allegation that his choice was specially directed to exclude my own friends is quite untrue. For one thing, he was much too fair-minded a person ever to have considered such an idea at all. And besides, even if he had, the adoption of such a course would have been incompatible with his determination to choose good men. My most intimate associates, I admit, are not perhaps very numerous, because, after all, one can only have close and constant relationships with a limited number of people; but my adherents are by no means restricted to them. On the contrary, any influence I may possess is derived from the fact that public life has brought me into touch with a wide range of good men. And so Pompeius, bent on selecting for this case the best judges he could find, and well aware that his own reputation was deeply involved in the choice, could not have failed to nominate people who felt warmly towards myself.

Moreover, Pompeius' strong desire that you, Lucius

Domitius,[14] should preside over the court demonstrates his single-minded intention to go for justice, authority, humaneness and integrity. As a preliminary he had enacted that the chairman must be of consular rank – evidently believing that it is the special function of our national leaders to stand up against the emotionalism of the crowd and the importunity of agitators. And out of all the consulars it was you upon whom his choice fell: for from your earliest years you have given ample proof of the disgust with which you view the excesses of agitators.

And now, gentlemen, we must come to the charge which is the reason for this trial. I have shown that confession of such a deed is not wholly without precedent. I have suggested that the only pronouncements the Senate has offered about our case were in complete conformity with what we ourselves should have wished. I have pointed out that the proposer of the law himself, even though there is no argument about the facts, desired the investigation to go further and look into the rights of the matter. And I have stressed that the judges and president chosen to conduct the action are personages whose deliberations will be both just and wise. It only remains then, gentlemen, for you to decide which of the two men involved laid the plot against the other. So as to help you to obtain a clearer view of the true circumstances, I will now give a brief account of what happened; and I ask for your close attention.

Publius Clodius was determined to use the post of praetor[15] to convulse the government by every sort of evil-doing. But the elections of the previous year had dragged on so pro-

14. L. Domitius Ahenobarbus, of the extreme right wing, was actually appointed president of the court by the Assembly – no doubt on the initiative of Pompeius.

15. Clodius had been aedile in 56 and according to the *Lex Villia* could have been elected praetor in 54.

tractedly that he saw his own praetorship would be restricted
to a period of no longer than a few months. Advancement in
rank, which appeals to other men, was not his object at all.
One of the purposes that carried more weight in his mind was
a strong desire to avoid having an excellent man like Lucius
Paullus as his colleague. But Clodius' main ambition was to
have an entire year to devote to the disruption of our state.
And so he suddenly abandoned the idea of being praetor in the
earliest year to which he was entitled, and transferred his candidature to the following year instead. His motive in so doing
was very far from involving the religious scruples which
sometimes cause people to take such a step. On the contrary –
as he himself admitted – what he wanted was to have a full
and continuous year for the exercise of his praetorship: that is
to say, for the subversion of the Republic.

All the same, in regard to the latter year as well, a worrying
thought continued to nag him. This was the consideration that
if Milo was elected to the consulate for that year his own
praetorship would once again be hampered and paralysed.
Indeed, as Clodius clearly appreciated, there was every likelihood of Milo becoming consul, and by the unanimous vote of
the Roman people at that. In this situation he attached himself to Milo's competitors, and did so in such a way that he
himself should have complete control of their electoral
campaigns – whether they liked it or not. That is to say, as
he himself frequently expressed it, his intention was to carry
the entire election upon his own shoulders. And so he proceeded to marshal the tribes, acting as a go-between in every
negotiation and mobilizing disreputable toughs who virtually
amounted to a new Colline tribe[16] in themselves.

And yet the more flagrantly Clodius' disturbances raged,
the stronger waxed Milo's position every day, until finally it
became evident to Clodius, through the unmistakable voice of
public opinion expressing itself in a series of popular votes,

16. The Colline tribe was composed of the lowest class of citizens.

that this courageous man, his inveterate enemy, was certain to become consul. And so Clodius, who was ready to stop at nothing, now began to operate openly: and he declared straight out that Milo must be killed.

Clodius had a gang of rustic and barbarous slaves whom he had recruited to ravage the national forests and harass the Etrurian countryside. These he now brought down from the Apennines – and you have seen the creatures yourselves. There was not the slightest concealment, for he himself asserted repeatedly and publicly that even if the consulate could not be taken away from Milo, the same could not be said about his life. Clodius frequently gave indications to this effect in the Senate, and he said it at mass meetings too. Moreover, when the gallant Marcus Favonius asked him what purpose all this violence could possibly serve while Milo was alive to resist it, Clodius replied that within three or, at most, four days Milo would be dead. And Favonius promptly reported this remark to Marcus Cato here.

Meanwhile Clodius became aware (and it was an easy enough fact to discover) that on 18 January Milo was under an obligation, prescribed by ritual and law, to proceed to Lanuvium. He held the local office of dictator[17] and it was his duty to make a nomination to the priesthood of the town. Equipped with this knowledge, Clodius left Rome without notice on the previous day. As subsequent events demonstrated, his plan was to take up a position in front of his own country manor, and set an ambush for Milo on that spot. Clodius' departure from Rome meant that he had to absent himself from a turbulent public gathering on that same day. His usual violent contributions were greatly missed at the meeting, and he would certainly never have failed to play his part had he not

17. 'Dictator' was an ancient title of office at Milo's home town Lanuvium, going back to its independent days and now limited to religious duties.

formed the deliberate intention to be punctually in the locality set for the ambush at the appropriate time.

Meanwhile Milo, on the other hand, attended the Senate on that day, until the meeting was concluded. Then he proceeded to his home, changed his shoes and his clothes, waited for the usual period while his wife got ready, and then started off at just about the time when Clodius could have got back to Rome if it had been his intention to return at all on the day in question. But instead he encountered Clodius in the country. The man was lightly equipped, not seated in a coach but riding on horseback, unimpeded by any baggage, with none of his usual Greek companions, and even without his wife who nearly always travelled with him. Milo, on the other hand, was sitting in a coach with his wife, wearing a heavy travelling cloak and accompanied by a substantial, heavily laden, feminine, unwarlike retinue of maids and pages.[18] And this was our so-called waylayer, the man who had allegedly planned the expedition with the explicit purpose of committing a murder!

And so at about five in the afternoon, or thereabouts, he found himself confronted by Clodius before the gates of the latter's house. Milo was instantly set upon by a crowd of armed men who charged down from higher ground; while, simultaneously, others rushed up from in front and killed the driver of the coach. Milo flung back his cloak, leapt out of the vehicle, and defended himself with energy. But meanwhile the people with Clodius were brandishing their drawn swords, and while some of them ran towards the coach in order to fall upon Milo from the rear, others believed he was already slain and began to attack his slaves who had been following behind him. A number of these slaves of Milo's lost their lives defending their master with loyal determination. Others, however, who could see the fight round the

18. Asconius says Milo was accompanied by a large number of slaves including gladiators.

coach but were unable to get to their master's help, heard from Clodius' own lips that Milo was slain, and believed the report. And so these slaves, without the orders or knowledge or presence of their master – and I am going to speak quite frankly, not with any aim of denying the charge but just exactly as the situation developed – did what every man would have wished his own slaves to do in similar circumstances.

The incident, gentlemen, took place precisely as I have described it. The attacker was defeated. Force was frustrated by force; or, to put the matter more accurately, evil was overcome by good. Of the gain to our country and yourselves and all loyal citizens, I say nothing. It is not my intention to urge that the deed be counted in favour of Milo – the man whose self-preservation was destined to mean the preservation of the Republic and yourselves. No, my defence is that he was justified in acting to save his life. Civilized people are taught this by logic, barbarians by necessity, communities by tradition; and the lesson is inculcated even in wild beasts by nature itself. They learn that they have to defend their own bodies and persons and lives from violence of any and every kind by all the means within their power. That being so, if you come to the conclusion that this particular action was criminal, you are in the same breath deciding that every other man in the history of the world who has ever fought back against a robber deserves nothing better than death – and that if the robber's weapons did not manage to produce this result, then you yourself would be quite prepared to bring it about! If Milo had been of the same mind, he would have done better to offer his throat to Clodius, who had already attacked him repeatedly, than to refuse the death-blow from Clodius merely so that it could be dealt him subsequently by yourselves.

If, then, you are all agreed that self-defence is not necessarily wrong, you need not trouble about the question *whether*

Clodius was killed. For we fully admit that he was. What you have to consider instead is that issue which has so frequently been raised in a variety of different cases – namely, whether the act was justifiable or not. That a plot existed is generally agreed, and indeed the plot is what the Senate has denounced as having been contrary to the national interests. But the point that needs to be settled is which of the two men was the conspirator, and this is the problem you were appointed to investigate. What the Senate censured was the deed itself, and not any particular individual; and the inquiry set up by Pompeius was intended to determine not the facts, but the question of justification. So quite clearly the only matter before the court is this: which man plotted against the other? If Milo plotted against Clodius, let him be punished; if Clodius plotted against Milo, then the only proper verdict is Milo's acquittal.

How, then, can it be proved that it was Clodius who laid the plot against Milo? When we are dealing with such an audacious and despicable monster as Clodius, it will surely carry conviction if we can prove that there was a strong incentive for him to kill Milo, and that he had high hopes and the prospect of great benefits from his death. We must consequently apply to the two men's characters that famous maxim of Cassius, *Who stood to gain?* [19] And to that it is only necessary to add that personal advantage will never drive a good man to crime, while a bad man will succumb even if the advantage is trivial. Now, if Milo had been killed, Clodius would have gained in two ways. First, he would not have been compelled to serve as praetor under a consul who would have made it impossible for him to indulge in mischievous behaviour. Secondly, the consuls who would have held office in Milo's

19. *Cui bono* was the maxim of L. Cassius Longinus, tribune of the people in 137.

place might have been expected by Clodius, if not actually to collaborate with him, at the very least to connive in allowing him a free hand to carry out his appalling designs. For no doubt he reasoned that, even if it were within their power to hamper his efforts, they would not be keen to do so since they were under such heavy obligations towards him. Besides, even if their intentions were obstructive, they might in any case scarcely possess the power to crush this loathsome creature's programme – so well established as it was, following a long list of previous outrages.

Judges: are you the only people who have no idea of what is going on? Are you strangers to our city – just here on a visit? Are your ears keyed to some far distant land, and entirely aloof, therefore, from the extremely persistent rumours about the laws Clodius intended to impose on us and brand upon the bodies of us all? If indeed laws are the right word for them, rather than fire-bombs for the destruction of the city or plagues to scourge our lives! Come, Sextus Cloelius, show us that file of your people's draft laws; we heard how you snatched them away to safety from Clodius' house, bearing them off like the Palladium[20] from amid the clash of weapons and the midnight multitude. For here, indeed, was a marvellous gift, a wonderful piece of tribunician apparatus, which you were in the happy position of being able to bestow upon anyone you could find who was prepared to become a tribune under your dictation.

I see Sextus has transfixed me with that famous glare that has become second nature to him on the occasions when he was screaming out menaces against all and sundry. And what a searing, terrifying flash it is – the selfsame blaze that plunged the Senate House in flames! But you cannot conceivably imagine, Sextus, that I could have any grudge against you: and I will tell you why. For you took the body of my bitterest

20. According to tradition the Palladium (image of Pallas Athene) had been rescued by Aeneas from the sack of Troy.

enemy and subjected it to far fiercer vengeance than I ever had the sternness to demand. You took the bloody corpse of Publius Clodius and hurled it out of doors. You flung it into the open street and left it there, denuded of funeral portraits[21] and mourners, bereft of its procession and valedictory speech, charred on a heap of ill-omened faggots, cast off to be torn to pieces by the dogs that prowl in the night. This was, indeed, such a shameful thing to do that I can find no words to defend it. And yet, since the victim of your ruthlessness was my own enemy, I can scarcely be expected to summon up as much indignation as I might!

So I have shown you, judges, how greatly it was to the advantage of Clodius that Milo should be killed. And now, please, think of the contrast presented by Milo's situation. What possible value could the death of Clodius have for him? Nothing in the world could have induced Milo either to do such a thing or even to want it done. Clodius, you suggest, presented an obstacle to Milo's candidature for the consulship. And yet Milo was clearly set for victory, in spite of the machinations of Clodius against him – or indeed all the more so because of them! Clodius helped to get him votes quite as effectively as I did myself. For the fact was, gentlemen, that you could not fail to be influenced by your recollection of Milo's services to myself and to our country. You were impressed by our appeals and our anxieties; I saw at the time how deeply they moved you. But most of all you were impelled by the dread of impending disaster. For it was impossible for any Roman citizen to envisage the prospect of Publius Clodius' unchecked tenure as praetor without feeling a harrowing apprehension that revolution was at hand. And unchecked you knew this praetorship would be, unless there was a consul who possessed both the courage and the power to keep it under control. Such a man the Roman people unanimously

21. Busts of ancestors who had held offices of state were carried in the funeral procession.

saw in Milo: and everyone, therefore, was eager to cast the vote which would dispel, at one and the same time, his own personal terrors and the perils that were besetting our whole nation.

Whereas now that Clodius is out of the way, Milo is reduced, for the defence of his position, to methods of a less dramatic kind. That special and unique renown, which his suppression of the demented violence of Clodius augmented every day, has been deprived of its field of activity, since Clodius is no more. You, for your part, have gained the inestimable benefit of no longer having to go in fear of any fellow-citizen. But he, on the contrary, has been deprived of the stage on which he was able to prove his valour – and win votes for his consulship. An exhaustible source of personal glory has been taken from his grasp. Milo's candidature, which remained as firm as a rock against every attack while Clodius was alive, has only begun to suffer damage now that he is dead. And so Clodius' death, far from being of any advantage to Milo, is actually doing him harm.

But it was sheer malevolence, you say, that prompted him to kill Clodius; he acted in rage and bitterness; he took upon himself to exact personal vengeance for a wrong, to satisfy his private grudge. Nothing could be further from the truth! Indeed, to say, as I might, that these motives were stronger in Clodius than in Milo would be a grave understatement. The fact of the matter is that they totally dominated Clodius, whereas in Milo there was no trace of them at all. For (apart from the public-spirited detestation we all feel for evil men) what reason could Milo possibly have had to hate Clodius, who was, indeed, the very root and base from which his own reputation had grown? As for Clodius, on the other hand, he had every motive for detesting my client. Here was a man who had been a strong supporter of my cause, who had opposed Clodius' desperate schemes, who had taken steps to crush his seditious activities, and who, finally, had announced his indictment in the courts: for Clodius, up to the day of his death, was facing a prosecution by Milo under the Plotian Law.[22] How do you imagine the tyrant felt about that? What a ferocious hatred he must have cherished! – and justly so, if 'just' is the right word for a man to whom justice was a total stranger.

There remains the suggestion that Clodius' character and habits speak in his favour, whereas those of Milo tell against him: that Clodius has never performed violent acts, whereas for Milo they have been habitual. Well, gentlemen, I ask you this: when I departed from this city – amid the grief of you all – what was my principal cause for anxiety? Was it a trial in the courts? No, it was not; the danger came from slave-gangs and weapons; in a word, from force. And indeed, how could my recall from banishment have been the just act that it was, unless that banishment itself had been the height of injustice?

For example, had Clodius, in proper form, ever served me with a writ for an action? Had he proposed a fine? He had not; I was under no treason indictment from Clodius. And yet you will not, I believe, be wanting to suggest that my case was a bad one – or, indeed, that its significance was limited to my own self. No, it was a splendid case, and it was yours as well as mine; I had nothing to fear from any trial. And yet, having laboured and hazarded my life to rescue my fellow-citizens from being savaged by impoverished thugs, I could not permit those very same citizens, in their turn, to expose themselves to peril on my own personal behalf. When the eminent Quintus Hortensius here, the shining light and ornament of the Republic, was acting in my support, I myself saw him being almost murdered at the hands of slaves; and in the same disturbances that fine Senator Gaius Vibienus, who was with him, was mauled so badly that he lost his life. From then onwards the dagger which Clodius had inherited from Catilina was

22. Clodius was indicted by Milo under the *Lex Plotia de vi* for rioting after Cicero's recall from exile (57), but was never brought to court.

never allowed to rest. That is the weapon which made me its target: and it was a weapon to which I felt I must not allow you to hazard yourselves as well. It plotted treachery against Pompeius; it caused the Appian Way – which bears the assassin's own name – to be deluged with the life-blood of Papirius. And then, after a certain lapse of time, the same blade was again directed against myself. For beside the Regia,[23] as I am sure you remember, it nearly made an end of me.

Now, when did Milo ever behave like that? He could not induce Clodius to face him in court, and such forceful measures as he employed were aimed solely at making it impossible for the man to plunge the city into chaos. If his intention had been to kill Clodius, he had frequent, first-rate, easy opportunities to do so. For when he was protecting his own home and his household gods from Clodius' aggression, could he not have hit back with ample justification? And at the time that his gallant and illustrious colleague Publius Sestius was wounded, might he not have done so again? Or again when the excellent Quintus Fabricius was driven away while proposing my recall from exile, and the Forum became the scene of an appalling massacre? And on yet another occasion when that brave, honest praetor Lucius Caecilius[24] had his home invaded? Or could he not very well have struck him down at the time of the bill which sanctioned my restoration? On that day the whole of Italy, as it flocked to Rome in anxiety for my safe return, would gladly have applauded the magnificent deed. In fact, even if the hand which dealt the blow had been the hand of Milo alone, the entire population would have been only too glad to claim the credit for itself.

That was, indeed, the moment for such an act. A valiant,

23. The Regia, on the Via Sacra, was traditionally regarded as the home of the legendary king Numa Pompilius. It contained the offices of the chief priest.

24. P. Sestius and Q. Fabricius were tribunes, and L. Caecilius a praetor, working for Cicero's recall from exile (57).

illustrious consul was in office. He was Publius Lentulus, the enemy of Clodius and avenger of his crimes, the champion of the Senate and defender of your rights, promoter of national harmony and initiator of my own recall. Against Clodius, and in favour of myself, were ranged no less than seven praetors and eight tribunes of the people. Furthermore, the prime mover and guiding spirit in my restoration was Cnaeus Pompeius, who loathed Clodius and advocated my cause by a powerful and eloquent pronouncement which won the Senate's unanimous concurrence. It was Pompeius again who exhorted the Roman assembly to take action. Moreover, the decree he sponsored in my favour at Capua initiated throughout the whole of Italy – in harmony with its own ardent desires, and its appeals that he should take the lead – the signal that there should be a general convergence upon Rome to work for my return. On that occasion, indeed, the longing for my restoration was so intense that every citizen blazed with hatred against Clodius. If anyone had killed him then, it would have been a question not merely of impunity but of a reward. And yet Milo still restrained himself. Twice he challenged Publius Clodius in the courts;[25] but he never challenged him to a trial of force.

Later, again, when Milo, a private citizen at the time, was obliged to defend himself before the people against Clodius' indictment,[26] Cnaeus Pompeius, while speaking on behalf of the defendant, was subjected to a physical attack. That, surely, was more than just a chance to kill Clodius: it was a thorough justification in itself. And recently, too, when Marcus Antonius[27] had caused all good citizens to entertain high

25. Of the first prosecution (which like the other was not brought to court) we have no direct account. The second was in 57 (n.22).

26. When Clodius became aedile at the end of 57 he retaliated on Milo, whose tribuneship was finished, by prosecuting him before the people. The prosecution was dropped.

27. M. Antonius, the future triumvir, had been sent from Gaul by Caesar to stand for the quaestorship.

hopes for the future of our country – when that young offspring of a noble house, gallantly taking upon himself a vital
task, already held the monster firmly entangled, struggle as he
might, in the noose of retribution: then, in the name of heaven, what an occasion, what a wonderful opportunity that
was! When Clodius had dived into hiding in a closet beneath
the stairs, it would have been the easiest thing in the world for
Milo to finish the pest off. If he had done so, no one would
have blamed him; and the result for Marcus Antonius would
have been glory. At elections in the Campus, too, Milo was
given any number of chances. Clodius had burst into the
voting enclosures and ordered his men to draw their swords
and start hurling stones. But then suddenly the sight of Milo
overwhelmed him with terror, and he made his escape in the
direction of the Tiber – while you and every other patriotic
citizen prayed that Milo might translate his valour into
action.

   If he had done so, everyone would have truly been delighted. And yet he still refused. So it is surely in the highest
degree unlikely that he should have deliberately planned to
perform precisely the same act at a juncture when objections
were inevitable. When justice, topography and circumstances
all favoured the killing of Clodius, and there would have been
complete impunity, he refrained. So is it in the least probable
that he would have chosen to slay the man, instead, at a juncture when all these factors were against him? Besides, gentlemen, this was the period when the struggle for the highest
office in the land was under way, and indeed the very day of
the election itself was imminent. I know only too well the
anxiety of a candidate's position, and the incessant worry of
the electoral campaign. It is a time when we are sensitive not
only to anything and everything that may be said against us
in so many words, but when we even dread people's vaguest
thoughts. All rumours, however false or silly, cause us profound alarm, and we nervously scan the expressions on every

face. For nothing in the world is so delicate and fragile and unstable and frail as the popular attitude and feeling towards men who are standing for an election. And it is not only a candidate who behaves badly that they take against; even if he has been a model of correctness they still have fault to find.

Here, then, was Milo, faced with the prospect of the long and impatiently expected day of the election. You surely cannot suppose that he intended to present himself at the solemn ceremony of the Assembly's auspices with bloodstained hands which openly and boastfully proclaimed a deliberate sin and crime. In Milo such behaviour is quite unthinkable. In Clodius, on the other hand, it would have been plausible enough, since he was convinced that Milo's death would provide him with the means of seizing autocratic power. Besides – and this is the vital point for malefactors – it goes without saying that the most powerful of all inducements to crime is the prospect of impunity. Now, which of these two men could anticipate such a benefit for himself? Not Milo, who, even as it is, has become the defendant in this trial – and for doing something, moreover, that was meritorious, or, at the very least, unavoidable. No, it was Clodius before whom that favourable prospect lay. He was a man whose one desire was to break the laws of god and man alike; and for courts of law, for the punishments they might inflict, he never showed anything but contempt.

But additional arguments, further discussions, are surely not necessary. I appeal to you, Quintus Petilius, as a fine and courageous citizen, and to you, Marcus Cato – the men who by heaven-sent good fortune are serving as judges today. You heard Marcus Favonius' report about the declaration of Clodius (who was still alive when Favonius told you) that Milo would be dead within three days. And indeed, just three days after he had spoken, the affair took place. Clodius does not seem to have been reluctant to disclose what he had in mind. Can you, therefore, feel any reluctance either, in assessing the action he subsequently took?

How did he manage to be so exactly right about the day? I have told you already. There was no difficulty about discovering the date fixed for the dictator of Lanuvium's sacrificial ceremonies. He appreciated that Milo would have to set out for Lanuvium on the actual day when, in fact, he proceeded to make the journey. And so Clodius got in first. It was also the day, as I mentioned before, of a hysterical public meeting at Rome, whipped up by a tribune in Clodius' pay. This was an occasion and a gathering and a riot which Clodius would never have allowed himself to miss unless he had been sent on some premeditated crime. So far, then, from having any pretext for the excursion, he would have had an excellent reason for remaining behind.[28] But Milc, on the contrary, could not possibly stay, since he had not merely a motive but an obligation to leave the city.

So Clodius knew Milo was going to be on the road on that day; but Milo could not even have suspected that Clodius would be travelling. For how, I ask you, could he have had the slightest idea of this? Whereas that is a question not even worth asking about Clodius. For even if you suppose that his close friend Titus Patina was the one and only person from whom he had inquired, he could easily have been aware that this was the date fixed for the appointment of a priest at Lanuvium by its dictator, who is Milo. There were any number of people who could have told him this, including anyone you like from Lanuvium itself. But whom, on the other hand, could Milo have asked about the date of Clodius' return? Let us even assume (and see what a concession I am offering you) that he bribed a slave, as my friend Quintus Arrius suggested. Even this would not have done any good – if the evidence of your own witnesses is to be believed. For

28. Asconius, however, says that Clodius had been attending a town council at Aricia (cf. p.247).

Gaius Causinius Schola of Interamna,[29] an intimate friend and companion of Clodius (whose evidence on an earlier occasion, incidentally, demonstrated that Clodius was simultaneously at Interamna and Rome!), declared that on the day in question Clodius had intended to remain at his place at Alba, but on learning unexpectedly about the death of the architect Cyrus he had suddenly decided to leave for Rome instead. This was confirmed by Gaius Clodius, another of Publius' companions.

You will note, gentlemen, the significant results which emerge from this testimony. In the first place Milo is absolved beyond all doubt from having deliberately set out to waylay Clodius *en route*, since there was evidently no reason to suppose that they would ever meet at all. And then I must mention a second matter – for I do not see why I should not do myself a good turn. Some people, you know, judges, while they were advocating the bill that established this court, suggested that although it was the hand of Milo that did the deed there was someone of greater importance behind the scenes. And actually, it was I myself, let me tell you, whom these abandoned scoundrels ventured to identify as the brigand and cut-throat in question. But they are refuted by their very own witnesses, who declare that Clodius never had any intention of returning to Rome if he had not received the news concerning Cyrus. I can breathe again; I am cleared. I need not be afraid of having based my plans on a situation which I would not conceivably have been able to anticipate!

And now let me pass on to the next question. For the argument I have put before you is countered by the objection that the same applies to Clodius: he, too, could never have planned any such plot, since he had fully intended to stay on at his

29. At the time of Clodius' trial for violating the rites of the Bona Dea (61) – at which, to Cicero's fury he bought his acquittal – C. Causinius Schola had sworn Clodius was at Interamna, 80 miles away, at the time. Causinius was with Clodius at the time of his death.

property at Alba. On the contrary! He left there with the specific purpose of committing the murder. It is perfectly clear that the messenger who is alleged to have brought the report of Cyrus' death did not really bring any such information at all, but instead conveyed the news that Milo was approaching. What unexpected bulletin could he possibly have brought about Cyrus, whom Clodius, on his departure from Rome, had left already at the point of death? I was with Cyrus myself, and Clodius and I were joint witnesses of his will. The will had been drawn up without any secrecy, and Clodius and myself had been named as heirs. At ten on the previous morning, he was already breathing his last. It would indeed be surprising if Clodius had to wait until four in the following afternoon to receive news of his death.

All right, let us suppose, for a moment, that it was so. But even so what possible reason could Clodius have to start for Rome at such an unnatural hour? Why must he be on his way in the depths of night? Did the fact that he was one of the heirs give him a motive for hurrying? But there was absolutely no need to hasten on that account. And, besides, even if there had been, what on earth was he likely to gain by arriving in Rome that night, or what could he lose by postponing his arrival until the following morning? Clodius, then, far from having a pretext for arriving during the night, had every reason to avoid doing any such thing. But Milo on the contrary, if you are supposing that he was the plotter, ought surely, when he heard of Clodius' imminent nocturnal arrival, to have concealed himself in some hiding-place to wait for him. He could have killed him during the night; he could have used any dusky bandit haunt appropriate for ambushes. If that is what he had done, his denials would have been accepted by everyone – in exactly the same way as everyone, now that he has admitted what actually happened, hopes he is going to get off. The burden of the charge would have fallen upon the locality itself, a den where robbers lurked. Its silent solitude would not have given Milo away; the blackness of night would never have shown him up. Furthermore, if the act had been accomplished in such a neighbourhood, suspicion would have fallen on all the many people whom Clodius had outraged and ravaged and ejected from their properties – and all others who went in terror of the same thing happening to themselves. Indeed, the whole of Etruria would have been in the dock!

Furthermore, on the day in question Clodius, on his way back from Aricia, undoubtedly called in at his house at Alba. Now let us concede, for a moment, that Milo knew he had been at Aricia. In that case he must surely have suspected that Clodius, even if he proposed to get back to Rome on the same day, would nevertheless make a stop at his Alban property, especially as this is right beside the road. Well, why, if that was so, did Milo not waylay him earlier, to prevent his getting to his place at Alba? Or, alternatively, why did he not wait for Clodius at some subsequent point where his intended victim, if he decided not to stop at Alba after all, would be likely to pass after dark?

Gentlemen, it all fits in. To Milo it was positively advantageous that Clodius should stay alive. But for Clodius, if he was ever going to attain his principal ambition, the death of Milo was very greatly to be desired. Clodius detested Milo, but Milo did not hate Clodius at all. Clodius had habitually and continually initiated violence, whereas all Milo had done was to resist aggression. Clodius had openly declared and proclaimed that Milo was going to die; but nothing of the kind was ever heard from Milo.[30] Clodius had known the day of Milo's departure, while Milo for his part had no knowledge whatever of the date when Clodius was likely to come back. Milo's journey was unavoidable, but Clodius' trip had no

30. But Cicero himself, in a letter to Atticus, reported that Milo had openly threatened to kill Clodius.

purpose, and was indeed positively inconvenient to him. Milo had openly announced that he would be leaving Rome on the date in question; Clodius had concealed the fact that he was going to return on the very same day. Milo made not the smallest change in his plans, while Clodius invented reasons to explain why his own movements were changed. And finally, Milo, if he was engaged in a plot, would have taken up his position near the city and waited until nightfall, whereas Clodius, quite regardless of any apprehensions he might have felt about Milo, still had every reason to be afraid of coming to the city after dark.

Let us now consider the question on which the whole matter hinges; and that means that we have to look at the spot where the confrontation took place. To which party did it offer better ground for an ambush? On this point, gentlemen, there is really no need for any doubt or reflection whatever. Surely Milo could not conceivably have imagined that he would be in a favourable position against Clodius in front of the man's own house – a mansion, moreover, with ludicrously exaggerated substructures in which there was room for at least a thousand able-bodied men. Nor could he possibly have chosen, of his own free will, to fight in precisely the vicinity where his opponent could make good use of an elevated and commanding position. No, it is perfectly evident that my client was the victim of the ambush which took place at that point, and that his aggressor relied on this favourable ground to launch a carefully planned attack.

Facts, gentlemen, are what carry conviction, and here the facts speak for themselves. Imagine that instead of listening to a narrative of events, you were looking at a painting which depicted them. Which of the two men was the plotter, which was guiltless of the slightest criminal design, would quite clearly emerge. See, there is one of them sitting in his coach, wrapped in a heavy cloak, with his wife by his side. Each and every one of these adjuncts – costume, vehicle, companion –

was a serious impediment. No man is equipped for battle if he is entangled in his cloak, imprisoned in his coach and hampered by the presence of his wife. And then watch Clodius, suddenly coming out of his house. Why? And in the evening, too. What was the need for that? And look how he is taking his time about it – a curious procedure, especially at that hour. We are told he was paying a call at Pompeius' country residence. Was this to see Pompeius? But he knew perfectly well that Pompeius was at his house near Alsium. Did Clodius call just to have a look at the place? But he had been there thousands of times before. What, then, was the significance of his detour? The answer is that its only purpose was to delay and take up time. Yes, he wanted to stay around until Milo appeared on the scene.

And now please compare the travelling methods of this unencumbered highwayman with Milo's heavily laden transportation. On previous occasions Clodius had constantly been accompanied by his wife; now she was not there. He had always travelled in a coach; now he was on horseback. Besides, wherever he went – even on those forced marches to his Etruscan encampments – he had invariably been surrounded by a retinue of little Greeks; now there was no sign of anything so unbusinesslike. By way of contrast Milo, who normally did not go in for that sort of thing, happened to have with him a boys' choir belonging to his wife, and a collection of female servants as well. Whereas Clodius, who was habitually escorted by whores and homosexuals and street-walkers, was not escorted on this occasion by any companions at all – except some individuals who were all of the same tough type, and looked as though each one had been hand-picked by the rest.[31]

Well, why, then, did Clodius get the worst of it? Because the robber does not always succeed in killing the traveller. Sometimes it is the traveller who wins instead and the robber

31. A method for the selection of volunteers.

who meets his end. Besides, although this was an encounter between one man who was prepared and another who was not, Clodius may be compared with a woman who had fallen among men.[32] Furthermore, Milo made a practice of never being totally unready for Clodius – at no time was an attack beyond the bounds of possibility. For Milo could never fail to bear in mind how useful his death would be to Clodius, how deeply Clodius detested him, and how Clodius was a man who stopped at nothing. For this reason, knowing that he could hardly call his life his own any longer (so enormous was the price that had been set upon it), he had formed the custom of not exposing himself to hazards without a measure of protection and precaution. And then take additional factors such as chance, the unpredictable outcome of a clash, and the even hand of Mars who often strikes down the victor even after the looting and shouts of triumph have already begun – overthrowing him by the hand of his apparently prostrate foe. Add, too, the fuddle-headedness of the principal gangster, who was drowsy from too much lunch and drink. He thought he had cut off his enemy from the rear, but quite forgot the extreme furthermost end of Milo's retinue. And so he landed in the midst of those followers, who, furious and despairing of their master's survival, exacted the vengeance which loyal slaves are wont to take in defence of their master's life.[33]

Then why, in that case, asks the prosecution, if the slaves were the guilty parties, did Milo give them their freedom? We are told he was afraid that they would prove unable to bear pain, and would talk;[34] that they would be induced by

32. A reference to the female disguise worn by Clodius when he broke into the rites of the Bona Dea (allegedly in order to make love to Pompeia, whose husband Caesar divorced her).

33. But it was believed, probably rightly, that Clodius, wounded by one of Milo's gladiators, was finished off on Milo's orders by his friend Saufeius.

34. The prosecution accused Milo of freeing slaves so that they should not be tortured into incriminating him. Free men could not be tortured.

torture to confess that they themselves had slain Publius Clodius on the Appian Way. But where is the need for any torturer to achieve that? For what do you want to discover? Whether Milo killed the man? But he did. Whether he was right to do so or not? But that is not the torturer's business; for facts are what can be elicited on the rack, whereas questions of justification, on the other hand, are a matter for courts of law. We, that is to say, are the people who have to track down what falls within the sphere of legal investigation – and what you want to find out by torture we already admit.

In asking why Milo freed his slaves, you are only showing that you have no idea of the best way to get to your enemy. What you ought really to be asking is why he did not reward them more amply still. Marcus Cato here, whose utterances are unfailingly resolute and courageous, declared to a riotous public gathering (at which order was restored by his own authoritative personality) that any slave who had defended the life of his owner emphatically deserved not only emancipation but the largest of all possible rewards as well. No recompense can be sufficiently generous for slaves like Milo's who are so staunch and devoted and true that their master owes them his life. And he owes them something more important still: it is due to them that this ferocious enemy is not now glutting his eyes and heart upon Milo's blood and wounds. If Milo had failed to liberate those slaves, he would have been compelled to surrender to torture the very men who had preserved their master from death, who had avenged the dastardly attempt on his life, who had saved him from destruction. In all his present misfortunes there is nothing which gives my client so much comfort as the thought that, if anything happens to him, at least his slaves have received the reward that they so richly merited.

And yet examinations of slaves – other slaves – are being held; and they are exercising a prejudicial effect on Milo's prospects. I refer to the examinations which have just taken place in the courtyard of the Temple of Liberty. Who, you ask, are being subjected to this inquiry? They are the slaves of Publius Clodius. Who has demanded their investigation? Clodius' nephew Appius.[35] Who produced the men? Appius again. From where? From Appius' house. Heavens, what could be more rigorous than this! Indeed, the examination of slaves against their own masters is forbidden, except regarding the infringement of divine law by incestuous practices – the crime for which Clodius himself was tried.[36] Clodius has practically been promoted among the gods – even more nearly so than when he broke into their actual presence – now that his death is investigated with the strictness appropriate to a sacrilegious violation of religious rites! All the same, what our ancestors ruled was that no slave must be examined in order to incriminate his own master. They made this decision, not because it is impossible to discover the truth by such a means, but because the attempt seemed unnatural and, indeed, even more deplorable than the death of the master himself. Well, is there, in that case, the smallest likelihood of getting at the truth when you actually examine the prosecutor's slaves for evidence against the defendant?

Anyway, let us see what the examination consisted of and how it was conducted. 'Now, Rufio' – to take a fictitious name – 'take care you don't tell lies. Did Clodius plot against Milo?' 'Yes.' The result is crucifixion for certain. Well, 'no', then. After that answer there is quite a possibility of freedom. What a peculiarly reliable sort of examination! Besides, normally slaves are taken off straightaway to be tortured, and

35. Ap. Claudius Pulcher and his brother of the same name, sons of C. Claudius Pulcher the elder brother of P. Clodius, were Milo's prosecutors.

36. Slaves could only bear witness against their masters for crimes against the divine law (e.g. incest, of which Cicero believed Clodius was guilty with his sisters). There follows yet another reference to his violation of the rites of the Bona Dea, which came under the heading of *incestum*.

yet even so the precaution is observed of isolating them in separate cells so that nobody can talk to them. Whereas these, on the contrary, had merely been in the custody of the prosecutor himself, for no less than a hundred days, and even after that it was the prosecutor himself who produced them. What a cast-iron, incorruptible method of investigation, to be sure!

The story of what happened is clear from every sort of conclusive evidence and proof. Yet if, even so, you are still not convinced that Milo returned to Rome with a completely clear conscience, free of the slightest taint of crime or fear or guilt, I urge you to recollect the rapidity with which he returned. As he came into the Forum – at the very time while the Senate House was in flames[37] – his attitude, his demeanour, his eloquence were all, you will remember, immensely impressive. He put himself at the disposal of the people and Senate and armed forces of Rome; and above all he entrusted himself to the man charged by the Senate with the entire government and man-power of Italy and all our national might. Milo would certainly never have placed himself in the hands of Pompeius unless he had been convinced of the justice of his own cause: especially as that personage heard everything there was to hear, saw reason to fear major perils ahead, entertained many suspicions, and felt convinced that not a few of them were justified. But Milo's action, gentlemen, illustrates the potency of conscience for good and evil alike. It ensures that those who have done wrong shall unceasingly have the threat of retribution before their eyes – and it frees an innocent man from fear.

Milo's cause has always received the approbation of the Senate; and there are rational grounds for this. For the Senators, in their wisdom, have appreciated his reasonable

37. This was the fire in the Senate-House when the followers of Clodius had brought his body into the building and cremated it there.

behaviour in the clash with Clodius, his ready presence of mind, and the courage he showed in defending himself. And you have not, I am sure, forgotten, gentlemen, how when we first heard of Clodius' death the enemies of Milo, as well as other people of deficient judgement, declared he would never come back to Rome at all. If they assumed he had acted in the heat of passion and had murdered his enemy in a paroxysm of hatred, their supposition presumably was that he must reckon even the loss of his country worth while provided only that Clodius was dead and he himself had been able to gorge his loathing with his enemy's blood. Or if, alternatively, they concluded that he had deliberately killed Clodius in order to set the country free, it no doubt seemed to them that a man of such outstanding courage, after he had risked his life to bring salvation to the Roman people, would not hesitate to submit to its laws. For he would do so in the consciousness of his own everlasting renown and of the salvation which it was our good fortune to enjoy because of what he had done. And yet at that time comparisons were actually made with Catilina and his monstrous gang. 'Milo will break out,' people said. 'He will seize some strong-point or other and begin a civil war.' Unhappy sometimes is the fate of a patriotic Roman, when men forget all about his exceptional services and suspect him of treacherous intrigues! These rumours could only have been true if Milo had been guilty of some action which he could not conscientiously and truthfully defend: and so it goes without saying that they proved groundless.

And then think of the vituperations that were afterwards heaped upon his head – slanders which would have paralysed anyone who had even the mildest of guilty consciences. Heavens, how nobly he endured those attacks! Endured them, yes, with contempt, and brushed them aside, in a way that no one, whatever his resolution, could possibly do if he were guilty; and indeed even an innocent man would not have been able to maintain so impervious an attitude unless his courage was altogether exceptional. There was a rumour, for example, that huge quantities of shields and swords and javelins and even bridles might be captured. It was claimed that every street and lane in the entire city contained a house rented by Milo; that weapons had been conveyed up the Tiber to his house at Ocriculum, that his home on the slope of the Capitol was crammed with shields, and that there were piles of incendiary arrows all over the place, intended for burning the city to the ground. And these stories not only went the rounds but almost seemed to carry conviction. It was only after investigation that their wholly fictitious character became clear.

I had to admire the exceptional vigilance of Cnaeus Pompeius.[38] But all the same, judges, in my opinion the gentlemen at the head of the government have to listen to too many reports, and indeed are given no alternative. It was even thought necessary to give a hearing to Licinius, the man from the Circus Maximus who cuts the throats of animals for sacrifice. He had a tale of slaves of Milo's having too much to drink at his shop and confessing that they were involved in a plot to kill Pompeius; and he added that he himself had later been stabbed with a sword by one of these same conspirators in case he should give them away. Licinius went to see Pompeius at his mansion and told him the entire story. In the consultations that followed I was one of the first to be called in, and in accordance with the advice of his friends Pompeius referred the matter to the Senate. Since the safety of our country and of myself so largely depended on Milo, the idea that he could have incurred such an atrocious suspicion could not fail to cause me serious concern. Nevertheless, it astonished me that people were believing what the slaughterer had said, and paying attention to confessions made by slaves, and letting the abrasion in Licinius' side, which looked like the scratch

38. Cn. Pompeius Magnus, who after Clodius' death had been appointed sole consul for 52.

of a needle, be magnified into the sort of wound that a gladiator might have inflicted!

As I see it, however, Pompeius was not giving way to panic but taking precautions, and extending those precautions beyond what gave manifest cause for alarm to everything else as well, his intention being to relieve your anxiety. For example, there was another rumour too, namely that the house of the illustrious and valiant Gaius Caesar had been in a state of siege throughout many hours of the night. The vicinity is much frequented, and nobody had heard or noticed anything wrong; and yet the story spread all the same. Cnaeus Pompeius is an immensely courageous man who could not conceivably be accused of timidity, and indeed, seeing that the responsibility for the entire government rests upon his shoulders, I agreed that in the circumstances no amount of precautions could justifiably be regarded as excessive. And then again, at a well-attended meeting of the Senate held lately on the Capitol, a Senator actually declared that Milo was carrying a weapon. Whereupon Milo then and there, in that most sacred temple, disproved the slander by tearing off his clothes. For since even the whole way of life of this outstanding individual and citizen was evidently not enough to bring conviction that the charge was untrue, the facts had to be allowed to speak for themselves, without his uttering a word.

And so it has been amply proved that all these stories are nothing but baseless, malicious fabrications.

But if, in spite of that, the concern about Milo's intentions still persists, what we on our side have to fear is no longer the charge of murdering Clodius at all. For what worries us now, Pompeius, and worries us very gravely – and here I am addressing you directly, with an emphasis particularly intended to catch your ear – is your own suspicion about what Milo proposes to do next. Let me consider this suspicion for a moment. Let us assume, for instance, that you truly believe this client of mine is now contemplating, or has contemplated, a criminal conspiracy against your life. Let us suppose that your recruiting officers are justified in their assertions that these call-ups of Italians and these weapons and these units on the Capitol and sentries and police, and the picked body-guard which watches over your own person and your home, are all specifically designed to resist an onslaught from Milo. Let us infer, then, that every one of those measures has been planned and organized and brought into effect against this single individual. But if so, if the selection of our outstanding general and the mobilization of the entire Republic are directed against this man alone, then surely his strength, his courage, his power and his resources must be on a most astonishing scale – far beyond the capacity of any one person!

It is, of course, generally understood that all the diseased or unsound elements in the state have been placed under your control, so that you may use these weapons of yours to bring them back to health and steadiness. And Milo, if he had been given the opportunity, would have proved to you in the most conclusive fashion that no man's affection for any friend, however great, could possibly exceed the devotion he feels towards yourself. He would have demonstrated that no hazard incurred in your interests has ever been too great for him to endure. He would have shown how, in defence of your renown, he has again and again opposed that pestilential scourge. He would have reminded you that, under your guidance, his whole tribuneship was directed towards my restoration from exile, a cause which you held very dear. He would also have recalled that you yourself had later spoken to defend him in an action affecting his civil rights, and had supported his candidature for the praetorship. He would have stressed that there are two men whose staunch friendship he always hoped to retain: yours because of the services you had performed on his behalf, and mine because of what he had done for me.

And if he could not convince you of this, if your suspicion of him proved to be too deeply ingrained for eradication, if the downfall of Milo, in short, is the only way for Italy to be rescued from mobilizations and Rome from all this array of weapons, then unhesitatingly, in keeping with his character and practice, Milo would have bidden his country farewell.

But before doing so, he would first have appealed to you, Pompeius whom we call Great. Indeed, that is what he does here and now; and I will tell you what he says. 'What changes and reverses are found in a single person's span of life! What inconstant and variable fortunes, what faithless friends, what pretences tailored to the exigencies of the times, what desertions by close associates in times of danger – and what faint hearts! Yet a time will assuredly come, a morning will at long last dawn (not, I hope, because of a disaster to yourself, but perhaps through one of those national crises of which we have such frequent experience) when you will look, and look in vain, for the support of a true friend, the loyalty of a dedicated man, and a spirit which for resolute determination has never had an equal.'

What the Senate charged Cnaeus Pompeius to do was to ensure that the state should come to no harm.[39] That is a concise formula, but it has always given the consuls sufficient power, even though it has placed no weapons in their hands. But it does not seem credible that a man with the expert legal knowledge, traditional sense and political skill of Pompeius, entrusted with an army and recruiting powers, need have believed he had to await the legal verdict of a trial before penalizing Milo, if it had really been true that what Milo intended was the violent abolition of all legal proceedings. And is not Pompeius' conviction of the falsity of these libels shown most clearly of all by his proposal of a special

39. The *senatus consultum ultimum* which conferred emergency powers. Before his appointment as sole consul Pompeius as proconsul had been authorized to levy troops throughout Italy.

measure? For, according to my interpretation, that law makes Milo's acquittal at your hands obligatory – or at the very least legitimate, as it would be impossible for anyone to deny.

There is also the question whether Pompeius intends to intimidate you into convicting my client. But surely that, gentlemen, is categorically denied by the way in which he is sitting there surrounded by a military bodyguard. Besides, Pompeius would never demean himself by coercing you to condemn a man whom ancient precedent and his own powers both entitled him to punish by himself. But in any case this escort is purely for his own protection. It emphasizes to you that you are entirely free, regardless of yesterday's mass gathering,[40] to return an unimpeded verdict in accordance with your true opinions.

However, the actual charge which Milo is facing causes me a minimum of concern. I am not so foolish, gentlemen, or so unperceptive of your reactions, or so ignorant, that your feelings about Clodius' death can escape me. Indeed, if I were not proposing to disprove the accusation – and indeed I have already done so – Milo might well with justification have boasted openly that it was he who committed the deed. And he could have gloried in the lie.

'Yes,' he would exclaim, 'the killing was done by me! And the man I killed was more than a Spurius Maelius who cheapened the price of corn, squandered his own resources, and became suspected of autocratic ambitions because he seemed too keen to win popular favour. The man I killed was more than a Tiberius Gracchus, who deposed a colleague[41] by seditious means, so that those who slew him earned worldwide renown. Yes,' he would have the courage to add,

40. On the previous day, when M. Claudius Marcellus had begun to cross-examine C. Causinius Schola, the uproar of the Clodian gangs standing round had compelled him to seek sanctuary with the president.

41. The fellow-tribune deposed by Ti. Sempronius Gracchus was M. Octavius (133). For Maelius cf. pp. 77, 221.

seeing that he had brought freedom to his country at the risk of his own life, 'this was an individual who had been caught by noble women, with their own eyes, in the act of a repulsive adulterous performance upon a consecrated couch! This was the creature whose punishment the Senate had again and again demanded, in order to purify the holy rites from this dreadful defilement. Moreover, as Lucius Lucullus[42] discovered from an investigation (and this he declared on oath), the man committed disgusting acts of incest with his own sister. And it was he again who, calling the weapons of slaves to his assistance, forced out of the country the citizen who had been pronounced by the Senate and the people of Rome and all the nations of the world to be the saviour of the city and all its citizens.

Clodius distributed whole kingdoms, or took them away;[43] he parcelled out the earth to whom he pleased. Repeatedly he plunged the Forum into bloodshed. By force of arms he imprisoned a fine, much admired Roman within his own four walls. To Clodius, no sin or lechery seemed too frightful. Here was the man who wanted to get rid of the public record of censors' registrations in the national archives; and so he burnt the temple of the Nymphs to the ground.[44] Statute, the law of the land, the boundaries of properties, meant nothing to him. In his covetousness of other men's estates, he got his way not so much by legal processes, however dishonest,

42. Clodia, the youngest sister of Clodius and of the notorious Clodia, was the wife of L. Licinius Lucullus.

43. Clodius, while tribune (58), had introduced laws making Brogitarus king of Galatia, deposing Ptolemy (brother of Ptolemy XII Auletes of Egypt) from the throne of Cyprus, and assigning the provinces of Macedonia and Asia to L. Calpurnius Piso Caesoninus and A. Gabinius (consuls 58) respectively, in defiance of the *Lex Sempronia* which empowered the Senate to make such appointments.

44. In his speech in support of Caelius, Cicero attributes this arson to Sex. Cloelius. The aim was probably to destroy evidence of election frauds.

not by spurious claims and suits,[45] but by vast military camps and armies and assaults. By his armed operations on this sort of scale he set out to expropriate the people of Etruria, for whom he had formed complete contempt. He also tried to expel the eminent, gallant Publius Varius, who is one of our judges today. A burden which many a person had to bear was the presence of Clodius and his architects roaming with their measuring rods round his country house and grounds. Clodius was not going to be content until the land he had grabbed reached as far as the Janiculum – and the Alps.

'When he had tried to induce that courageous and distinguished knight Marcus Paconius to sell him an island on Lake Prilius, and Paconius refused, Clodius forthwith transported whole boat-loads of timber, lime, stone and sand to the island, and under the owner's very eyes (for he was watching across the water) proceeded at once to erect a building on this land which did not belong to him. He also had the nerve to threaten a man of the calibre of Titus Furfanius – not to speak of a poor woman like Scantia, and the young Publius Apinius, who were both told they would be killed unless they evacuated their properties in his favour. Well, Clodius had the effrontery to tell Furfanius that, if he did not hand over a stipulated sum, then he himself would plant a dead body in the man's house, a scandal which would have been the end of such a blameless gentleman. Clodius even took advantage of the fact that his own brother Appius, a very loyal friend of mine, was absent from his estate – and evicted him from it altogether! Furthermore, he planned to build a wall through the forecourt of his sister's house, with the foundations laid in such a way as to prevent his sister from getting into her own forecourt or even, indeed, from entering the house at all from the street.'

45. In a property dispute the claimants first made their formal claim before the praetor and then deposited a sum of money to be forfeited by the loser.

These outrages fell impartially upon the Republic and private individuals, upon people near and far, upon his own relatives and persons quite unconnected with himself. All the same, as long as matters rested at that, we somehow contrived to put up with it all. Our people, who are extraordinarily patient, became deadened and resigned. But the things that were due to come next, the things that were already impending, would have been as impossible to tolerate as to avert. For just imagine what would have happened if Clodius had gained his praetorship and the military powers it confers! About the fate of our allies, of foreign nations, of kings and tetrarchs, I say nothing. Indeed, you would actually have been praying that he should make them his targets instead of your own lands and your houses and your money. Money, did I say? Heaven knows, his uncontrollable lusts would not even have spared your own children and your wives. Do you suppose I am just inventing all this? But every word that I am saying is plain fact, universally known and established by proof. Do you believe I am fabricating his intention to mobilize armies of slaves here in Rome so as to gain control of the government – and thereby seize the property of every private individual in the country?

So let us picture Titus Annius Milo raising his bloodstained sword above his head, and crying out: 'Come, citizens, and listen to what I have to say! I have killed Publius Clodius. With this blade, with this right hand, I have saved you from the frenzied violence of this creature whom we failed to curb by laws and courts. And so, by this deed, I, and I alone, have made it possible for justice and fairness and law and freedom and honourable, decent behaviour to abide in this country of ours.' If Milo spoke in those terms, would he need to worry how his fellow-citizens might react? For, as things are today, the entire community praises and admires what he has done. The whole population declares and believes that Titus Annius is unique in human history because of the benefit he has conferred upon his country, the joy he has brought to Rome and all Italy and every nation of the world.

I am not in a position to measure the occasions which caused Romans of ancient times to rejoice. But our own age, too, has seen many glorious victories won by generals of the utmost distinction; and yet none of these triumphs brought such enduring or outstanding satisfaction as what has happened now. In times to come, I trust that you and your children will live to see many blessings, in a well-conducted state. But remember this: as each of them comes your way, reflect that if Publius Clodius had lived you would never have seen any of them at all. Optimistically I feel, and I believe my optimism is justified, that this very year, under this exceptionally great consul who is with us today, is going to bring significant benefits to Rome. Turbulence is going to be put down and evil passions subdued; the authority of the law and its processes will be supreme. Now nobody, surely, can be demented enough to suppose that these happy results would have been obtainable if Clodius were still alive! Besides, consider your own private possessions: what guarantee of their permanent tenure could have had the slightest value under a madman's tyrannical regime?

Gentlemen, the suggestion that my attack on Clodius looks as though I am giving vent to my own personal animosity, and showing greater zest than fair-mindedness in the process, would not worry me at all. It is true that I had every right to abominate him. Since, however, he was the detested enemy of all the world, my own hatred scarcely even rose above the general average. No words would be strong enough to express the capacity for crime and destruction that was in Publius Clodius. No thoughts could even conceive its appalling magnitude.

Or look at the matter in this way, gentlemen. We are engaged in an investigation into the circumstances of his death. But since our thoughts are at liberty to conjure up what

they will – just as our eyes are free to select the objects within
their line of vision – imagine, for a moment, that I am pre-
senting you with this alternative to our present situation.
Suppose I can induce you to let Milo off, but only on the condition that Publius Clodius comes back to life again. You look
terrified at the prospect! Yes, because you know just how you
would be feeling if he were alive, since even when he is dead
a mere idle fancy causes you such alarm. Or let us consider
Cnaeus Pompeius himself. His talent and fortune have
continually enabled him to perform feats such as have never
been achieved before. Let us pretend, then, that Pompeius
was offered the choice between appointing this inquiry into
Clodius' death and summoning him up again from the dead.
Which of these courses do you feel he would have chosen?
Even if on account of their friendship he had wanted to call
him back to life, for the sake of our country he would have
refrained from doing so. Here you are in this court, then, to
avenge the death of a man whom you would refuse to bring
alive again even if you knew you had the power to do so!
Your inquiry was proposed by a special law which would
never have been put forward if its corollary were that he should
live again. If, therefore, this was the sort of man Milo killed,
why should my client, who admits the deed, have to go in fear
of punishment at the hands of the very persons he has rescued?

The Greeks bestow divine honours upon those who have
slain a tyrant. At Athens and other cities of Greece I have seen
remarkable spectacles celebrating such heroes with religious
rituals and the singing of laudatory hymns. They are vene-
rated in a manner which scarcely falls short of the reverence
due to the immortal gods themselves. So what a dreadful
contrast it will be if you, so far from conferring even the
smallest honour upon the man who has saved his country
and avenged a grave wrong, actually permit him to be haled
off for the ultimate punishment! If the deed had been inten-
tional, he would confess it – confess, I say, confidently and

cheerfully that to vindicate the freedom of the entire Roman people he had performed an action which could justify not merely a confession but the proudest of boasts. And indeed if he freely admits the killing in self-defence, and in return asks for nothing but a pardon, why should he not have unhesitatingly avowed the deliberate act (if he had done it) since this would have deserved the most enthusiastic applause? Unwillingness, on his part, to make that confession would mean he was suggesting that you would be more likely to be gratified by his preservation of his own life than of yours! For indeed, if you valued even his present admission at its true worth, you would now be loading him with rewards. And if what he has done should fail to gain your approbation – though how could any man forbear to praise what has saved his life? – still, if the valour of a very courageous man does not succeed in winning the appreciation of his fellow-citizens, then he would go with pride and resolution from his ungrateful country. For he could not fail to regard it as the very depth of ingratitude that everyone else should be able to rejoice, and that the one and only mourner should have to be the man who has made all this rejoicing possible.

Besides, consider our custom. When there were traitors to suppress, we have always recognized that, since ours would be the glory, we must not shirk the peril and unpopularity either. I, during my consulship, should not have merited any praise for all the hazards I underwent on behalf of yourselves and your children had I not realized that my endeavours would involve me in a desperate struggle. If there were no peril to fear, any woman would be brave enough to kill an evil and destructive citizen. The real hero is the person who, faced with opprobrium and death and vengeance, nevertheless moves manfully to his country's defence. It is the duty of a grateful nation to recompense its benefactors – and, conversely, it is up to a brave man not to let even the danger of a death penalty make him regret his valorous deed. Titus

Annius, then, might have made the same confession as Ahala, Nasica, Opimius, Marius and myself. If his fellow-citizens were grateful, there would be joy in his heart; and if they were ungrateful, still amid his misfortunes he would be comforted by the knowledge of a good deed done.

For this blessed thing that has happened, gentlemen, we must thank the fortune of Rome, your own propitious star, and the immortal gods. For no other conclusion is possible, if you agree that a divine power and force exists; if you are stirred by the grandeur of our empire, by the radiance of the sun, by the movements of the sky and the heavenly bodies, by the alternation and order which prevail in nature, and (most significant of all) by the wisdom of our forefathers who piously observed, and handed down to us their descendants, the worships and rituals and auspices of our religion.

And such a power does assuredly exist. The presence, in these frail bodies of ours, of something which has activity and consciousness is linked with the existence of a similar force in the vast and splendid revolutions of the universe. To disbelieve in this force because we cannot see or apprehend it ourselves would be illogical, since, after all, we are equally unable to discern the nature or location of our own minds, and yet we owe to them our senses, and our capacity to plan, and the actions we perform and words we speak.

That, then, is the power which has again and again showered unbelievable blessings and resources upon our city, and which has now uprooted and removed this pernicious menace. It contrived his destruction by disposing him to provoke and challenge with violence and the sword a man whose bravery is exceptional. As it happened, the intended victim got the better of him. But if the issue had gone the other way, the aggressor would have remained unpunished and uncontrollable for evermore.

It was not a mere human design, gentlemen, that prompted

this outcome. No, it was heavenly providence; but not even heavenly providence of any familiar order either. For assuredly it seemed as if the very sacred places themselves, the places which witnessed the monster's downfall in their midst, had taken action on their own account to claim their rights upon his body. Hills and groves of Alba,[46] hear my appeal and prayer! Hear me, demolished altars of the Albans, partners and coevals of the sacred rites of Rome itself, altars which this frenzied lunatic, hewing down their holy glades and levelling them to the ground, has overwhelmed beneath the vast, preposterous substructures of his mansion! Yours was the wrath, yours the hallowed force which showed its might, yours the strength which prevailed against all the pollutions with which he sought to blot it out. And it was you from your lofty hill, sacred Jupiter of Latium,[47] after your lakes and woods and boundaries had been befouled by all his filthy immoralities and crimes, who at long last opened your eyes to his enormities and brought down retribution upon his head.

All these were the powers, and it was before their very gaze, to which vengeance was paid, late indeed, yet just and fitting all the same. For you surely cannot attribute it to mere blind chance that the very chapel of the Good Goddess, which stands on the property of the worthy and accomplished young Titus Sertius Gallus – this Good Goddess herself, I repeat, was close beside the place where Clodius started the fighting and received the first wound that brought him to his shameful death. Here indeed was proof that the iniquitous court of law before which he once came for judgement had not really acquitted him as it seemed to do, but was saving him up, after all, for this stern penalty.

46. The Alban Mount was the ancient religious centre of the Latin League.
47. Jupiter Latiaris, the god of the Latin League, had his temple on the Alban Mount.

And it was the same anger from on high which deranged the minds of his satellites. For they gave the dead Clodius no funeral image, no dirges or games, not a trace of a procession or lamentation or panegyric or ceremony. Besmeared with blood and dirt, bereft of that final solemnity which even foes habitually concede, his corpse was charred and tossed out into the street. Evidently it was the will of heaven that the effigies of his glorious ancestors should be nowhere at hand to grace this abominable murderer; and that in death his body should be mauled on the selfsame spot where in life he had been condemned.

I had begun to believe, I assure you, that the Fortune of the Roman people was pitiless and harsh, since for so many years past she had allowed this individual to trample our Republic underfoot. Here was a man who defiled the most sacrosanct of our rites with sexual orgies, shattered into fragments the most solemn Senatorial resolutions, blatantly bribed the judges who were examining his conduct, and as tribune of the people subjected the Senate to countless persecutions. Furthermore, he was actually able to reverse measures that had been taken, by universal consent, for the safety of our state. For he succeeded in compelling me to leave the country,[48] setting fire to my house and tormenting my children and my wife.

Against Cnaeus Pompeius he had proclaimed an impious war. State officials and private citizens alike succumbed to his violence. He burnt down my brother's home; he devastated all Etruria; he ejected a host of victims from their homes and lands. Fiercely he pressed on. The whole Republic, all Italy, the provinces, the kingdoms of our allies – in none was there space enough to contain his demented projects. Within his home, men were already at work engraving laws which would subject us to our own slaves.[49] Whatever property he

48. Cicero was exiled in 58 by a law of the tribune Clodius.
49. There were probably rumours that Clodius was planning a law conferring freedom on a number of slaves.

fancied, whoever were its owners, he vowed it should be his within the year. Now, there was one man, and one man only, who obstructed all these schemes, and that was Milo. There was also, it is true, a great personage who had the power to block them; but he regarded himself as tied by his recent reconciliation with the man. As for Caesar's influence, Clodius claimed it was at his own disposal. He had shown very clearly, over the issue of my exile, how little concern he felt for anything respectable citizens might do. But Milo stood up against him – Milo and nobody else.

It was at that point, gentlemen, that the immortal gods implanted into his degraded, unhinged brain the idea of forming a plot against my client. Now this, as it happened, was the one way in which the obnoxious Clodius could be eliminated. For the state, by its own powers, would never have given him the punishment he deserved. Can you see the Senate keeping him under control when he became praetor? Even in the days when such control was normal, and when Clodius was still a private citizen, its efforts in this direction had failed. Was there the slightest chance, then, of the consuls proving any more effective if they tried to restrain their praetor? Besides, if Milo had been killed, Clodius would have had consuls who were his own partisans.[50] But in any case what consul would have dealt resolutely with a praetor who, even in the days when he was merely a tribune, had already played havoc with consular authority? His oppressions, confiscations, annexations, would have descended upon the entire community. He had even prepared a revolutionary bill – discovered in his house with the rest of the Clodian legislation – which would have plucked our slaves from out of our households and made them into freedmen depending upon himself. In a word, if the powers of heaven had not instilled into that effeminate creature the proposition that he should put this

50. Milo's competitors for the consulship had been Q. Caecilius Metellus Pius Scipio and P. Plautius Hypsaeus.

most valiant of gentlemen to death, today the Republic would be no more.

For if he had lived to become praetor with the consulship to follow; if, while he lived, these temples and walls had remained standing long enough to see him as consul; can you really suppose that the living Clodius would have done no mischief? Why, even after his death he was able to burn the Senate House down, through the agency of his henchman Sextus Cloelius. This was the most appalling, and horrible, and saddening spectacle that has ever been seen. For here was the very shrine of holiness and majesty and wisdom and states-manship, the centre of the city's life, the sanctuary of our allies and haven of every nation, the habitation reserved for one single Order by the agreement of the entire commonwealth of Rome. Such was the building that was plunged in flames, destroyed, and desecrated by the presence of a corpse! Nor was this the work of an ignorant mob, which would have been tragic enough; it was the act of one single individual. If a mere cremator of corpses, on his own, had the nerve to do all this for his dead chief, the mind reels at the outrages he would have committed as gang-leader for the living boss himself.

But, meanwhile, the edifice into which he chose to throw the body was, of all places, the Senate House itself. So Clodius, in his death, was able to burn to the ground the very place that, alive, he had done everything in his power to overthrow. And yet there are people who are quite prepared to moan about what happened on the Appian Way, but have not a thing to say about these events in the Senate House. There are those who seem to imagine that the Forum could have been defended against him if he had lived, though the Senate House itself could not even stand up to his dead body!

Would you really like to raise him from the dead, if you possessed the power? But since you can scarcely cope with the ferocity of his unburied corpse, how on earth would you resist his onslaughts if he were still alive? You did not succeed in stopping the men who ran into the Senate House with lighted torches, who burst into the Temple of Castor waving demolition tools, who brandished their swords from end to end of the Forum. You saw the Roman people massacred. You were witnesses of a public meeting broken up at the point of the sword. Its audience was listening with silent attention to Marcus Caelius,[51] that tribune and determined statesman who is so resolute in the defence of his friends – a dedicated champion of loyal causes and senatorial authority, and in Milo's present predicament (or, one might rather say, in his singularly glorious fortune) a man of wonderful, immortal loyalty.

I have said enough about the charge itself. About matters extraneous to it perhaps I have said too much. If, while we all weep, you have seen no tears from Milo,[52] if you have noted that his expression is unchanged and his voice and speech remain steady and unfaltering, you should by no means on that account feel any the less willing to acquit him. Indeed, I feel this is actually a reason why you should help him all the more. In fights between gladiators, involving the fates of the lowest sections of humanity, we find it natural to dislike timorous suppliants who whine to be allowed to keep their lives, whereas we feel eager, on the other hand, to save spirited and courageous fighters who dauntlessly expose themselves to death. The men who have our sympathy are not the ones who beg for it but those who do nothing of the kind. And by the same token our attitude should be the same, with all the greater emphasis, when it is the life of a valiant Roman citizen that is at stake.

51. Cicero's friend M. Caelius Rufus (see the speech in his support) was tribune in 52, resisted Pompeius' special courts, and defended M. Saufeius who was thought to have led the band which killed Clodius.

52. Milo's lack of tears (which were expected from a Roman defendant) was an embarrassment to his cause and to Cicero.

As for myself, judges, I am paralysed with misery when, day after day, I hear the sad words of Milo perpetually ringing in my ears. 'Farewell, my countrymen, farewell!' he cries. 'May all prosperity and safety and happiness be yours! May this city and this beloved land of mine be filled with ever-lasting glory – however badly it has treated me. May my fellow-citizens be vouchsafed full enjoyment of a tranquil public life, not in my company, since I am not to be allowed to enjoy it with them – though it is only because of me that this blessing shall be theirs. As for myself, however, I shall depart and be gone, and even if it be not granted me to stay here long enough to see a good government, at least I shall be spared from continuing to live under a bad one. And so I shall rest – in the first free and well-regulated community I can find.

'My labours have all been in vain, my hopes dashed. My dreams have not come true. When I held the office of tribune, the government was being badly harassed. And so the Senate, which I found at the end of its tether, and the knights, who were desperately enfeebled, received my services; and I placed myself at the disposal of all the patriotic citizens whose position in the country the weapons of Clodius had blasted. Could I, in those days, ever have believed that these same loyal citizens would fail to come to my aid in their turn? And when I had restored you, Cicero, to your homeland' (for thus he has repeatedly spoken to myself), 'could I possibly have imagined that this same country would one day have no room left for myself? Where is the Senate whom we have both so staunchly backed? What has become of those knights of yours? Where is all that enthusiastic support in the towns of Italy? What has happened to the applause in which every Italian joined? And where, in particular, is that eloquent ad-vocacy of yours, Marcus Tullius, which has been of assistance to so many? Am I, who have so often hazarded my life on your behalf, to be the only man denied the help of your voice?'

As he pronounces these words, gentlemen, I weep. Yet he does nothing of the kind. No, his countenance remains unmoved – just as you see it now. For he knows that the citizens, on whose behalf he did this deed, are not men of ungrateful disposition; though he admits that encompassing perils had made them anxious and alarmed. And as for Clodius' proletarian mob which menaced your security, Milo reminds us that in order to keep your lives safe he did everything in his power to control them by his authoritative personality. To soothe their turbulence, he even sacrificed three properties he had inherited.[53] The shows which were paid for from these funds succeeded in appeasing the populace. How much more, then, would he have expected that you, too, would be won over – by his remarkable services to the state. The Senate's friendly feelings towards him, he says, he has often had occasion to appreciate, especially during these difficult times; and whatever fate may have in store for him for the future, he will always remember the visits which you and other members of your Orders have paid to his house, and your sympathy and friendly speech.

Another thing he can never forget is the situation regarding his candidature for the consulship. For everything was complete except just the herald's announcement of the result. And that, too, had become an unnecessary formality. For in effect he had already been declared consul, by unanimous popular vote – which was the height of his ambition. And finally, he has the satisfaction of knowing that, even if the present trial turns out in his disfavour, what really stands against him will not be the charge for which he is arraigned at all. No, the objection to Milo will be something quite unconnected with it – and only a vague suspicion at that.

*

53. Milo, a Papius by birth, had been adopted by his maternal grandfather T. Annius: hence perhaps a second patrimony. (He was said to have taken the name Milo from the famous Greek athlete of Crotona).

Milo also points out, and he is certainly right to do so, that men who are brave and wise do not generally perform a noble act merely for the sake of the reward; they undertake it for its own sake. He himself, he ventures to think, has had a uniformly glorious career – if it is agreed that the most glorious thing a man can do is to free his country from the perils which endanger it. Enviable above all other men, he will admit, are those who, having accomplished such achievements, are honoured for them by their fellow-citizens. All the same, the very fact of having outdone all others in the magnitude of the actions themselves automatically makes a man greatly enviable, quite regardless of any reward.

But if we must take rewards into account, the noblest recompense a great deed can have is renown. Indeed, this is the one and only thing which makes up for the shortness of our lives. It perpetuates among future generations the memory of what has been done; it ensures that though absent we are present, that in death we remain alive. It is glory, in fact, that places men on the ladder to heaven. 'I am convinced,' declares Milo, 'that the people of Rome and all the nations of the world shall continue to speak of me for evermore. After aeons of time, their voice shall still not be mute. Even at this very moment, when all my enemies are kindling every slander of which hostile tongues are capable, nevertheless, wherever people are gathered together, wherever one man is conversing with another, they are thanking and congratulating me for what I have accomplished.'

I say nothing of the festivities celebrated or planned throughout Etruria. It is, I believe, the hundred and second day since Clodius' death. During the intervening period the tale of what Milo did has spread to the furthermost boundaries of the empire – and so have the celebrations. It is therefore all one to him, says Milo, where his body may sojourn upon this earth, since there is no land that does not glorify his name and will not cherish it for all eternity.

When you and I have been together, Milo, and these gentlemen have not been with us, you have often spoken to that effect. And now, in their hearing, I have this to say to you in my turn. I admire your resolution immensely. Your qualities, which exceed merely human standards, would make my grief all the keener if we had to be parted. Moreover, if you were torn from my side I should not even have that last poor consolation of being able to feel anger against those who had dealt me such a sorrowful wound. For the men who had wrested you away from me would not be my foes at all but my closest friends: not people who have ever treated me badly before, but my helpers on all occasions.

I can think of no blow that could possibly afflict me more sorely. And yet even that terrible stroke, gentlemen, would not make me oblivious of the high esteem in which you have always held me. And if you, for your part, have forgotten that this has been so, or if you have taken offence against me in some way, I beg you to exact reprisal not from Milo but from myself. If I die before I see him suffer such a fate, I shall feel I have not lived in vain.

Meanwhile, Titus Annius, one thing and one thing only brings me consolation. That is the thought that I have given you every service of affection and support and friendship that is in my power. On your behalf I courted the hostility of the great; to your enemies' weapons I continually exposed my body and my life; for your sake, before a host of different people, I prostrated myself in supplication. In order to be with you in your adversity I have risked all my property and my possessions and my children's as well. On this very day, moreover, if violence is to be your fate, if a life and death struggle lies ahead, I demand that I too should not be spared. What, then, can still be done? What further recompense can I offer in return for all your services to myself, except to demand an equal share of whatever fortune awaits you? I will not shrink from the challenge; it shall not be refused. And consequently I entreat you, gentlemen, crown all the kindnesses you have ever done me by acquitting my client today. Or note very clearly that, if you choose to destroy him instead, all those kindnesses shall go for nothing.

Milo, however, is not moved by all these tears. His reserves of spiritual strength are unbelievable. There is no such thing as exile, he maintains, except where virtue finds no place; and death is a natural termination, not a penalty. Thereby he shows his inborn disposition. But you, gentlemen, what will your disposition be? You cannot help retaining the memory of Milo in your midst; and do you really propose to expel the man himself? And yet nowhere is there a land which should more readily harbour his noble personality than the very place which brought it into existence. Judges, you are men of well-tested valour, who have spilt much blood in the defence of your country: and I appeal to you. And to you also I appeal, centurions and soldiers. For a man and a citizen of invincible courage is facing his ordeal. Before your very eyes, despite all the weapons in your hands, in a court enjoying your protective care, are we going to see this magnificent figure evicted from our city, and cast into banishment?

What a desperate personal tragedy that would be for me! For it was you, Milo, with the help of these gentlemen here, who was able to secure my return to our homeland.[54] It would be terrible to think that, by the judgement of these same arbiters, I had failed to prevent you from having to go away yourself. For how, if that happened, could I ever reply to the questions of my children, who regard you as a second father? How could I answer you, my brother Quintus, who are now far away but were the partner of those dangerous hours? It would be shameful to have to explain that, by reason of a decision made by the very same men who saved myself, I in my turn had failed to bring protection to Milo –

54. The judges are spoken of as representative of those who voted for the law which recalled Cicero from exile.

and protection in a cause applauded by every nation that exists. Protection from whom? From people who were, in fact, more delighted than anyone else that Publius Clodius was dead! And who was pleading his cause? I myself. Did I then commit such a dreadful deed, gentlemen, such an abominable crime, when I tracked down the conspiracy that threatened the destruction of our nation,[55] when I disclosed it and brought it out into the light and annihilated the whole evil plot? Well, that was the source of all the sorrows which have since then afflicted me and mine. Was that why you wanted me to be back with you – merely so that I should have to watch the banishment of those who had enabled me to return? The day of my departure was bitter, but do not, I implore you, make my homecoming even harder to endure. For how can I think of myself as recalled in any true sense of the word if I am torn apart from the very man who made my restoration possible?

If only heaven had arranged – forgive me, Rome, for what I am now about to say, for the wish I am expressing in Milo's interests may, I fear, be criminally harmful to your own. But I am obliged to pronounce the wish that Publius Clodius had lived after all! And had not only lived but become praetor and consul and even dictator – anything rather than that I should have survived to see what I am seeing today. For Milo, heaven knows, is a truly valiant man: a man whom you will do well to preserve. He himself, it is true, speaks in different terms. Of Clodius he says it is good that he received the punishment he merited. 'But as for myself,' he goes on, 'let me, if I must, be punished as well – though I have done nothing whatever to deserve it.'

Milo was born to serve his country. Surely, then, it cannot be right that he should be forbidden to die within its bounds – or at least while continuing to fight on its behalf. The reminders

55. The reference is to Cicero's suppression of the Catilinarian conspiracy.

of his heroism will always be with you – and yet do you really propose to allow him no corner of Italian soil for the burial of his body? If Milo went into exile, he would be welcomed by every other city in the world. How, then, could anyone venture to vote for the banishment of such a man as that? Blessed is the land which shall give sanctuary to this hero! Ungrateful Rome, if it shall cast him out! Unhappy Rome, if it shall be bereft of him!

But enough. Tears choke my voice; and my client does not want a tearful defence. What I am asking you, gentlemen, and asking you urgently, is that when you come to cast your votes, you should be brave enough to act as you really think is right. If you do, believe me, your fearlessness, impartiality and integrity will meet with sincere approval from the person who, in picking the judges, has permitted his choice to fall upon men who are conspicuous for their loyalty and their wisdom and their courage.

CHAPTER SIX

IN SUPPORT OF
MARCUS CLAUDIUS MARCELLUS

The inevitable Civil War between Pompeius and Caesar took place, and Cicero – who had just been intensely bored by his governorship of Cilicia – with great gloom and hesitation supported Pompeius (though he would not fight). Caesar had often been kinder than Pompeius, and had lent him money, but Cicero made his choice because Pompeius had arranged to have him brought back from exile – and because he seemed slightly the less likely of the two to bring about the final overthrow of the Republic if he won. After the defeat of Pompeius at Pharsalus (48), followed by his death, Cicero did not join the Pompeian forces which Caesar subsequently put down in Africa and Spain, but returned to Italy where after a miserable year at Brundisium (Brindisi) he accepted the offer from Caesar, now dictator and autocrat, of pardon and return. In 46 he broke his silence to deliver this speech in the Senate. It concerns the stiff-necked, ineffective but cultured Republican Marcus Marcellus who had held the consulship in 51, joined Pompeius, and after Pharsalus lived in retirement at Mytilene. His case was brought up in the Senate by Caesar's father-in-law Lucius Calpurnius Piso Caesoninus, and the Senate unanimously asked Caesar for his recall, which was granted (46).

Cicero buried the past sufficiently to stand up in the Senate and express thanks to the dictator for his gesture. There was no vote or issue to worry about, and the orator could devote himself to a demonstration of rich eloquence, a model (on the lines of the speech about Pompeius' command) for formal panegyrics of the future. His account of why he had joined Pompeius, stressing the personal link instead of his fear of Caesar's autocracy, is disingenuous. But only those who have lived under a dictatorship can have a clear apprecia-

tion of the problem this speech presented to Cicero. It is easy, and right, to be shocked at this fulsome praise of the autocrat against whom Cicero had sided and on whose death he was shortly to gloat. Nevertheless the speech does very ingeniously pass on to a firm request that the dictator should not consider his task complete until he had done a thousand things to set his house in order. He never did most of them, because he was murdered. But even if he had not died, he was about to leave on a prolonged eastern expedition; so it is at least open to doubt whether he was as keen on patient organization as on more spectacular glory – in which case Cicero put his finger on the crucial problem. His speech is a fascinating example of how a Republican, his cause destroyed, could yet bring himself to flatter the autocrat in the hope of guiding him to do the many things that needed doing; though he finally gave up the project of writing a whole essay to Caesar on the same subject.

Marcellus, learning of his pardon, wrote to Cicero – whom like most of his class he probably considered an upstart – in dignified yet by no means affectionate terms. He was in no hurry to return, but by May 45 had reached the Piraeus, where he was stabbed to death by a member of his staff. Some said that Caesar was responsible, but Cicero and Brutus were probably right in declaring the suspicion unjustified.

During this recent period, Senators, I have maintained a long silence,[1] due not to fear but to a combination of sorrow and diffidence. Today that silence comes to an end, and I now begin to resume my old custom of frankly expressing my hopes and thoughts. For it would be quite impossible for me to refrain from commenting on this remarkable leniency, this un-accustomed and indeed unprecedented clemency, this unique moderation on the part of a ruler whose power is supreme, this unbelievable and almost superhuman wisdom. Moreover, I venture to point out that this decision reuniting Marcus Marcellus with yourselves, gentlemen, and with our national

1. Cicero had not spoken in the Senate for two years.

life, means that the Senate and the state are able to regain and resume the use not only of his own voice and influence but of my own as well. For I had found it a source of profound pain and grief, Senators, that a man of this calibre, who had supported the same cause as I, should have suffered so different a fate. And so I could not bring myself – I should not have thought it right – to continue in that career we once shared, seeing that he, my competitor and emulator and indeed partner and companion in those pursuits, had been torn from my side.

And so now, Gaius Caesar, what you have done is to allow my old occupation, from which I had been severed, to be thrown open to me again; and to all other Senators, likewise, you have raised aloft a signal of hope for the future of Rome. For one thing has become very clear to me from the experiences of numerous people and most of all from my own; and it has of late become universally apparent, now that after explaining your grievance against him[2] you have vouchsafed Marcus Marcellus to the Senate and commonwealth of Rome. I refer to the fact that the authority of this Order and the greatness of our nation evidently take priority, in your mind, over any resentments or suspicions which you yourself may harbour.

This fulfilment of the Senate's unanimous desire, by means of your own authoritative and weighty decision, has today granted Marcus Marcellus the supreme reward for his entire career; and when it is so blessed to receive, you can see how glorious it is to give. Marcellus, moreover, is going to derive a very special satisfaction from the fact that the delight with which he himself will learn of his recall is scarcely greater than the universal rejoicing inspired by the news. And nothing could be more fully deserved, more amply justified! For Marcellus is a man whose character is as outstanding as

2. Caesar had at first pointed out the hostility that M. Marcellus, unlike his colleague, had shown to him during his consulship of 51.

his birth. His learning rivals his integrity; he shines in every field.

As for your own deeds, Gaius Caesar, no genius could be abundant enough, no pen or tongue sufficiently eloquent and fluent, to embellish them or even to describe them. Nevertheless I maintain, with all deference, that the glory you have gained today is greater than any you have ever won before. I am continually aware, and I constantly tell others, that all the exploits of Roman generals and foreign powers combined, all the achievements of the most potent nations and illustrious monarchs in the world, fall short of what you have achieved: so enormous was the magnitude of your enterprises, and the number of your battles, and the lightning rapidity with which you acted, and the immense diversity of the military operations involved. No one else upon this earth could have traversed all those widely separated lands with the amazing speed with which you marched – or rather, I should say, with which you conquered.

If I failed to declare that these triumphs virtually defy every effort of description or imagination, I should be an idiot. And yet – there are others still greater to record. For it is not unknown for people to make light of martial success, withdrawing the praise from the generals and distributing it instead among every member of their army, so that the commanders shall have no monopoly.[3] And indeed it has to be admitted that in warfare there are other important factors – the courage of the fighting man, for example, and the occupation of advantageous ground, and the support available from allies or the sea, and the efficient provision of supplies. Besides, the greatest part of all is almost automatically claimed by chance, which is inclined to take the credit for every favourable development.

3. E.g. this sentiment is expressed by Euripides, _Andromache_, l. 696.

This fame, on the other hand, which you have gained for yourself by your present act, Gaius Caesar, is shared with nobody. It is enormous, and it is all yours. Centurions, prefects, cohorts, squadrons – not a fraction of the merit belongs to any of them. Indeed, here is a case when even Fortune, who rules over the destinies of men, does not demand a share in your glory. She renounces all praise in your favour; she admits it is entirely your own. For where true wisdom dominates, chance can play no part. When the intellect is in charge, the role of accident disappears.

You have conquered nations of barbarous ferocity, immeasurable population, endless extent, gigantic and varied resources. And yet there was something in the nature and condition of those lands which made them amenable to conquest, seeing that no power on earth is mighty enough to be able to avoid becoming undermined and broken by a sufficient power of weapons. But to conquer one's own heart, to curb one's anger, to show restraint in victory – to raise up a prostrate enemy of splendid family and talent and character, and raise him up in a way that actually enhances the greatness that was his – the hero who acts in this way I do not venture to compare to the greatest of mankind, because he seems to me to resemble a god.

Your fame in war, Gaius Caesar, will be celebrated by the literature and eloquence of our own country and, one may almost add, of every nation in the world. There will never be a time when your praises are no longer sung. And yet, somehow or other, such deeds, even when one reads about them, are apt to be drowned by the shouting of soldiers and the sound of the trumpet's blast. But when, on the other hand, we hear or read of some act of mercy, kindness, justice, moderation and wisdom, especially if it is performed under stress of anger which is inimical to good counsel, and especially also if it takes place in the moment of victory which by its very nature is haughty and proud, then, whether the tale is of fact or of fiction, what enthusiasm fills our hearts! – so that we come to feel, very often, the deepest devotion towards men we have never seen.

But you, Caesar, we are able to gaze on face to face. We perceive your thoughts, and your emotions, and your countenance. They reveal to us your determination that whatever remnants of our political system the fortunes of war have allowed to survive shall henceforward be preserved. So what terms could be superlative enough to express the compliments, the devotion, and the gratitude that we want to shower upon you? I swear I see the very walls of this Senate House yearning to thank you because, so soon, the noble presence of Marcus Marcellus shall again grace the abode which he and his ancestors adorned before!

When, like yourselves, I witnessed the tears of our good friend Gaius Marcellus,[4] whose devotion to his family is so strong, the memory of all the other holders of his name came flooding into my mind. Even when they are beyond the grave, Caesar, your restoration of Marcus has meant that they, too, are restored to their ancient dignity: through your act that most noble house, dwindled to a mere handful of members today, has practically been rescued from extinction. And so you will have every right to esteem this day even more highly than those of all the magnificent festivals that have been held on innumerable occasions in your honour. For here is an exploit which belongs to Gaius Caesar and to Gaius Caesar alone.[5] Other actions performed under your leadership have been marvellous indeed, but they were triumphs which you shared with a multitude of others. In this present feat, on the

4. M. Marcellus' cousin C. Marcellus (not Marcus' brother of the same name), consul in 50, hostile to Caesar who had tried to transfer his great-niece Octavia, wife of Marcellus, to Pompeius. He precipitated the Civil War but like Marcus took no actual part in it.

5. But Cicero's son-in-law P. Cornelius Dolabella, the third husband of Tullia, had acted as go-between in negotiations with Caesar about M. Marcellus' return.

other hand, you are not only the leader: the entire deed is your own.

One day, your trophies and monuments will be no more. For there is no work of human hands which time does not eventually wear away and reduce to dust. But what you have accomplished now is something so outstanding that the memory of your just and merciful spirit shall wax ever more vigorously as day succeeds to day. What time chips away from your monuments it shall add to your renown! You had already outdone all previous conquerors in civil war by your fairness and leniency; and today you have outdone even yourself. Indeed, I would like to put it like this – though I am afraid I may not express very clearly the thought I want to convey. It seems to me that what you have done is to vanquish Victory, since everything that Victory had placed in your hand you have let the vanquished have back. By the law of conquest, we on the losing side could well have perished. But by your mercy you have deliberately saved us. You are therefore invincible in the most accurate sense of the word, since you have conquered the savage law of Victory itself.

And note, gentlemen, the immense repercussions of the decision which Gaius Caesar has taken. For the result of it is that all those of us who were prompted by some unhappy, lethal destiny to involve ourselves in that war, even if we must be called guilty of some human error, have at least been absolved of any crime. Moreover, when Caesar in response to your appeal saved Marcellus for his country, and when on an earlier occasion, even before an appeal was made, he restored me also – to the state as well as to myself – and when he gave back all those other distinguished men to themselves and to Rome (and you see them here today, gathered together in full force and dignity), it was by no means the case that he was introducing enemies into the Senate House. No, he had decided that most of them had entered the war because of a mixture of ignorance and unjustified, baseless anxiety, rather than from any motives of a selfish or vindictive kind.

I myself, throughout the whole course of the war, invariably believed that peace proposals should be given a hearing. I was continually sad that peace, and even recommendations in favour of peace talks, met with rejection. Neither in this civil war nor in any other did I myself take part. My policy was invariably directed towards peace and the arts of peace, and never towards war and violence. The leader I followed received my support in his individual capacity, as a man to whom I possessed personal obligations, and not because of any political link. The memory of what he had done for me required a grateful recompense, and so, without regard for my own interests and indeed even without any hope, I plunged voluntarily, with my eyes open, to destruction. And there was nothing secret about my policy. For before war had broken out I argued at length in favour of peace, and after hostilities had started I still maintained the same attitude – at the risk of my life.

Now, in relation to these matters, even the most biased interpreter of events could feel no doubt regarding Caesar's attitude to the war. For, while retaining a measure of resentment against others who had joined the opposite side, he unhesitatingly decided that those of us who had argued in favour of peace should be restored. This moderation was not, perhaps, so remarkable while the result of the war still hung uncertainly in the balance. But the man who in the hour of victory favours those who had spoken up for peace reveals that he himself would have preferred not to have fought in the first place rather than to have fought and won.

And, in this same connexion, I can testify to the attitude that Marcus Marcellus adopted; for our opinions were invariably identical in time of war, just as they had already coincided in peace. Often, with sorrowful sympathy, I have seen him exhibit the deepest apprehension about the arrogant intransigence of certain individuals in his own camp – and about the ferocity which victory for their side could have let loose.

This, Gaius Caesar, is a reason why we, who have been through these experiences, are all the more grateful for your mercy. For we are in a position not only to match cause against cause, but to consider how the one victory would have compared with the other. As for you, we have seen your triumph reach finality when you prevailed in battle – inside the city, on the other hand, we never had to witness a sword drawn from its scabbard. The citizens we lost were destroyed by the fury of Mars and not by the victor's rage, and it should be clear to everyone that if Gaius Caesar were able to summon them up from the dead he would do so in numerous cases, since, as it is, he saves as many of the survivors as he can. But with regard to that other side, I will only say this: its victory would have been quite as ruthless as we all feared. For we heard some of those people threatening not only their enemies in arms but on certain occasions non-combatants as well, and claiming that the relevant point was not a man's political opinions but where he had been. Well, the immortal gods, who stirred up so terrible and tragic a civil war, were evidently exacting retribution from the Roman people for some sin it had committed. But now they are at last appeased or glutted, and have concentrated all their hopes for a happy future upon the clemency and wisdom of the conqueror.

So you have the utmost reason to congratulate yourself, Caesar, on this wonderful situation. Make the most of your good fortune and renown! And make the most, above all, of your own natural character, a thing in which every sensible man finds the principal source of his strength and happiness. When you recollect all your other exploits, you will have cause very frequently to thank your own talents, in addition to the fortune with which you have often been blessed. But whenever your attention turns in the direction of ourselves, whom you have welcomed as your associates in public life, you will have every reason to be proud of your outstanding acts of kindness, your extraordinary generosity, and your remarkable wisdom. And these are things which I have no hesitation in describing as the chief and indeed the only good things in life. For true merit, greatness of heart, and dis-interestedness shine out so brilliantly that they have the ap-pearance of gifts bestowed by virtue itself, while all else is but a loan borrowed from chance.

So be tireless, I beg you, in your task of rescuing good citizens, and particularly those who lapsed not from any selfish or evil motives but because they had conceived an in-terpretation of their duty which was perhaps foolish yet surely not criminal – and because, also, they had a certain theoretical idea of what seemed to them to be in the public interest. If some people have feared you, the fault is not yours. On the contrary, it is highly to your credit that the majority realized there was so little cause to be afraid of you after all!

Now I pass to certain suspicions which you have entertained: and you have expressed them in the severest terms. These are suspicions which make vigilance an imperative duty not only for yourself but for the entire citizen body, and most of all for us who owe you our preservation. Your suspicions are, I trust, unfounded; but nothing will induce me to make light of them. For precautions taken on your behalf are taken on behalf of us all, and if we have to exaggerate in one direction or the other I should rather be too careful than too negligent.

But who is the madman you have in mind? Is it one of your own supporters? But that term now needs redefining, since no one could now support you more strongly than the men you granted a salvation for which they had not even dared to hope. So let me be more explicit, and ask if you are thinking of one of the people who were your associates? Only a madman would value the life of the leader, who has given him his heart's desire, any less highly than he prizes his own life. Clearly, then, your friends cannot possibly have any such abominable intentions. So should you look for them instead among your enemies? But who on earth can these be? For all the men who have been your enemies in the past have either lost their lives through their own stubbornness or have kept them owing to your mercy. Either they are dead, or if they have survived they are now your staunchest friends.

And yet, since the hearts of men contain dark corners and obscure recesses, it is by no means in our interest to soothe your suspicions. We ought instead to intensify them; if we do we shall intensify your vigilance as well. For no one in the world, however naïve and ignorant of politics, however unperceptive of what is the right thing for himself and his country, could possibly fail to appreciate the extent to which his own welfare is bound up with yours, with the result that the survival of the whole community depends upon the survival of yourself alone. As I think of you day and night – and it is only proper that I should do so – my anxieties are concentrated upon the risks of mortal life, the uncertainties of health, the frailness of mankind. Our country should be immortal; and so I am unhappy that its future should depend on the breath of a single man. And if the hazards of the human condition and the precariousness of human health are supplemented by sinister and treacherous conspiracy, it becomes hard to see how even a god, if he wanted to, could rescue our country from disaster.

It is for you and you only, Gaius Caesar, to revive all you see lying in ruins around you, inevitably shattered and overthrown by the violent shock of war. Law courts have to be reorganized, credit re-established, licentious passions checked, the birthrate raised.[6] Everything that is now in a state of disintegration and collapse needs to be knit together by rigorous legislative measures. It was only to be expected that a civil war of such dimensions, accompanied by such ferocious feelings and formidable combats, would deprive our nation, whichever side won, of many of its elements of greatness and safeguards of stability. For the leaders of both parties alike were bound to do things under arms which they would not have allowed in times of peace. All these are the war wounds that you have to heal – and no one can heal them but yourself.

That is why I was so distressed to hear your remark, sage and splendid though it is, 'Whether for nature or for glory, I have lived long enough.' Long enough perhaps for nature, if you like, and even for glory, if you must have it so: but certainly not long enough for your country, and that is the most important point of all! So let us hear nothing, please, of that famous wisdom of the philosophers who talk slightingly of death: do not, by being wise yourself, imperil us! Word often reaches me that this observation about having had a long enough life is too frequently on your lips.[7] I know you are sincere, but I would only accept such a statement if it were for yourself alone that you are living and were born to live. As it is, on the contrary, the welfare of every Roman citizen and the whole state has become dependent on what you do. And so far are you, to this day, from having completed your greatest achievements that you have not even laid the foundations of all that needs to be planned.

How, then, can you venture to determine the length of your life according to your own peace of mind instead of by the interests of your country? If that is what you are going to do, are you even sure that this life of yours will be sufficiently

6. Caesar gave financial aid to large families.

7. These ideas inspired by Epicurus corresponded with the known views of Caesar.

glorious? And for glory you must admit that, wise though you are, you feel an intense ambition. 'What!' I can hear you saying. 'Do you mean that the achievement I shall leave behind me is going to be as insignificant as all that?' No, it would be large enough for other men, indeed for a whole host of other men added together. It is only for you that it will fall short. For everything you achieve, however enormous, cannot fail to be too small for you so long as something greater remains. If then, Gaius Caesar, the outcome of your mortal deeds is that, after crushing your enemies, you propose to take your leave of the commonwealth while it is still in the condition in which it finds itself today, you will run the risk, for all your superhuman exploits, of gaining astonishment rather than glory as your reward: if, that is to say, we are right to interpret glory as meaning a brilliant, universal renown earned by mighty services to one's fellow-citizens and one's country and the world.

This phase, then, still awaits you. This act of the drama has not yet been played. This is the programme to which you must devote all your energies: the re-establishment of the constitution, with yourself the first to reap its fruits in profound tranquillity and peace. And then, if you wish, after you have paid your country what you owe her, after you have fulfilled your debt to nature itself, after you have really had your fill of life – then and then only you may talk of having lived long enough. And in any case what does the word 'long' signify, if it carries the implication of an eventual end? For when that arrives, all the pleasures of the past are in any case of no account, because there are no more to come. Besides, your great spirit has never been satisfied with the narrow limits by which nature bounded our lives, since it has always blazed with a passion for immortality. You would be wrong to identify your life with the mere confines of body and breath. For your true life, I insist, is the one which shall wax in the memory of all ages to come, cherished by every future generation of mankind and preserved to all eternity. This is the life for which you must put forth your endeavours and display your real greatness. Mankind has long had reason to be amazed by your achievements. But now it is looking for deeds which it may praise.

Posterity will be staggered to hear and read of the military commands you have held and the provinces you have ruled – Rhine, Atlantic, Nile – battles without number, fabulous victories, monuments and shows and Triumphs. And yet unless you now restore this city of ours to stability by measures of reorganization and lawgiving, your renown, however far and wide it may roam, will never be able to find a settled dwelling-place or firm abode. For among men still unborn, as among ourselves, there will rage sharp disagreements. Some will glorify your exploits to the skies. But others, I suggest, may find something lacking, and something vital at that, if you do not extinguish the conflagration of civil war, bring salvation to your country, and thereby prove that whereas those hostilities were caused by fate their remedy must be credited to your own deliberate act. Work, I pray you, for a verdict from the judges who are to pronounce it many ages from now. Their decision is likely to be more unbiased than our own, since they will be judging without partisanship or self-interest, without rancour or animosity. And even if, as some falsely believe, you will be beyond the reach of this judgement when it comes, still it is vital for you, here and now, to act so as to make quite sure that your fame shall never be overtaken by oblivion.

The purposes and standpoints of our citizens have been divergent and opposed. Not only were we sundered by differences about policies and ideals, but we had even taken up arms among ourselves and were split apart into two camps. The situation was highly confused. Two famous generals were at war with one another. Many people could not make up their minds which side to support, which side it was in their interest to support, which side it was their duty to support – and, in certain cases, which side it was even legally permissible to support. Yet our country got through this horrible war it was fated to undergo. The winner, however, was not the sort of man whose enmities were fomented by success: on the contrary, his natural kindliness favoured their mitigation. If people had earned his resentment, he did not necessarily believe they must be deserving of exile or death. Some of his foes laid down their weapons, others had them torn from their hands. But any man who is freed from the menace of arms and yet still remains armed within his soul is being ungrateful and unjust. Even he who has fallen in battle, shedding his life-blood for his cause, is better off; for although some would attribute his fate to obstinacy, in the eyes of others he has acted bravely.

But now all dissension has been suppressed by the verdict of war – and extinguished by the fairness of the victor: so that all men with even a minimum of wisdom or commonsense must obviously be united in their present political views. For our safety depends on your safety, Gaius Caesar, and on your continued adherence to the policy you have chosen to adopt hitherto, and above all today. And consequently all those of us who are devoted to the welfare of our country urge and entreat you to take good care of your life and your personal safety. Moreover, I know I am speaking for my colleagues when I add a further conviction of my own. Since you feel there is some hidden danger to guard against, we promise you sentinels and bodyguards. And we swear we will protect you ourselves with our own breasts and bodies.

But let me end on the note upon which I began. Gaius Caesar, we offer you our profoundest gratitude – and even that does not do justice to what is in our hearts. For as you have been able to appreciate from the pleas and tears of us all, our feelings are unanimous. There is no need for everyone to stand and speak, but it is at everyone's wish that I am telling you these things; and I have a very special obligation to do so. The official response which should fittingly follow your restoration of Marcus Marcellus to this Order and the Roman people and the state is, I understand, being conveyed. For I know very well that the joy we all feel reflects the belief that it is not merely one single individual who has been granted salvation, but our entire community.

My special friendship towards Marcus Marcellus has always been well known. Indeed, in this respect, I would scarcely yield place to his good and devoted brother Gaius, and certainly to no one else. While the recall of Marcus was still in doubt I gave constant proofs of this dedication by my anxious, unremitting efforts on his behalf, and now that my anxiety and worry and sorrow are at an end, I particularly want to demonstrate again how profound my affection is. And that is why I am offering you my thanks, Gaius Caesar. I owe you my preservation in every sense of the word: and to preservation you have added honour. Today, however – though I would never have thought such a thing to be possible – your numberless acts of kindness on my behalf have actually been exceeded by this latest deed of yours which magnificently crowns the rest.

CHAPTER SEVEN

THE FIRST PHILIPPIC AGAINST
MARCUS ANTONIUS

After the murder of Caesar his assassins had apparently thought that the Republic would automatically revive. But it rapidly became clear that this was not so, and Marcus Antonius, who had been Caesar's deputy (Master of the Horse), showed his intention of seizing dictatorial power for himself. Within a month of the menacing popular manifestations at Caesar's funeral, Brutus and Cassius had found it prudent to leave Rome, to which they never returned, sailing east from Italy in August 44 B.C. With the field apparently to himself (the young Octavian, Caesar's personal heir, not yet being regarded as a serious threat) Antonius exploited his possession of Caesar's papers, recruited troops, and irregularly secured a tenure of Transalpine and Cisalpine Gaul for five years.

Cicero had left the capital, to the accompaniment of much criticism, notably from his best friend the knight Titus Pomponius Atticus, and from Brutus. When he finally returned on 31 August from a despairing, abortive journey towards Greece, Antonius assailed him in the Senate on the following day for failing to attend. On 2 September Cicero put in an appearance and delivered the present speech. It was the first of a series of fourteen attacks on Antonius which were called Philippics (first by Cicero himself, half jokingly) in imitation of the speeches which the Athenian orator Demosthenes had delivered against King Philip II of Macedonia (351–341 B.C.).

The Second Philippic is the most ferocious and famous,[1] but this first speech (which, unlike it, was actually delivered in something approaching its present form) is interesting because its tone is moderate and reasonable and avoids scurrilities. Yet it earned a violent riposte, and the battle was joined.

1. Translated in *Cicero: Selected Works*, Penguin Classics, 1960.

Because of his Philippics Cicero has often been regarded through-out the ages as the champion of liberty, and it is true that he ex-presses in them that perfectly authentic devotion to non-autocratic forms of government which is his finest and also his most unvarying quality. When so hesitant and peace-loving a person as this rises to the occasion it is a remarkable achievement. Here, 'spurred to desperate action,' as Sir Ronald Syme remarks, 'by the memory of all the humiliations of the past', Cicero rises to the occasion more vigorously than ever before in his life. He was prepared to risk any-thing to try to restore his beloved Republic and his own freedom of speech and action, and the attempt did, indeed, cost him his life.

Although the Republican consuls, together with the young Octavian, defeated Antonius at Mutina (Modena) in April 43 B.C., neither consul survived, and Octavian joined Antonius and Lepidus in the Second Triumvirate, a committee of joint dictators. Antonius ensured that the lengthy list of their proscriptions should include Cicero's name. He decided to escape across the Adriatic, but changed his plans many times. His servants did not betray him (as his brother Quintus was betrayed), but on 7 December 43 B.C. the agents of the triumvirs came upon him near Formiae. They cut off his head, and the hands which had written the denunciations of Antonius; then Fulvia, wife of Antonius and widow of Clodius, thrust a hair-pin through his tongue. In 42 Brutus and Cassius fell at Philippi in Macedonia, and the Republic was no more. Eleven years later Octavian, soon to be Augustus, overwhelmed Antonius; and a new order, which Cicero would not have enjoyed, was on the way.

Senators, before I offer the views on the political situation which the circumstances seem to me to demand, I will briefly indicate to you the reasons, first why I left Rome, and then why I turned back again.

As long as it still seemed possible to hope that you had re-sumed your control and authority over the government, I felt determined, as consul and Senator, to remain at my post.

And so, from the day when we were summoned to meet in the Temple of Tellus,[2] I made no journeys and never lifted my eyes from public affairs. In that temple I did all that was within my power to lay the foundations of peace. I reminded members of the ancient precedent created by the Athenians[3] – making use in my oration of the Greek term which that state then employed to calm down civil strife – and I moved that every memory of our internal discords should be effaced in everlasting oblivion.

Marcus Antonius made a fine speech on that day, and his intentions were excellent. It was, indeed, he and his children[4] who made it possible for peace to be established with the greatest of our fellow-citizens. What followed was in harmony with these beginnings. He held consultations on the national situation at his home, and invited the political leaders to attend. He offered admirable recommendations to the Senate. At that stage nothing was disinterred from Gaius Caesar's notebooks except matters that were generally known already. In his reply to every question Antonius was completely direct. Were any exiles recalled? One,[5] he said, and nobody else. Were any tax-exemptions granted? None, he replied. He even wanted us to accept the proposal of the illustrious Servius Sulpicius[6] that no announcement should be posted of any decree or favour attributed to Caesar which had originated subsequently to the Ides of March. Of the many other excellent measures of Marcus Antonius I will say nothing, because I want to pass immediately to one particular

2. The Senate had met in the temple of Tellus (Earth) on the Esquiline on 17 March 44.

3. The restored Athenian democrats under Thrasybulus granted the oligarchs an amnesty in 403.

4. Antonius sent his two-year-old son M. Antonius (Antyllus) to the Capitol as a hostage.

5. With Cicero's reluctant agreement, Sex. Cloelius had been recalled from exile.

6. The famous lawyer Ser. Sulpicius Rufus, consul in 51.

admirable step that he took. The dictatorship, which had come
to usurp virtually monarchical powers, was completely
eliminated from the Roman constitution by his agency; we
did not even debate the question. He brought us a draft of the
decree he wanted the Senate to adopt,[7] and when this was
read out we accepted his proposal with the utmost enthusiasm,
and passed a highly complimentary vote of thanks in his
honour. The prospect ahead of us now seemed brilliant. For
we had won liberation from the tyranny under which we
had been labouring and, what is more, from all fears of
similar tyranny in the future. Although there had often been
legitimate dictators in the past, men could not forget the perpetual dictatorship of recent times, and by abolishing the
entire office Marcus Antonius gave the state a mighty proof
that he wanted our country to be free.

And then again, only a few days later, the Senate was delivered from the peril of a massacre when the runaway slave
who had appropriated the name of Marius was executed and
dragged away on a hook.[8] All these deeds were performed
jointly with his colleague; other things, later, were done by
Dolabella alone, but I am sure that if his colleague had not
been away these also would have been matters for collaboration. For during this period a most pernicious trouble was in-
sinuating itself into the city and gaining strength day by day.
The same men who had organized that travesty of a burial
were now building a funeral monument in the Forum.[9]
Every day an increasing number of ruffians, together with
their equally degraded slaves, menaced the dwellings and
temples of the city with destruction. But these impudent

7. In the Third Philippic Cicero criticizes this accelerated procedure.
8. The bodies of executed criminals were dragged by a hook to the
top of the Scalae Gemoniae and then down into the Tiber.
9. The agitator was Herophilus (Amatius), a veterinarian (or oculist)
by profession, who after several days' rioting was executed by Antonius
without trial before mid-April. He had put up an altar to Caesar; and a
column had also been erected near by.

criminal slaves, and their loathsome and infamous counterparts who were free, met their deserts from Dolabella when he pulled that accursed column down. So determined was his action that I am amazed by the contrast[10] between that day and all the others which have followed.

For by the first of June, the date fixed for our meeting, you can see how everything had been transformed. Nothing was any longer done through the Senate, many significant measures were passed through the Assembly of the people – and others, what is more, without even consulting the Assembly, and against its wishes. The consuls elect[11] declared they did not dare come into the Senate at all. The liberators[12] of our country, too, were excluded from the very city which they had rescued from servitude – though the consuls simultaneously kept on praising them at public meetings and in private talk. Moreover, ex-soldiers claiming veteran rights, on whose behalf this Senate had shown great solicitude, were being egged on to cherish hopes of new plunder in addition to what they already possessed.

I came to the conclusion it was less disagreeable to hear of these things than to see them for myself; and, besides, I was entitled to go travelling on a special mission.[13] This being so, I left Rome with the intention of being back by the first of the following January – which seemed the earliest likely date for a meeting of this body.

And so those, Senators, were the circumstances which prompted my departure. I will now indicate briefly the motives behind my return – which no doubt gives greater cause for

10. The sudden transformation is a dramatic exaggeration, as Cicero's own letters show.

11. The consuls elect were C. Vibius Pansa and A. Hirtius.

12. The liberators (assassins of Caesar) Brutus and Cassius had left Rome before mid-April.

13. At this period Senators wishing to leave Italy sought an honorary mission (*legatio libera*) which enabled them to travel at public expense.

surprise. After avoiding Brundisium and the usual route to Greece – as it was only sensible to do[14] – I arrived on the first of August at Syracuse, since the crossing from there to Greece was well spoken of. But although I was associated with that city by the closest ties,[15] I could not allow it to detain me for more than a single night, despite its desire to do so, because I was afraid that my sudden arrival among my friends there might arouse suspicion if I lingered. And so I proceeded with a fair wind to Leucopetra, which is a promontory in the district of Rhegium, and there I embarked to cross over to Greece.

But I had not gone very far when a southerly gale blew me back to my embarkation point. It was the middle of the night, and I stopped at the house of my friend and associate Publius Valerius. On the next day, while I was waiting there in the hope of a favourable wind, a number of citizens of Rhegium came to see me, including newcomers from Rome. They supplied my first news of Marcus Antonius' speech, which pleased me so much that after reading it I first began to consider the idea of returning to Rome. A little later the manifesto of Brutus and Cassius arrived,[16] and it seemed to me – perhaps because I esteem them as national figures even more highly than as personal friends – a model of fair-mindedness. But bearers of good news have the habit of inventing additional points to give their message an even better welcome than it would otherwise receive, and so my informants added that an agreement[17] was about to be reached, that there would be a

14. The legions which Antonius intended to transport from Macedonia to Gaul were due to disembark at Brundisium. Cicero's letters show his many changes of mind.

15. Cicero had won many Sicilian friends as quaestor at Lilybaeum (75) and prosecutor of Verres (70).

16. Towards the end of July Brutus and Cassius, dissatisfied with the duties of superintending the corn-supply of Rome which had been assigned to them (5 June), issued a manifesto requesting Antonius to allow them to resign the commission.

17. i.e. an agreement between Antonius and the Liberators.

well-attended meeting of the Senate on the first of August, and that Antonius was going to drop his bad advisers, renounce his governorship of the Gallic provinces, and resume his allegiance to the authority of the Senate.

On hearing this I felt so enthusiastic to come back that no oars and no winds were speedy enough to satisfy my impatience – not that I imagined I would fail to return in time, but I was eager not to waste a moment in offering the government my congratulations. I made a quick passage to Velia, where I saw Brutus; though I found this a sorrowful meeting.[18] I for my part was overcome by shame at the idea of returning to the city which Brutus had just left, and consenting to live there in security when he could not do the same. However, I did not find him as upset as I was myself. For he was exalted by the consciousness of his superb and magnificent deed. And he had no complaints to make about his own fate – but many about yours.

It was he who gave me my first information about Lucius Piso's[19] speech in the Senate on August the first. Piso had received little support, Brutus said, from the people who ought to have backed him. And yet in Brutus' opinion – which is the most authoritative view you could have – and according also to the complimentary comments of everyone I have spoken to since then, his effort was evidently a noble one. And so I hastened back to lend him my aid. My purpose was not so much to accomplish anything concrete, for such a thing I neither expected nor, in fact, achieved. But this is a time when many things contrary to the order of nature and even against the ordinary course of fate seem likely to happen at any moment, and, in case the doom that is common to all of us

18. Brutus mentioned, and agreed with, the widespread criticisms of Cicero's absence.

19. L. Calpurnius Piso Caesoninus (violently attacked by Cicero in 55, and leader of the move for Marcellus' recall in 46), evidently took a bold and independent line in the speech to which Cicero refers.

should come my way, I wanted to bequeath our country the sentiments I am now expressing, as a testimonial of my eternal devotion to its welfare.

Well, those, Senators, were the motives for my two successive courses of action, and I trust I have explained them to your satisfaction. And now, before I begin to speak about the political question, I feel obliged to enter a brief protest about the injustice Antonius did me yesterday. I am his friend, and, because of a service he rendered me,[20] I have always insisted on maintaining that this is so. Then why, I should like to know, did he show such unpleasantness in endeavouring to drag me to yesterday's Senate meeting? Was I the only absentee? Were the numbers of those present lower than on many previous occasions? Did the matter under discussion attain the degree of gravity which has sometimes in the past meant that even sick men had to be carried to meetings? Are you telling me that Hannibal himself was at the gates?[21] Or perhaps we were considering the question of peace with Pyrrhus – since that, tradition records, was the debate for which the great Appius, blind and old, had himself carried into the Senate.[22] But no: the motion was about public thanksgivings, and that is a subject for which Senators are not usually in short supply. Securities need not be called for to guarantee their attendance, since this is ensured by their eagerness to show goodwill to the proposed recipients of the honour; and the same applies when a Triumph is being discussed. On such occasions the consuls can afford to be so indifferent that a Senator is virtually free to attend or not as he pleases.

I knew that this was the practice; and I was tired after my

20. Antonius claimed that he had saved Cicero's life at Brundisium in 48. In any case, he had treated him courteously.

21. Hannibal's dash for Rome in 211 had become proverbial.

22. Ap. Claudius Caecus persuaded the Senate to reject Pyrrhus' peace terms after the latter's victory at Heraclea (280).

journey, and not very well. So for friendship's sake I sent a
message to inform Antonius. Whereupon he declared, in
your hearing, that he would come to my house with a
demolition squad. This was a remarkably ill-tempered and
immoderate way to talk. Whatever sort of an offence did he
suppose he was penalizing by this harsh declaration, in the
presence of the Senators, of his intention to use state employees
to demolish a residence that had been erected at state expense
in accordance with a decision of the Senate?[23] Never has
compulsion been applied to a Senator by any sanction as
severe as that. Indeed, the only known penalties are a security
or a fine. Besides, had he known the opinion I should have
expressed if I had in fact attended, I am sure he would have
wanted to relax the rigour of his coercive attitude quite a bit!

For you cannot imagine, gentlemen, that the decree you
yesterday passed so unwillingly would have had my support.[24] For that decree involved the confusion of a thanksgiving with a sacrifice in honour of the dead, and the
insertion of sacrilegious procedures into the state religion –
for such was the effect of proclaiming a thanksgiving in honour
of a man who was no longer alive. The question of his identity
is neither here nor there. Even if he were that famous Brutus[25]
himself, the man who by his own hand liberated the country
from the tyranny of royal rule, whose descendants have
maintained the same tradition of active heroism for very
nearly five hundred years, still nothing would induce me to
equate a dead human being with the immortal gods by
awarding him a public thanksgiving when he should instead
have had honours rendered to him in his grave. No, the vote I

23. Cicero's house on the Palatine was rebuilt at public expense after
his return from exile (57).

24. Perhaps Antony's proposal was that at the end of every thanksgiving to the gods prayers should be offered to Caesar, whose deifi-
cation Cicero refused to accept.

25. L. Junius Brutus was the quasi-legendary hero of the expulsion of
the Tarquins (c. 510).

should have cast would have been one capable of justification
to the Roman people in case some outstanding catastrophe
such as a war or a plague or a famine overtook the country.
For some of these disasters have already actually come about;
while the rest, I fear, are impending. But as it is, all I can do
about yesterday's decree is entreat the gods to pardon the
people of Rome, who in any case do not like the measure –
and to pardon the Senate that only passed it with reluctance.

Well, as regards our other political ills, am I permitted to
offer my observations? For I regard myself at liberty (and
always shall) to fight in defence of my own position, and to
think nothing of death; and that will always be my attitude.
Only give me free access to this place, and I am prepared to
express my thoughts whatever the risk.

Well, gentlemen, I wish after all it had been possible for
me to attend on August the first! Not that it would have been
any use, but then at least there would not have been, as there
was, only one isolated consul whose behaviour lived up to his
own high rank and his country's needs. How sad that the
men who had received Rome's greatest favours failed to support Lucius Piso in his truly admirable motion! Was it for
this meagre result that the people of Rome made us consuls?
Were we supposed to enjoy the highest position that the state
is able to confer, and yet remain entirely oblivious of the
national interests? For not one single former consul supported Lucius Piso either by word of mouth or even by the
expression on his face!

Curse it, do you have to be voluntary slaves? I grant you that
a measure of servility may formerly have been unavoidable.
And I am also prepared to concede that my criticism need not
apply to every consular speaker indiscriminately. For I
distinguish between certain people whose silence I excuse[26]
and others who I feel are under an obligation to speak out.
The latter category, I regret to say, has incurred suspicion in

26. e.g. L. Julius Caesar, uncle of Antonius.

the eyes of the Roman people. This is not so much because they are frightened, though such a thing would certainly be shameful, but because for whatever reasons – and these are various – they have fallen short of what their eminent status demands.

First of all, therefore, I want to express the warm gratitude I feel towards Piso, who was undeterred by the practical limitations of what he could achieve for his country, and thought only of what his duty demanded that he should attempt. And then, as to my next point, Senators, I realize you may not feel sufficiently intrepid to support the point of view and course of action which I am now going to urge upon you. Nevertheless, I ask you to continue to listen with the same goodwill that you have shown me up to this point.

To begin with, then, I hold that the acts of Caesar ought to be retained. I say this not because I approve of them: for who could do that? No, I say it because I attach supreme importance to peace and tranquillity. I wish Marcus Antonius were here today (though I should prefer his advisers[27] to remain elsewhere!). But I suppose he has the right to be unwell – even if yesterday he did not allow it to myself. If he were here, he would tell me, or rather he would tell you, Senators, what line he adopts as regards the justification of Caesar's acts. The point is this: are the acts we are being asked to ratify the ones that are jotted down in scrappy memoranda and handwritten scrawls and notebooks produced on the sole authority of Antonius – or rather not even produced but merely quoted – whereas the acts that Caesar himself engraved on brass tablets, with the intention of preserving the national Assembly's directions and definitive laws, are to be totally disregarded? My own view is that nothing forms such an indissoluble part of Caesar's acts as the laws which were adopted on Caesar's proposal. But if, on the other hand, he once made some

27. An ironical reference to Antonius' bodyguard.

promise or other to somebody, does that also really have to be regarded as irrevocable, even though he was never able to give effect to it himself? It is true that in his lifetime he offered many promises which he did not, in fact, fulfil. But these promises of his which have been dug up after his death are so immensely numerous that they exceed the entire total of the favours he actually dispensed for services rendered, or as free gifts, during all the years of his life.

All the same, it is not by any means my intention to tamper with any of those items; I do not even propose to touch them. On the contrary, I am an enthusiastic defender of his excellent acts. For example, I sincerely wish that the funds he collected in the Temple of Ops[28] were still there this day. Blood-stained that money certainly was, but since it cannot be restored to its owners we could make good use of it today. However, let us put up with its dissipation – if it is a fact that this is what his acts laid down.

But surely the most important of all the acts of a civil officer of state, conducting the government through the powers vested in his person, are the laws which were passed on his initiative. Look for the acts of Gaius Gracchus;[29] you will find the Sempronian laws. Consider the acts of Sulla; the Cornelian laws are what you see. Or think of the third consulship of Pompeius[30] – what acts did that produce? Surely his legislation again. If you asked Caesar himself to describe his acts at Rome and in civil life, he would answer that he had sponsored many first-rate laws. But his handwritten notes, on the other hand, he would either regard as provisional and liable to emendation, or he would omit to

28. From early April onwards (or earlier) Antonius gradually embezzled Caesar's treasure in the Temple of Ops (harvest, plenty) on the Capitoline Hill.

29. C. Sempronius Gracchus, tribune 123.

30. Pompeius' third consulship: laws as sole consul in 52 (see speech in support of Milo).

produce them at all, or even if he produced them he would not wish for their inclusion among his acts. However, that is a point on which I am prepared, in certain instances, to give way and turn a blind eye. But the most important aspect of the matter relates to his laws, and in so far as they are concerned I am by no means ready to tolerate the annulment of Caesar's acts.

Take, for example, that exceptionally salutary and valuable law, frequently longed for in the happy days of the Republic, which provides that former praetors should not govern provinces for longer than a year, and former consuls for not more than two. Suppress this law, and how can you still speak of preserving Caesar's acts? And then again this bill that has been published about a third panel of judges[31] – surely it rescinds Caesar's entire legislation relating to those panels. If you are going to abolish Caesar's laws how on earth can you say you defend his acts? For it is totally illogical to suggest that everything he jotted down in a notebook to help his memory, however unjust and useless, must be regarded as part of his acts, whereas what he actually had passed by the people, voting in its Assembly of Centuries, is not going to be included among them at all.

But let us see what this new third panel is. It consists of centurions,[32] Antonius says. Well, they were authorized to serve as judges, were they not, by a Julian law, and before that by Pompeian and Aurelian laws. So they did serve: and not only in cases concerning a centurion but a Roman knight as well – and so it has come about that gentlemen of great valour and repute, former commanders of troops, have served as judges in the past and still do so to this day.[33] 'But those are

31. In 46 Caesar had suppressed the panel of tribunes of the treasury created by the *Lex Aurelia* (70) and *Pompeia* (55) (see pp. 28, 140).

32. Obscure. Perhaps the reference is to ex-officers who had served under Caesar.

33. The minimum age for a judge, earlier thirty, may now have been thirty-five.

not the men I am concerned with,' he continues. 'I want everyone who has ever commanded a unit of a hundred men to be a judge.' Even if you applied this principle to everyone who had served as a knight, which is after all a more distinguished rank, the argument would still be totally unconvincing. For when you appoint a judge it is perfectly proper to be guided by considerations of property and rank. 'But such qualifications do not interest me,' answers Antony. 'Indeed, I am proposing that judges should be taken from another category also: from private soldiers of the Legion of the Lark.[34] For without such a measure our supporters are sure they will suffer victimization.' But what an insult to these people whom (though nothing was further from their thoughts) you are proposing to mobilize as judges! For what your law implies is that the third panel is going to consist of members who will not dare to produce impartial verdicts. But, heavens, what a miscalculation on the part of the people who thought up the law! For what in fact will happen is that people of no standing who are now to be included among the judges will try to force themselves up out of their obscurity by producing the strictest possible decisions – calculating that these can get them promoted to grander panels instead of the undistinguished one to which, quite rightly, they had been allotted.

Another bill that has now been published rules that men convicted of violence and treason shall have the right to appeal to the Assembly. But, I ask you, is this a law at all – is it not rather a law to end all laws? And anyway, who cares nowadays whether this bill is persevered with or not? For there is not, in fact, one single person today awaiting trial under the laws concerned with those offences.[35] And I do not suppose

34. Cicero passes over this surprising assertion so lightly that it may be an exaggeration or only a rumour. The Legion of the Lark had been raised by Caesar in Narbonese Gaul.

35. The *Leges Juliae* of Caesar against riot and treason respectively.

that there will be anyone in the future either – since acts perpetrated by people under arms will clearly never be brought into court!

But the measure, we are told, is a popular one. What a good thing it would be if you really had something popular in mind![36] For in our present circumstances, Roman citizens are unanimous in their estimate of the country's political needs. So I cannot understand your enthusiasm to propose a law which, far from being a source of popularity, is bound to earn you discredit. For it is in the highest degree discreditable that a man who has committed violence and treason against the Roman people, and suffered condemnation for those offences, should forthwith be allowed to relapse into precisely the same violent behaviour which was responsible for his conviction. However, it is a waste of time to go on arguing about the proposed law. For obviously its real concern is not with the question of appeal at all. Its object, and your object in bringing it forward, is to prevent any and every prosecution under the laws in question. For how could one ever find a prosecutor idiotic enough to secure a conviction and thus expose himself to hostile crowds on someone else's payroll, or a judge rash enough to pronounce a sentence which will get him dragged before a gang of bribed toughs?

No, the bill is not really designed to give a right of appeal. What it does instead is to hand over two particularly useful laws and courts to suppression. In other words it offers young men a clear invitation to become riotous, seditious, pernicious citizens. One hesitates to think of the ruinous excesses to which rabid tribunes will be encouraged to go when these two courts for violence and treason are no more. Besides, the measure will also have the effect of superseding the laws of Caesar which rule that men convicted of the two offences in

36. Cicero plays on the political meaning of *popularis*, indicating a 'democrat' who acted through the Assembly of the people rather than the Senate.

question become outlaws banned from water and fire. Because, surely, to allow people condemned for these crimes to appeal[37] is tantamount to declaring that these acts of Caesar are abolished. Although I personally was never in favour of his acts, gentlemen, I nevertheless maintained that for unity's sake they ought to be kept intact. That is why I maintain that nothing should be done at this juncture to annul the laws he sponsored in his lifetime – or even, for that matter, the ones you now see published and posted after his death.

It is true that exiles are recalled from banishment – by a man who is dead. A dead man, again, has conferred citizenship, not merely on individuals but on entire nations and provinces.[38] A dead man has wiped out national revenues, by unlimited grants of exemption. And yet, even so, I assert my willingness to defend these measures, even when they are only guaranteed by a single individual's authority (a substantial authority, admittedly) and produced from his own house. But, if this is accepted, how on earth can we simultaneously urge the suppression of laws which Caesar himself read out in our presence and published and proposed, laws about provinces and about courts which he was well content to sponsor and considered indispensable to our national interests? When laws are publicly announced, as those were, at least we are afforded a chance to complain if we want to. But when we merely have to rely on hearsay to discover that a law has been passed at all, no such opportunity exists. And the laws produced by Antonius were passed without any prior advertisement whatever: we were not even shown a preliminary draft.

There is no reason, it is true, Senators, why I myself, or any of you, need have the slightest fear of bad laws being adopted so long as good tribunes are available. And we do possess such tribunes, men ready to apply their veto, ready to

37. An outlaw had no right of appeal to the people.
38. Antonius published a scheme of Caesar to grant Roman franchise to Sicily.

use their sacred office in defence of the constitution. Obviously we ought, then, to lack the slightest grounds for apprehension. 'But what is this veto,' asks Antonius, 'what sacred office are you talking about?' The answer is that the right of veto, and the office to which I refer,[39] are institutions fundamental to the security of the state. 'That does not impress us at all,' Antonius comments. 'We regard it as old-fashioned and stupid. What we shall do is to barricade the Forum and close all its entrances; detachments of armed men will be posted at numerous points.'

And then, I suppose, what is transacted in that fashion will be law. And you will give orders to have bronze tablets engraved with the legal formula 'the consuls by right of law put the question to the people'. But how can you call this the same right of putting the question which our forefathers handed down to us? The formula continues, 'and the people by right of law passed the measure'. Which people? The ones who were shut out? And what right of law? The law which armed violence has obliterated out of existence?

These observations are intended as guidance for the future – since it is the duty of a friend to offer advance warning against things that can still be avoided. If these unfortunate occurrences never materialize, then my comments will automatically be refuted. The bills I am talking about are ones which are going to be published in due form, and there is nothing to stop you from proposing whatever you like. But as for myself, I consider it my duty to forecast possible flaws and ask you for their removal – to denounce, in other words, armed violence, and to demand its elimination!

When patriotic motives impel me, Dolabella, to offer such suggestions, I am justified in hoping that you consuls will not take it amiss. I do not imagine that you yourself will be angry,

39. Tribunes possessed the right of veto against all officials except a dictator.

since I know what a good-tempered man you are. But people
are commenting that your colleague Marcus Antonius, as he
luxuriates in his present position which he regards as so fine
(though I would hold him more fortunate, to put it mildly, if
he modelled his consulship on those of his grandfathers and
his maternal uncle),⁴⁰ has taken offence. Now it is far from
agreeable, I can see, when a man who has something against
you holds a weapon in his hand – especially now that swords
can be used with such impunity. But I will propose a pact: it
seems to me a fair arrangement and I do not believe Antonius
will turn it down. That is to say, if I utter one single insulting
remark about his private life or his morals I shall not object to
him treating me as a bitter enemy. But if, on the other hand,
I merely adhere to the custom of my entire political career and
pronounce my frank opinion about national issues, first of all
I beg him not to be indignant with me, and next, if that plea
fails, I at least urge that his indignation should only be that of
one fellow-citizen against another. Let him by all means
employ an armed guard if this is needed, as he claims, for self-
defence; but do not let their weapons be used on people who
are expressing their views on public affairs. Now, what could
be a fairer request than that? However, if any and every
speech which goes against his wishes causes him to take
umbrage even though it may contain not a trace of an insult –
and some of his friends have told me that this is what happens
– then we shall just have to put up with our friend's disposition
and leave it at that. But these same henchmen of Antonius
also advise me, 'You as an opponent of Caesar will not be
allowed the same indulgence as Piso, who was the father of
his wife.'⁴¹ And at the same time they give me a word of

40. Antonius' grandparents were M. Antonius Orator and L. Julius
Caesar (consuls 99, 90), and his maternal uncle was L. Julius Caesar
(consul 64).

41. L. Calpurnius Piso Caesoninus was the father of Caesar's widow
Calpurnia.

warning which I do not propose to neglect, and it is this: being ill has not served me as an excuse for absence from the Senate – but I shall have a better excuse if I am dead!

You are my intimate friend, Dolabella; and, when I see you sitting there, heaven knows I find it impossible to keep silent about the mistake that you are both making. Each of you is a nobleman with lofty aims, and I must part company with those who maintain, in their excessive credulity, that it is money you are after; for that is something which men of true greatness and renown have always despised. I refuse to believe that what you want is wealth acquired by violent means, or the sort of power that Romans would find intolerable. Yours, I am convinced, is the very different ambition of gaining the love of your fellow-citizens and winning a splendid reputation. Such a reputation means praise won by noble actions and by great services to one's country, and endorsed by the testimony of national leaders and the whole population. And I would be prepared to enlarge further, Dolabella, on this subject of the rewards won by splendid deeds, did I not see that in these recent times you yourself have shown that you appreciate this very matter even better than anyone else.

For you can surely remember no happier occasion in all your life than the day on which, before returning home, you cleaned up the Forum, dispersed that concourse of blasphemous scoundrels, punished the ringleaders for their loathsome designs, and rescued the city from incendiarism and the menace of massacre. All members of the community, whatever their rank or class or station, pressed forward to compliment and congratulate you. Indeed, loyal citizens were even thanking and congratulating me as your proxy; because they believed your deed had been instigated by myself. Cast your mind back, I urge you, Dolabella, to that unanimous demonstration in the theatre when the entire crowd of spectators, dismissing from their minds what they had held against you previously, revealed that your recent action on their behalf had made them put aside all recollection of their earlier grudges.[42]

And so it distresses me deeply, Dolabella, that after winning such great respect you should now be prepared to cast this all aside with complete equanimity.

And as for you, Marcus Antonius, you are not with us now, but I have an appeal to address to you all the same. That one day, on which the Senate met in the temple of Tellus, must surely have happier memories for you than all the subsequent months in which so many people (greatly differing from me) have accounted you fortunate. For what a splendid speech you made about national unity! When you renounced your hostility towards your fellow-consul and forgot the unfavourable auspices which you yourself as an augur of Rome had declared to be an impediment to his election: when you accepted him for the first time as your colleague, and sent your infant son to the Capitol as a hostage, your words freed the ex-soldiers from all apprehensions about their position, and indeed delivered our entire nation from its anxieties. Never has there been more rejoicing than there was on that day, both in the Senate and among the whole people of Rome – which was gathered together in numbers such as had never been seen at any public meeting before. At that juncture it finally and definitely seemed true that the action of those most valiant citizens had brought us our liberty, because their wish had come true, and the outcome of liberation was peace.

And then again on the next day and the second and the third and those that followed, you daily continued to confer some fresh gift upon your country; and the greatest of all these benefits was your abolition of the title of dictator. For

42. In 47 Dolabella as tribune had proposed a general abolition of debts and of rent, and subsequent bloody riots had been put down by Antonius.

that was the time when you (of all people) branded the dead Caesar's memory with ineradicable infamy. In a bygone age the crime of a single Marcus Manlius[43] caused the Manlian family to decree that no patrician Manlius should ever again bear the first name of Marcus. And now, by the same token, the detestation felt for a single dictator caused you to suppress the name of dictator altogether.

But then, after these outstanding services that you had contributed to the nation, whatever can have happened? Did you regret the good fortune and illustriousness and glory and renown you had won? I wonder how that sudden transformation came about. I cannot bring myself to suspect you were corrupted by financial considerations. Let people say what they like, one is not forced to believe them: and I have never found anything squalid or mean in your character. It is true that the people in a man's home sometimes deprave him – but I know very well that you are a strong-minded person. I am only sorry that your freedom from guilt is not equalled by your freedom from suspicion.

But what frightens me more than such imputations is the possibility that you yourself may disregard the true path of glory, and instead consider it glorious to possess more power than all your fellow-citizens combined – preferring that they should fear you rather than like you. If that is what you think, your idea of where the road of glory lies is mistaken. For glory consists of being regarded with affection by one's country, winning praise and respect and love; whereas to be feared and disliked, on the other hand, is unpleasant and hateful and debilitating and precarious. This is clear enough from the play in which the man said, 'Let them hate provided that they fear'.[44] He found to his cost that such a policy was his ruin.

43. After his success against the Gauls M. Manlius Capitolinus was believed to have fostered sedition and been condemned to death (c. 385–4).

44. The words of Atreus, in Accius' tragedy of that name. He was killed by his nephew Aegisthus.

It would have been so much better, Marcus Antonius, if you had kept the record of your grandfather before your eyes. You have heard me speak of him at length and on numerous occasions. Do you think *he* would have regarded his claim to immortality as being best served by terrorizing people with armed gangs? No, what life and good fortune meant to him was to be the equal of everybody else in freedom, but their superior in his honourable way of life. About his glorious successes I shall say nothing now; but I want to record my conviction that the last tragic day of his life was preferable to the tyranny of Lucius Cinna[45] who brutally slew him.

However, I see no hope of influencing you by what I say. For if the end that befell Gaius Caesar does not persuade you that it is better to inspire affection than terror, no words that anyone could utter will have the slightest effect or success. People who say Caesar was enviable are profoundly misguided. For no one can be said to have a happy life when its violent termination brings his slayers not merely impunity but the height of glory. So change your ways, I entreat you. Remember your ancestors – and govern our country in such a way that your fellow-citizens will rejoice that you were born. For without that there is no such thing as happiness, or renown, or security.

Your fellow-Romans have furnished you both with ample warnings, and it worries me that they fail to impress you sufficiently. Think of the clamour raised by countless citizens at gladiatorial shows, think of all the versified popular slogans, think of those endless acclamations in front of the statue of Pompeius,[46] think of the two tribunes who are against you![47] Surely these are sufficient indications that every Roman speaks

45. L. Cornelius Cinna held four successive consulships (87–84).

46. It was at the foot of the statue of Pompeius, in the hall of his theatre, that Caesar had fallen.

47. Tribunes hostile to Antonius were Ti. Cannutius and L. Cassius Longinus; Cicero also mentions Dec. Carfulenus.

with a single voice! And then again did you attach no importance to the applause at Apollo's Games?[48] – or rather I should call it the testimony and judgement of the entire Roman people. What an honour for the men who were prevented by armed violence from being present in person – though they were present in the hearts and emotions of the people of Rome! Or did you really suppose that all that approval was meant for the playwright Accius – that his tragedy[49] was winning a belated prize sixty years after its first performance? No, Brutus was the man for whom the cheering and the prize were intended. He could not himself attend the games that were displayed in his name, but the Romans who witnessed that sumptuous show paid their tribute to him in his absence, and sought to comfort the sadness which they felt because their liberator was not with them by incessant cheers and shouts of sympathy.

Personally I have always despised applause of this kind – when its recipients are the sort of men who will do anything to win popularity. All the same, when the cheering comes unanimously from the highest and middle and lowest classes of the community alike, and when the politicians who used to bow to the popular will are suddenly found going in the opposite direction, that seems to me to constitute not merely applause but a verdict!

Or if you regard that as a trivial matter – although it is actually most significant – do you also attach no importance to the proof you have seen of Rome's loving solicitude for the health of Aulus Hirtius?[50] It was already a very notable fact that Roman people esteem him as they do, that unique

48. The Games of Apollo (July) should have been undertaken by the city praetor Brutus, but in his absence were organized by Antony's brother Gaius, with financial aid from Atticus.

49. The play was the *Tereus* of Accius.

50. The consul elect A. Hirtius (politically still hesitant) had been seriously ill.

affection is lavished on him by his friends, that his family hold him so exceptionally dear. But now, in his illness, is there anyone in the memory of mankind who has been the object of such profound anxiety among all good citizens, and of such universal alarm? Nobody has ever been favoured with such demonstrations before. And so does it not occur to you that the people who are so deeply concerned for the lives of those they hope will serve the state may start having thoughts about your own lives as well?

Senators, the rewards I hoped to gain from my return are now mine. For the views I have expressed to you today are a guarantee that, whatever may happen in the future, my determination shall be on record. Moreover, you have given me an attentive and sympathetic hearing. If, without peril to myself and you, I am allowed further opportunities to speak, I shall use them as often as I can. If not, I shall work to the best of my ability for the welfare not of my own self but of our country. Meanwhile, I can say that my life has now lasted long enough, by the measure of years and fame alike. If an additional span is now to be vouchsafed to me, I shall again not devote it to my own interests, but it will be placed, as before, at the disposal of yourselves and Rome.

APPENDIXES AND INDEX

APPENDIX A

KEY TO TECHNICAL TERMS[1]

AEDILES. Officials ranking above quaestors and below praetors (*q.v.*), concerned with the care of the city of Rome, its corn-supply and its Games.

ALLIES. Term applied not only to allies outside the empire but to 'free' treaty-bound communities within the empire and to the ordinary provincial subjects of Rome.

AUGURS. The official Roman diviners; one of the four Orders of Priesthood. They took the auspices (*q.v.*) at the request of an official.

AUSPICES. Certain types of divination – particularly from birds – officially practised at elections, inaugurations of office, entrances into a province and the conduct of wars.

CENSORS. Officials appointed every five (earlier every four) years to draw up and maintain the list of citizens (*census*) and revise the list of Senators.

CENTURIES. The units of one hundred men by which voting was organized in the Assembly for some of its most important business, notably the election of the principal officials. (The century was also a military unit.)

CENTURIONS. The principal professional officers in the Roman army, sixty to a legion, selected during the Republic from ordinary soldiers.

COHORTS. Military units of infantry, ten to a legion.

FREEDMEN. Liberated (manumitted) slaves.

GAMES. Annual or occasional formal sports and representations, generally of religious origin.

KINGS. Traditionally the earlier rulers of Rome (to 510 B.C.).

1. For the Assembly, judges, knights (*equites*), lawcourts and Senate, see the Introduction.

LEGIONS. The principal military units, 6,000 strong.

PRAETORIANS. During the last two centuries of the Republic these were the bodyguards of Roman generals.

PRAETORS. The state officials, now eight in number, who were next in importance to the consuls; largely concerned with the administration of justice.

PREFECTS. Commanders of cavalry squadrons.

QUAESTORS. The lowest state office in the Senator's career; now twenty in number.

SQUADRONS. Cavalry units, ten to a wing.

TAX-FARMERS. The *publicani*, who (in addition to other functions) were organized into corporations controlled by knights, and formed contracts with the government for the collection of taxes in the province of Asia.

TRIBES. All Roman citizens were registered in one of thirty-five territorial tribes (four urban and the others 'rustic'), which were the units of voting for certain matters in the Assembly (e.g. the election of tribunes of the people).

TRIBUNES (OF THE PEOPLE) possessed ancient, revered 'democratic' powers entitling them to 'protect the people' by intercessions and vetos directed against officers of state. (For the obscure Tribunes of the Treasury, see p. 140).

TRIUMPH. The processional return of a victorious Roman general, when he sacrificed to Jupiter on the Capitol. Triumphs were awarded by the Senate.

TRIUMVIRS. The informal First Triumvirate was established by Pompey, Crassus and Caesar in 60–59 B.C., and the Second Triumvirate, with formal autocratic powers, by Antonius, Octavian (the future Augustus) and Lepidus in 43 B.C.

VESTAL VIRGINS. The priestesses, normally six in number, serving the goddess Vesta whose worship at her temple near the Forum was symbolical of the greatness and eternity of Rome.

FURTHER READING

F. E. ADCOCK, *Roman Political Ideas and Practice*, Ann Arbor, 1959

L. ALFONSI (etc.), *Marco Tullio Cicerone*, Rome, 1961

D. R. S. BAILEY, *Cicero: A Biography*, London, 1971

K. BÜCHNER, *Cicero*, Heidelberg, 1964
Das Neue Cicerobild: Denker, Weger der Forschung 22, 1973

J. CARCOPINO, *The Secrets of the Correspondence of Cicero*, London, 1951

CICERO, *Letters to Atticus* (ed. D. R. S. Bailey), London, 1978

CICERO, *Letters to his Friends* (ed. D. R. S. Bailey), London, 1978

CICERO, *Murder Trials* (ed. M. Grant), London, 1975

CICERO, *On the Good Life* (ed. M. Grant), London, 1971

CICERO, *On the Nature of the Gods* (ed. H. C. P. McGregor), London, 1974

CICERO, *Selected Works* (ed. M. Grant), London, rev. ed., 1971

C. J. CLASSEN, *Recht, Rhetorik, Politik*, Darmstadt, 1985

P. R. COWELL, *Cicero and the Roman Republic*, London, 2nd ed., 1962

T. A. DOREY (ed.), *Cicero*, London, 1964

A. E. DOUGLAS, *Cicero* (Greece & Rome, New Surveys in the Classics, No. 2), 1968

M. FLECK, *Cicero als historicker*, 1993

H. FRISCH, *Cicero's Fight for the Republic*, Copenhagen, 1946

M. FUHRMANN, *Cicero and the Roman Republic*, 1992

M. GELZER, *Cicero*, Oxford, Blackwell, 1973

M. GELZER, *The Roman Nobility*, Oxford, 1969

M. GRIFFIN, *Cicero and Rome*, in *Oxford History of the Classical World*, Oxford, 1986

P. GRIMAL, *Cicéron*, Paris, 1984

A. HEUSS, *Ciceros Theorie vom romischen Staat*, Göttingen, 1975

H. J. HASKELL, *This was Cicero*, New York, 1942

L. HUTCHINSON, *The Conspiracy of Catiline*, London, 1966

A. H. M. JONES, *The Criminal Courts of the Roman Republic and Principate*, Oxford, 1972

G. KENNEDY, *The Art of the Rhetoric in the Roman World 300 B.C.–A.D. 300*, Princeton, 1972

C. KUBICHT, *Cicero der Politiker*, Munich, 1990
Cicero the Politician, Baltimore, 1990

W. K. LACEY (ed.), *Cicero and the End of the Roman Republic*, London, 1978

A. W. LINTOTT, *Violence in Republican Rome*, Oxford, 1968

P. MACKENDRICK, *The Philosophical Books of Cicero*, London, 1995
The Speeches of Cicero, London, 1995

H. D. MEYER, *Cicero und das Reich*, Köln, 1957

T. N. MITCHELL, *Cicero: The Ascending Years*, New Haven, 1979

U. ORTMAN, *Cicero, Brutus and Octavian: Republicans and Caesarians*, Bonn, 1988

P. PERELLI, *Il pensiero politico di Cicerone*, Florence, 1990

T. PETERSSON, *Cicero: A Biography*, Berkeley, 1920, 1963

M. RAMBAUD, *Cicéron et l'histoire romaine*, Paris, 1953

E. RAWSON, *Cicero: A Portrait*, London, 1975, 1993

E. RAWSON, *Cicero* in T. J. Luce (ed.), *Ancient Writers: Greece and Rome*, New York, 1982

G. C. RICHARDS, *Cicero: A Study*, London, 1935

R. SEAGER (ed.), *The Crisis of the Roman Republic*, Cambridge and New York, 1969

R. E. SMITH, *Cicero the Statesman*, Cambridge, 1966

D. STOCKTON, *Cicero: A Political Biography*, Oxford, 1971

R. SYME, *The Roman Revolution*, Oxford, 1939, 1960

D. TAYLOR, *Cicero and Rome*, London, 1973

L. R. TAYLOR, *Party Politics in the Age of Caesar*, Berkeley, 1949

S. L. UTCENKO, *Cicerone e il suo tempo*, Rome, 1975

T. WEDERMANN, *Cicero and the End of the Roman Republic*, Bristol, 1994

L. P. WILKINSON, *Cicero* in *Cambridge History of Classical Literature*, II, *Latin Literature*, Cambridge, 1982

T. P. WISEMAN, *Roman Political Life 90 BC–AD 69*, Exeter, 1985

N. WOOD, *Cicero's Social and Political Thought*, Berkeley, 1991

ANCIENT ROME

○ Blocks of flats owned by Cicero
— City-wall

Flaminian Way

CAMPUS MARTIUS

Theatre of Pompey
(Caesar murdered)

CAPITOLINE
HILL

Temple of Ops

IANICULUM HILL

R Tiber

CITADEL

Temple of Concord
Rostra
Senate-House
Sacred
Way
Tullianum FORUM
Temple of Castor
Temple of Jupiter Stator
PALATINE
HILL

ESQUILINE HILL
Temple of Tellus

Temple of Vesta and Regia

Cicero's House

Temple
of Bona Dea
AVENTINE
HILL

CIRCUS
MAXIMUS

Appian Way

THE ROMAN

GALLIA COMATA

ALLOBROGES
GALLIA
NARBONENSIS

GALLIA
CISALPINA

MASSILIA

ILLYRICUM

GALLAECIA

Numantia

S P A I N

ITALY

Rome

LUSITANIA

SARDINIA

Corduba

SICILY

①

NUMIDIA

Carthage
AFRICA

MAURETANIA

EMPIRE 51 B.C.

- - - Boundaries of provinces
── Boundaries of the empire

BOSPHORUS

BLACK SEA

R. Danube

M O E S I A

DARDANIA

BITHYNIA PONTUS

Zela

A R M E N I A

A S I A

Pessinus

CAPPADOCIA

CILICIA

Antioch

②

PAMPHYLIA

CYPRUS

SYRIA

CRETE

E G Y P T

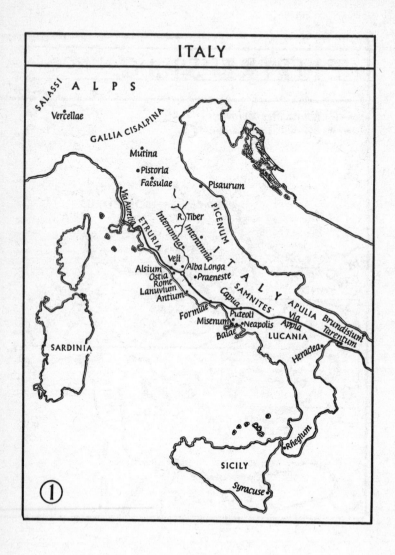

ITALY

SALASSI
A L P S
Vercellae
GALLIA CISALPINA
Mutina
Pistoria
Faesulae
Pisaurum
PICENUM
Via Aurelia
R. Tiber
ETRURIA
Interamnia
Interamnia
I T A L Y
Veii
Alsium
Alba Longa
Ostia
Praeneste
Rome
SAMNITES
APULIA
Lanuvium
Antium
Capua
Via
Formiae
Puteoli
Appia
Brundisium
Misenum
Neapolis
Tarentum
Baiae
LUCANIA
SARDINIA
Heraclea
Rhegium
SICILY
Syracuse

①

GREECE AND WEST OF ASIA MINOR

EPIRUS

MACEDONIA

Philippi

Pydna

THESSALY

Pharsalus

Pelion

AETOLIA

ACHAIA

PELOPONNESE

Corinth

Athens

Piraeus

Salamis

Delos

AEGEAN SEA

Sigeum

Tenedos

Troy (Ilium)

Cyzicus

MYSIA

Mytilene

Pergamum

LYDIA

Chios

Colophon

Samos

ASIA

CARIA

Cnidus

②

INDEX OF PERSONAL NAMES